Art Classics

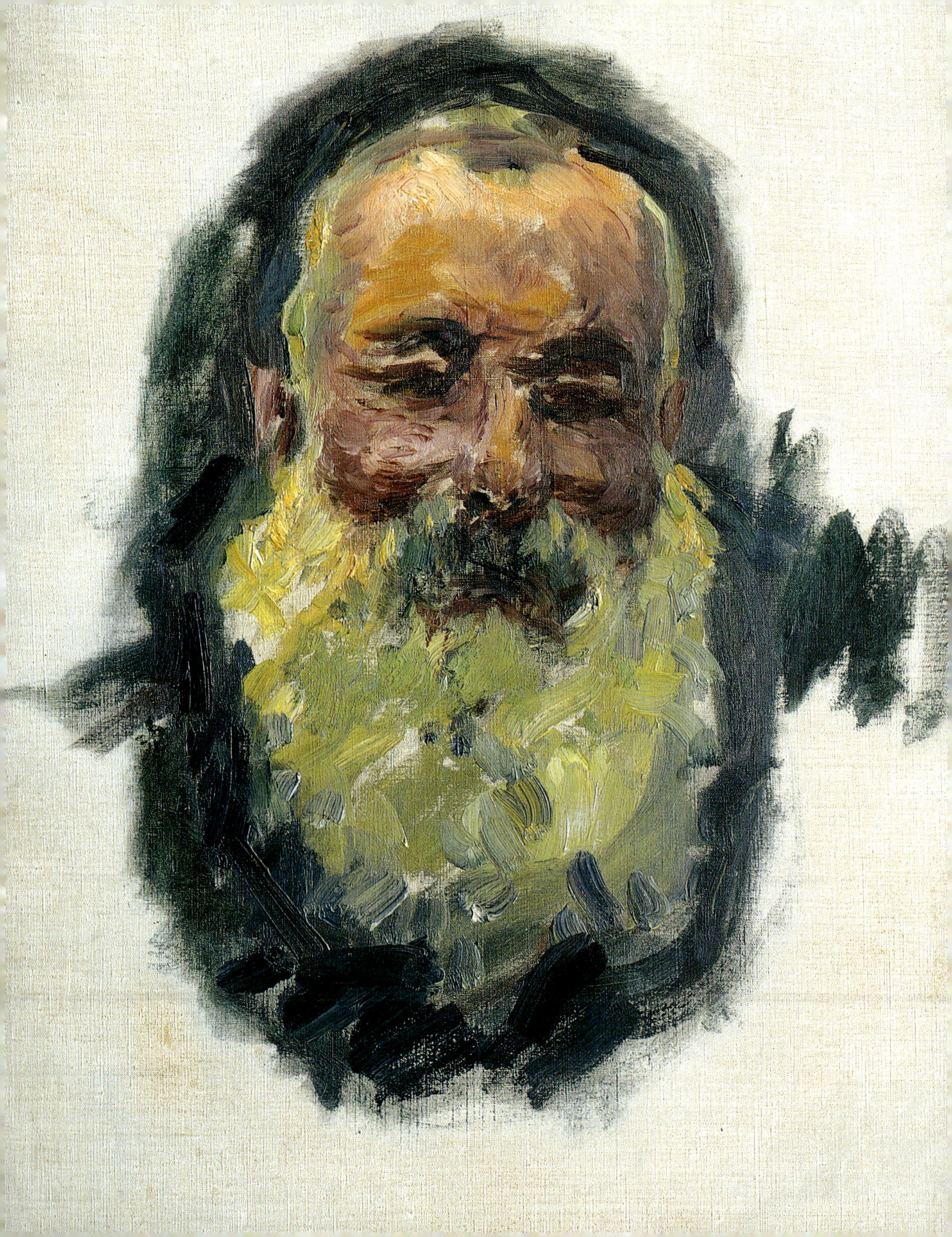

MONET

Preface by Roberto Tassi

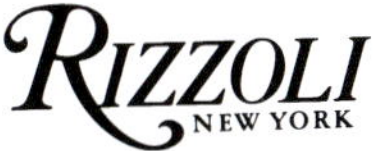
RIZZOLI
NEW YORK

Art Classics

MONET

First published in the United States
of America in 2005 by
Rizzoli International Publications, Inc.
300 Park Avenue South
New York, NY 10010
www.rizzoliusa.com

Originally published in Italian by
Rizzoli Libri Illustrati
© 2004 RCS Libri Spa, Milano
All rights reserved
www.rcslibri.it
First edition 2003
Rizzoli \ Skira – Corriere della Sera

2005 2006 2007 2008 2009 /
10 9 8 7 6 5 4 3 2 1

Printed in China

ISBN: 0-8478-2728-3

Library of Congress Control
Number: 2005922008

Director of the series
Eileen Romano

Design
Marcello Francone

Translation
Timothy Stroud
(Buysschaert&Malerba)

Editing and layout
Buysschaert&Malerba, Milan

cover
Women in the Garden,
1867
Paris, Musée d'Orsay

frontispiece
Self-Portrait
(detail), 1917
Paris, Musée d'Orsay

The publication of works owned by
the Soprintendenze has been made
possible by the Ministry for Cultural
Goods and Activities.

© Archivio Scala, Florence

Contents

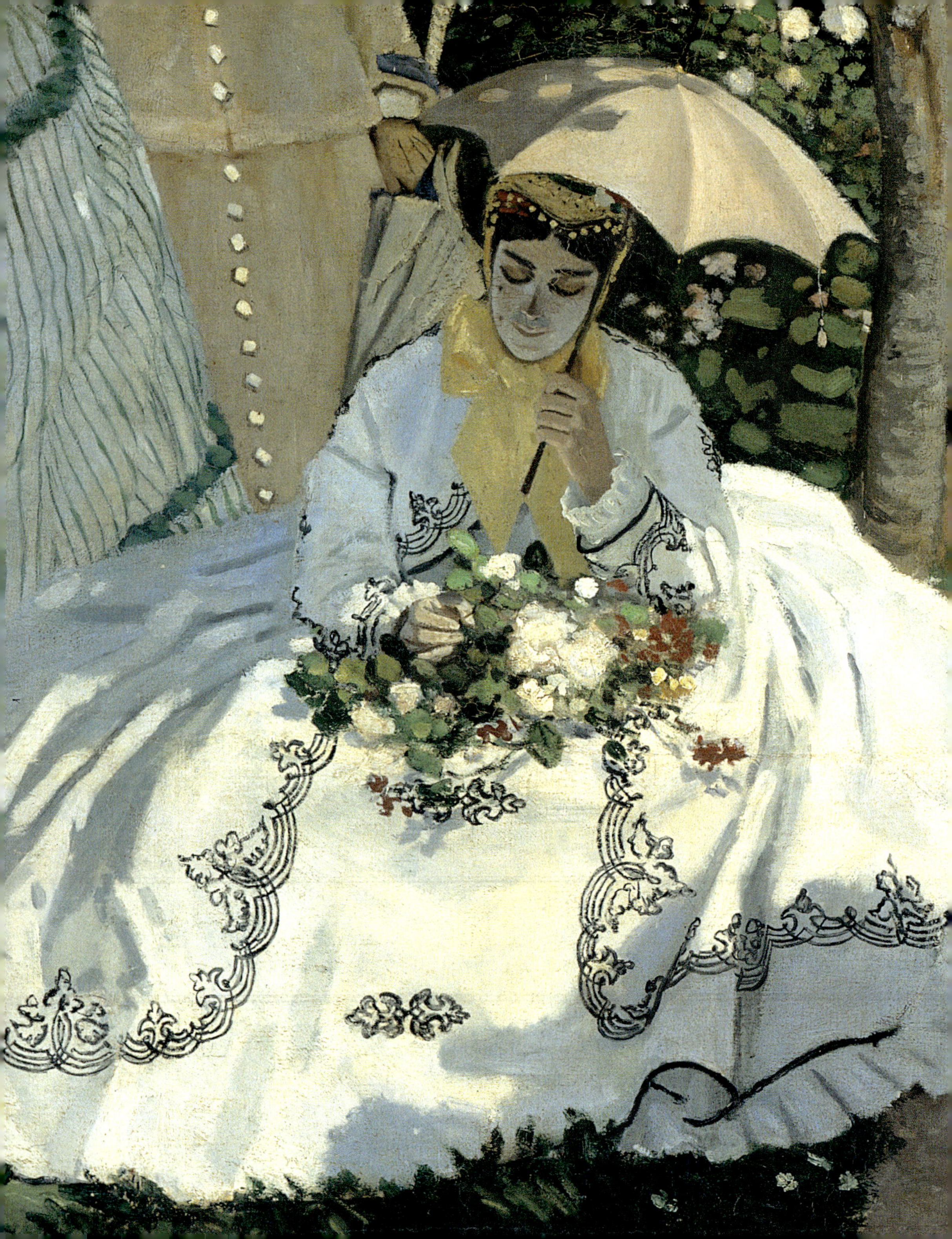

Monet's Studio
Roberto Tassi

In April 1880 in Vétheuil, a village on the right bank of the Seine where he was living at the time, Claude Monet received the journalist Emile Taboureux who was to interview him for *La Vie Moderne*. When the interviewer asked if he could see the artist's studio, Monet replied, "My studio! I have never had a studio, and I cannot understand how it is possible to shut yourself up in a room." Then, gesturing to the Seine and surrounding countryside, he said "There is my studio."

This comment encompasses the whole truth of Monet's work, the uninterrupted evolution of his life to create that truth, and the sense of his working method that merged his life and work—his presence in the world and his need to paint—in such a singular manner that it seemed there had never been an artist like him before. Critics have interpreted this gesture as pompous, rhetoric, or even a means of presenting his life as an epic, whereas it was in fact the statement of a complete truth that arose from a sudden intuition, one that gives weight and breadth to the sense of every word. It brings to mind a similar statement by Caravaggio, "When the most famous statues by Phidias and Glycon were shown to him so that he might study them, he gave no other answer than to point to a multitude of men, hinting that Nature had provided him sufficiently with masters."

The two gestures, which were so similar in terms of the idea they represented, indicate, some centuries on, the practice inherent in nature painting, or in painting nature, though with an awareness of the differences that exist between the two. But the underlying intention was the same, that of painting reality, nature, life, people, water, and sky. Two complete revolutions were announced and brought about by these gestures. Monet's work represented a revolution; based on a concept of existence which—with that "I cannot understand how it is possible to shut yourself up in a room"— modified Pascal's idea to mean that all things bad will come to those unable to leave a room, unable to abandon the studio, unable to live and paint *en plein air* (outdoors). This vital need to paint in nature and its ethical sense give Monet's method and resulting work an authentic greatness and diversity compared to that of other artists. No painter had ever been so extreme or so sure, as though it had been the ineluctable hand of fate that kindled and supported him, rather than his own determination and obsession.

Many artists throughout time would leave their studios to go out and draw people, motifs, and views directly from nature, though mostly to jot things down or make sketches. However, some also went out to paint, from as early as the first, though rare, landscape painters of the seventeenth century. This number increased during the eighteenth century and achieved an almost unstoppable growth during the century of naturalistic painting, so that by the time Monet began his artistic career a long and established tradition had been created. For example, both Joseph Vernet (the grandfather of Horace Vernet) in the eighteenth century and Turner in the nineteenth had had themselves tied to the mast of a ship during a storm to be able to study its effects. Constable and Boudin indicated the day, time, and weather conditions on their sheets, the first on his "cloud studies" and the second on his watercolors of the sea. There had also been Valenciennes with his *études d'après nature* made in Rome, Théodore Rousseau who contemplated and painted trees in the forest of Fontainebleau, Daubigny who lived on a *bateau-atelier* (boat-cum-studio) he had designed himself, and Corot who painted in the woods. Consequently, painting *en plein air* already existed. Monet discovered it by following Boudin's example: "...One day Boudin said to me, 'Do what I do, learn to draw well and admire

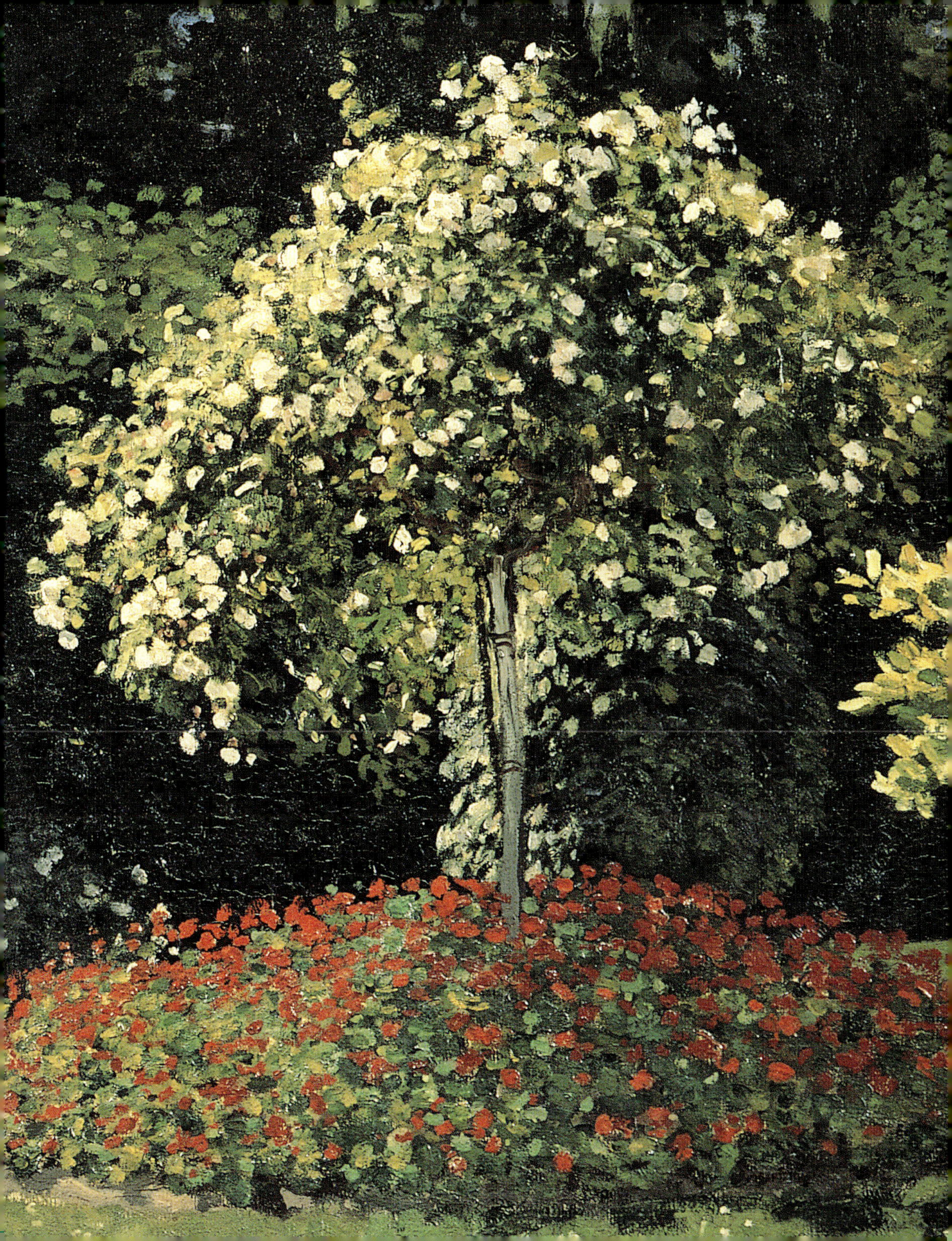

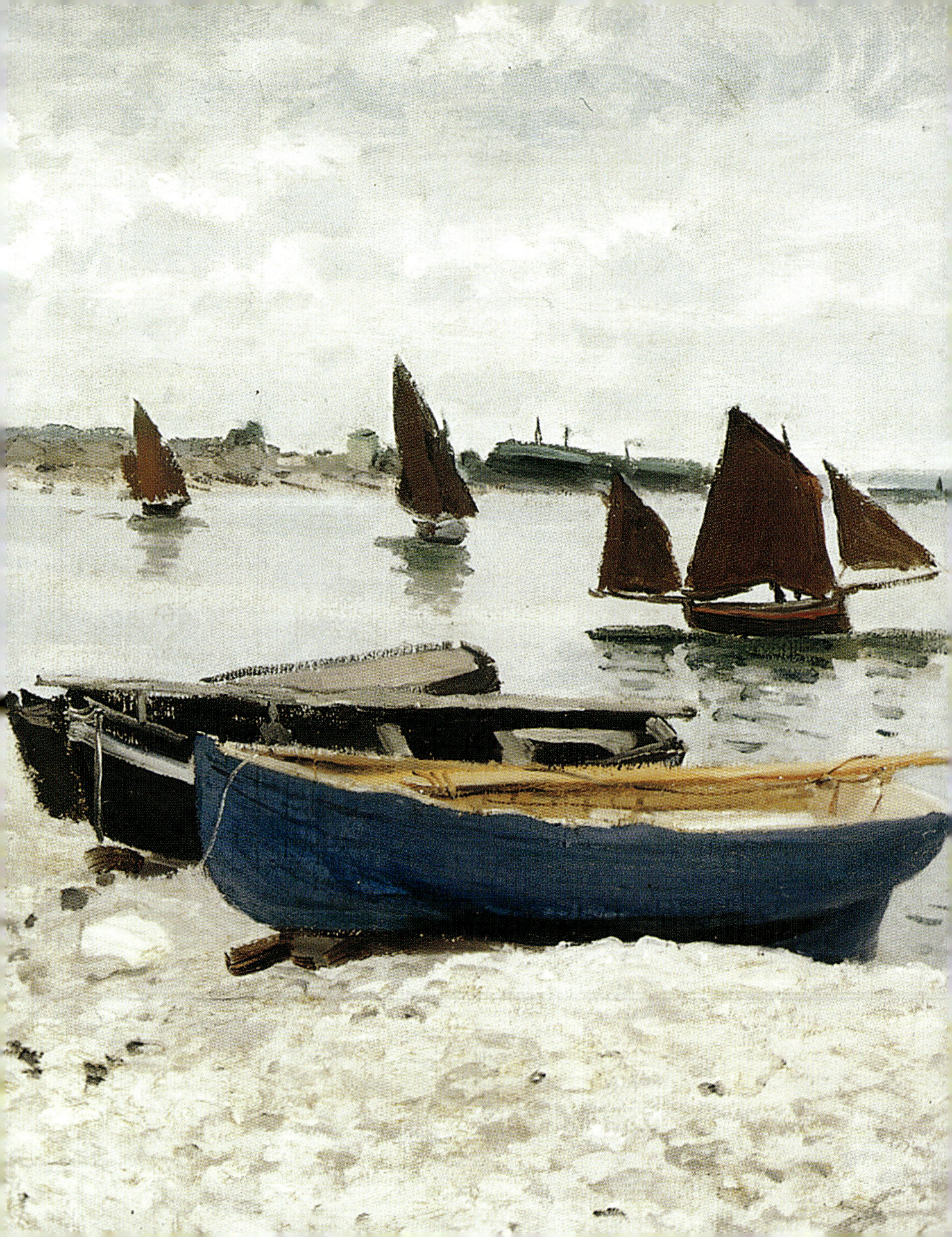

the sea, the light and the blue sky.' I followed his advice and together we took long walks during which I did not cease painting nature. That is how I learned to understand it and to love it passionately."

But Monet's *en plein air* is different in substance, spirit, and meaning from anyone else's, even that of his impressionist colleagues Renoir, Sisley, and Pissarro with whom he formed *l'école du plein air*. Unlike the others, Monet produced his entire work outside by making nature his studio. Certain writers, who were his friends, recognized the value of his painting but this depth of appreciation did not continue far into the twentieth century and is only now beginning to return. Maurice Guillemot: "His studio is nature." Octave Mirbeau: "The open air is his only studio." Clemenceau: "His garden was, in short, [...] an open-air studio." And Manet said: "Monet? His boat is his studio." It took a real freedom of judgment, which was acute in only a few individuals due to the general incomprehension and scandal that surrounded Monet, to understand the totalizing essence of that fact.

All his life Monet painted while immersed in nature, often taking with him many canvases in addition to his usual equipment, as if each time he were taking his studio along. Then, when he found the right spot, he would recreate it. His studio was formed by light, the movement of the air, the wind, water—whether still, slowly flowing, or lightly ruffled—rivers, fog, snow, trees, meadows, hills, and flowers: everything that not only met the painter's eyes but that came into contact with his body and senses, that brushed against him, encircled him, soaked him with dew at dawn, the strong sea wind, the winter cold, the northern frost, the southern heat, the warmth of the grass, the smells and buzzing of the insects in the gardens, the flashes the sunlight shot into the August sky, and the chiaroscuro that trembled mysterious in the woods. Monet needed not just to see nature with his eyes to paint it, but to feel it and all its phenomena around and through him; he needed total physical immersion and abandonment and the difficulties, pleasures, discomforts, and sensations that it brought him and which he needed to overcome. His studio, which altered every time the scenery, subject, or viewpoint changed, was the most unstable, varied, and ephemeral possible. It changed every minute as he painted, with the movement of light, air, and clouds, and with the imperceptible passing of time. When Monet chose a spot to paint in the countryside, along the Seine or on the beach, his studio would miraculously evolve around him.

It was always like this, from that moment in 1859 when, at Boudin's advice, he began to paint the sea at Le Havre and felt that his destiny as a painter was imminent, until his final years when he invented the "series" and the "decorations" of the lilies in the last, vast, paradisiacal studio he created over a long period, with effort and dedication: his garden at Giverny. In this way the history of Monet's painting became the history of his lovely, meteorological, ever-changing studios.

The great adventure of the series of *Water Lilies* moved toward an unknown destiny. In August 1897 the journalist Maurice Guillemot spent a whole day at Giverny and published an account of it in *La Revue Illustrée* the following year. After describing the famous lily pond, he wrote, referring to its flowers, "they are models for a decoration of which he has already begun the studies, large panels that he showed me afterwards in his studio." The history of Monet's adventure, which lasted until his death twenty-nine years later, began with that article, but it remained unacknowledged as his undated "studies" were dispersed and, when they reappeared, were considered to have been made very late in the artist's career as the conception of space was so revolutionary: just a few scattered leaves and flowers suspended over an abyss of gradations and nuances of color, with no sky, no banks, and no perspective. But the correct dating to 1897 by Daniel Wildenstein has revealed the true course of that exceptional history.

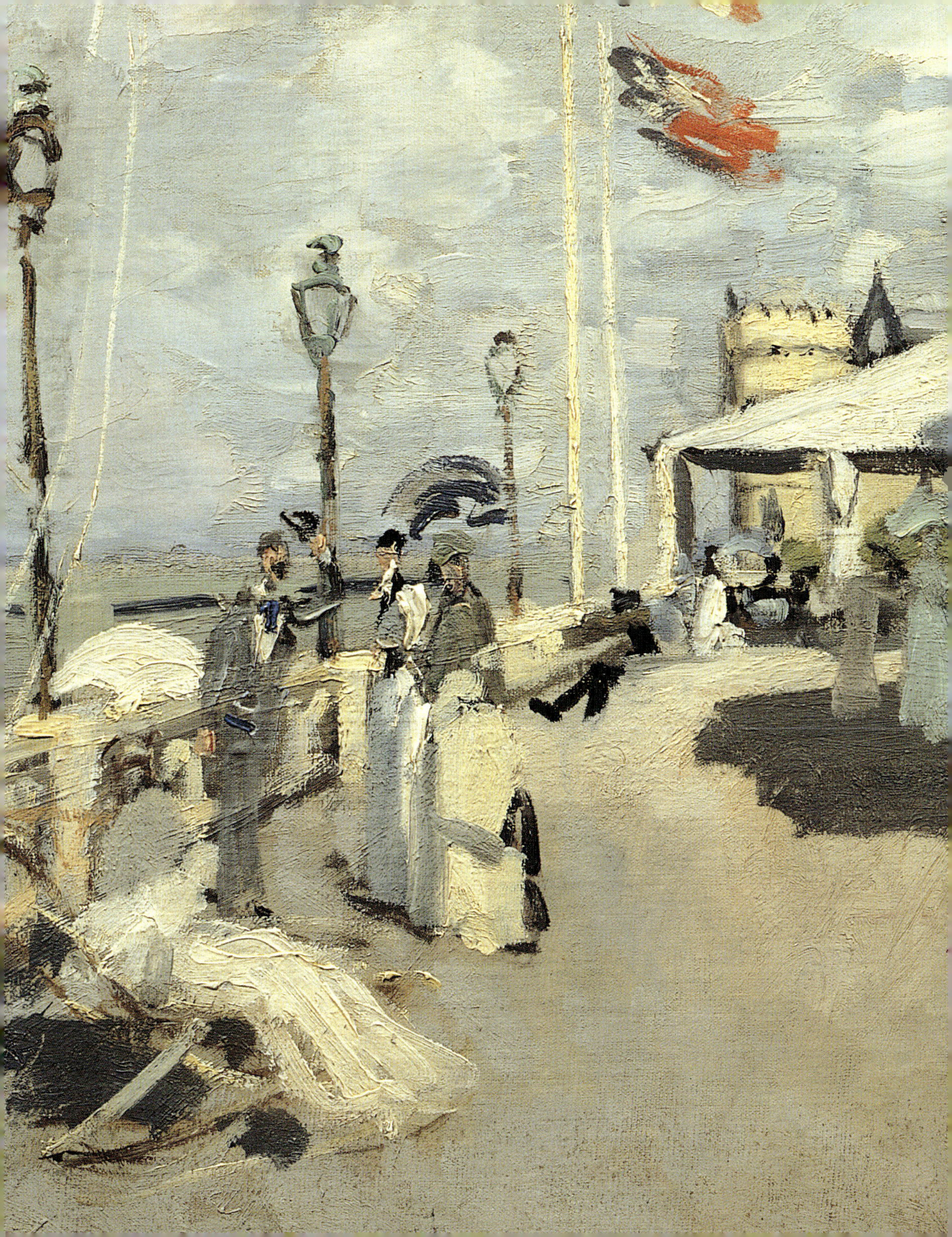

The result was an enormous and heroic undertaking that has no equal in the art of the nineteenth and twentieth centuries, a period that it helped to unify. Monet painted two hundred and fifty works, including the huge decorative panels of his last years that, despite numbering just forty, represent three hundred and fifty square meters of canvas. They are a sort of "Sistine Chapel of impressionism," as the painter André Masson commented, though perhaps it would be better to term them a "Sistine Chapel of naturalism." All the paintings in the cycle are unified by a single conception and a single aim, thereby turning them into a unified work. From the start Monet intended to create a "decoration" but this gradually grew and proliferated into something immense that went quite beyond decoration to become profound, involving, the musical and the poetic. The cycle is divided into groups: after the group of "studies" of 1897 came that of *Le bassin aux nymphèas* (The Waterlily Pond) which formed the core of the exhibition held in 1900 by Durand-Ruel. Still we see in that phase a space to a large extent based on reality, with the pond that stretches away, the "Japanese" bridge that crosses it, the clumps of irises on either bank and the large, deeply shadowed wall of trees that closes the horizon and embraces the branches, stems, wooden fences, and their reflections in the water in a green radiance. On the water—like natural, garlanded rafts—float islands of lilies, some white, the odd one pink, further away a few reds, depending on the species, the angle of the light, and the time of day.

These paintings already seemed to represent a peak of experimentation until the next group was exhibited by Durand-Ruel in 1909 with the title *Les Nymphèas – Série de paysages d'eau* (Water Lilies – A Series of Water Views). In these paintings, every horizon has disappeared. No longer are there the banks, the trees, the ground or the bridge; we see only water, unbounded except by the edge of the canvas, water that merges the gradations of the light with the moving, mixed colors of the depths and the even more variable and vague reflections of the bushes, trees, sky, and clouds. Yet on all this mysterious, transient trembling, this highly realistic fiction, on this inverted space, the elliptical floating flowerbeds represented by the leaves and flowers of the lilies invest the surface with truth, but one so contradictory to our senses, compared to the space beneath them, that they seem suspended in the air, to *fleurir en plein ciel* (bloom in the sky). It is a miracle created by an image that is both deceptive and real, and which fluctuates between the two: in the water the mother-of-pearl tones of dawn are softened to brilliant grays and dark violets, sunset enflames it with reds and oranges, at midday the immobile, serene blue reigns supreme, and the shadows of evening are represented by trickles of indigo. Like an altar created by nature, over all these variations in color bloom the yellow, pink, white, and red of the flowers, isolated and regal. No one had ever painted the passing of time, changing of the seasons, or advance of the hour with such melancholic happiness.

Monet painted in his enchanted garden with an ardor and absent-mindedness that had made him forget his early plans for a "decoration." Then, in 1914, he came across his 1897 studies by chance and the sense of the purpose of all that painting of lilies suddenly came back to him. By this time he had overturned space in the third group of paintings and he had to continue from that point. He then began a gigantic tussle with the dimensions of his paintings, which became increasingly larger, longer, and more absorbing. He no longer knew any limitations and built an enormous studio able to hold all his immense canvases. The older he grew, the more he was sustained by his own energy; nor did his eyes or mind dim, rather they became more vigorous, delicate, and acute. In a period of ten years he painted all his great panels and, on the same motif, innumerable individual paintings that he used as "studies" or new variations in a constant shuttling between the pond and his studio—as though the walls he had just had built existed purely to protect the canvases from the elements and

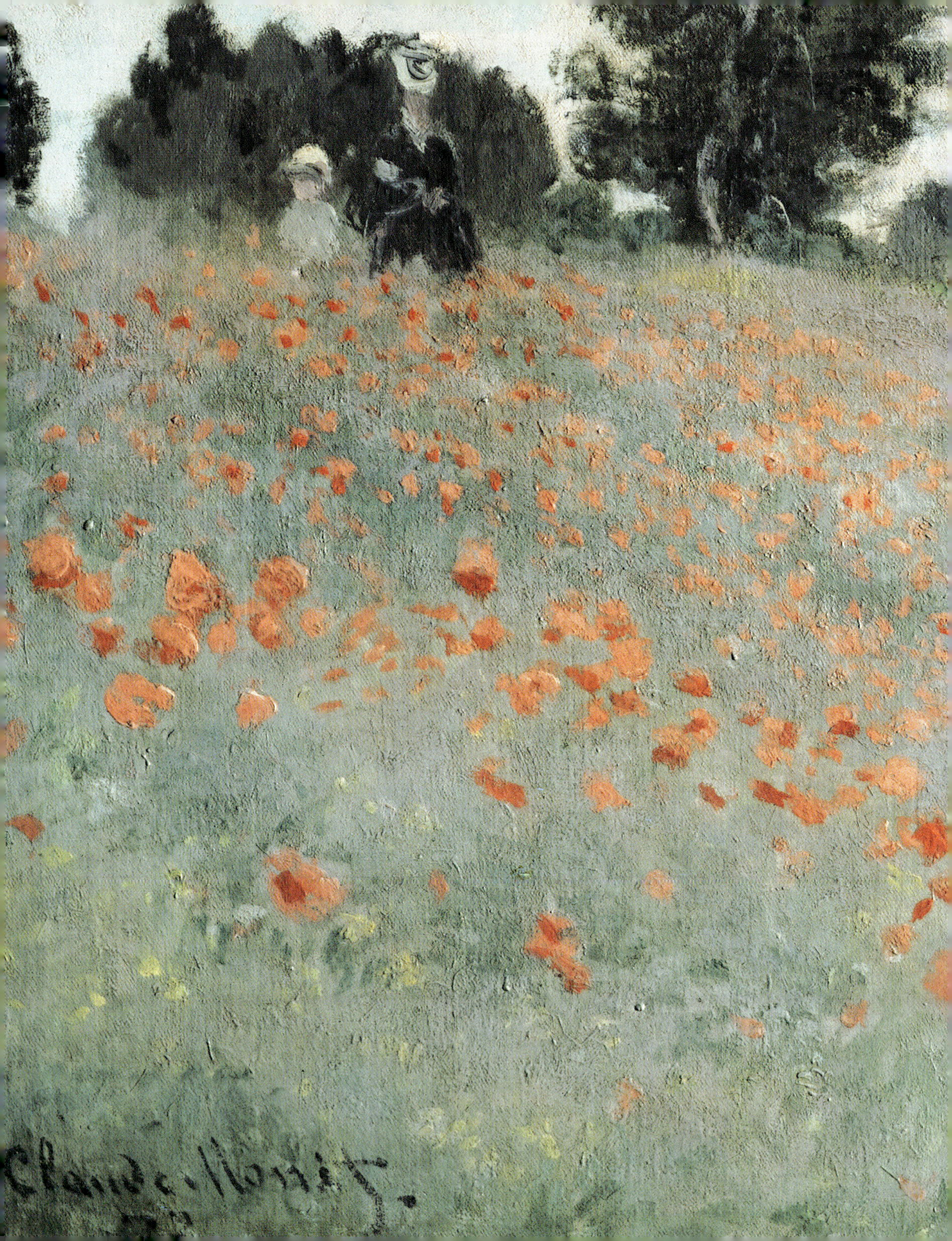
Claude Monet.

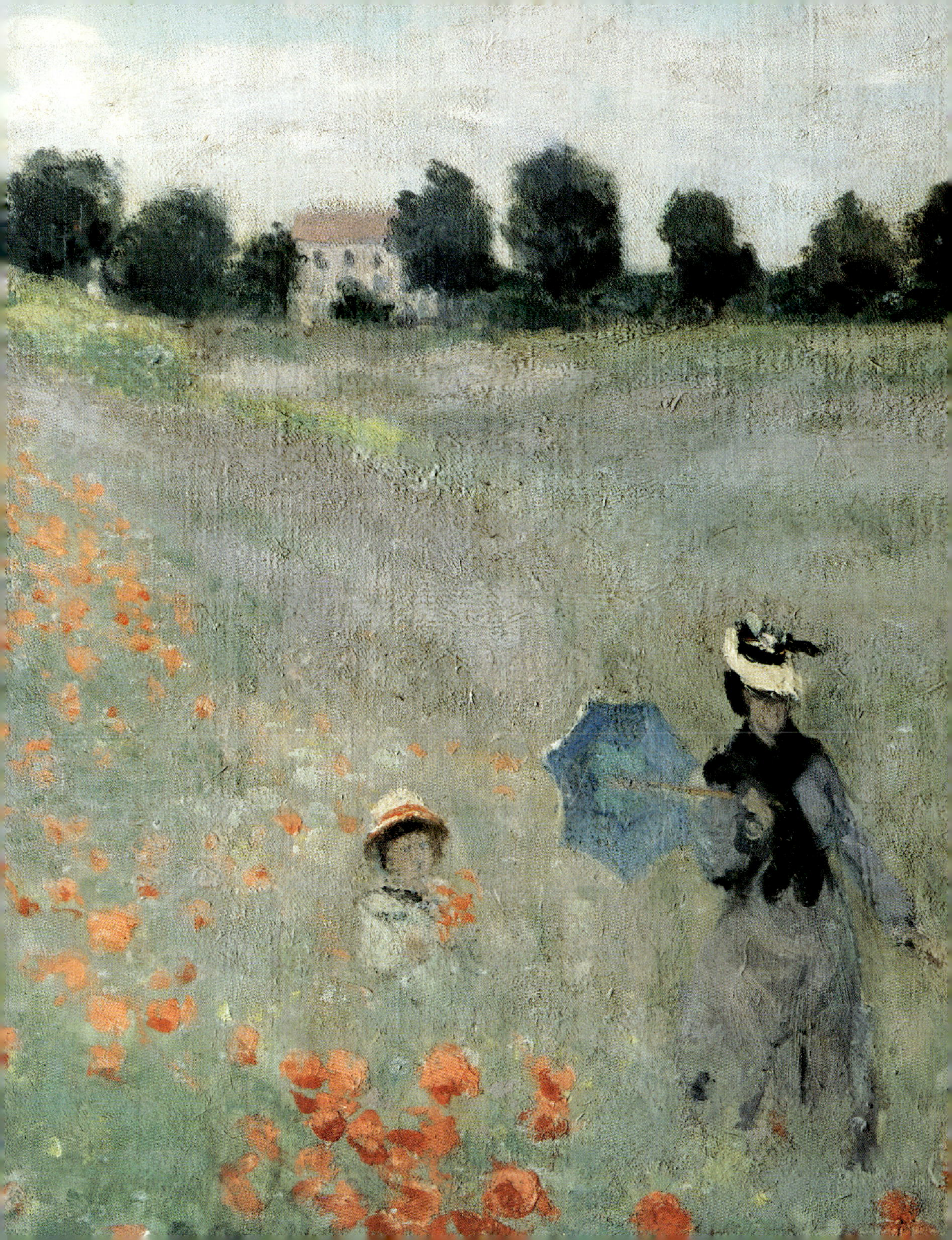

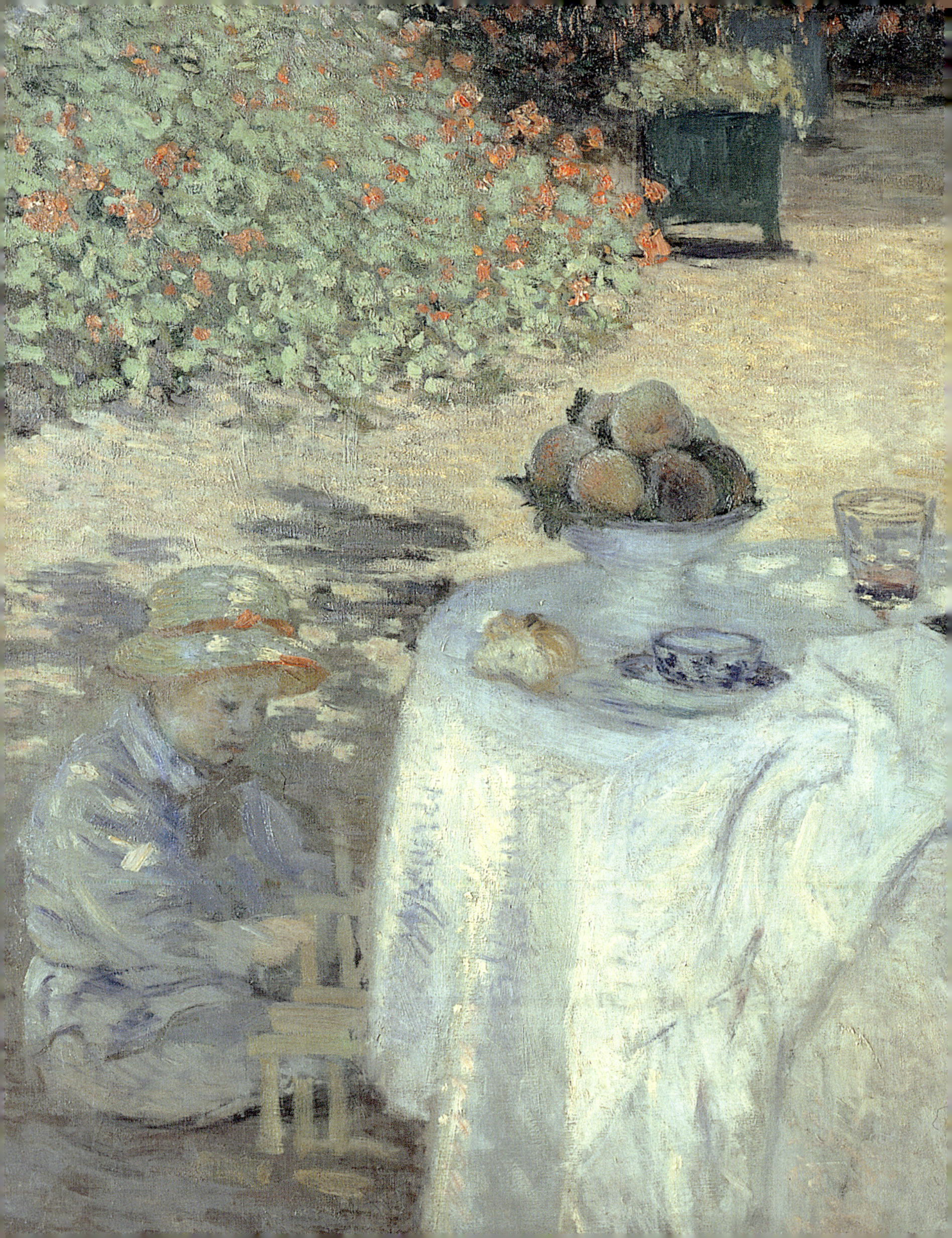

the garden remained his real studio, a place where his manner of seeing, feeling, and painting continued to be immersed.

Those panels, which an illustrious Italian critic considered Monet's great error, instead became the supreme summation of his work and life: all the infinite variations of color and light in the world, insubstantial, undetermined things, the delicacy and strength of nature, its hidden life, his great love of water, the variation in the thickness of the paint on the canvas, each of these things is apparent in the great panels and helps to make them a monument to painting. Although he seems to abolish space, Monet actually expands it endlessly, and thus involves the observer to the maximum degree. With the twenty-two panels that were later hung to form a circle in the Orangerie, he demonstrated that his aim was to create a sense of encirclement, to place the observer at the center of a natural flow created by the atmosphere, air, light, and the harmony of shadows, reflections, and colors that surround one on all sides and which draw the observer into nature. In this way Monet allowed the viewer to share a sense of identity with himself, placing him at the center of nature in the same way the artist had experienced it. The formula "nature into art" used by John House as the subtitle to his book should in fact be inverted: if we really need a formula, we would have to say that Monet's work was "art into nature."

Monet's panels brought to a magnificent conclusion the subversive intuition that had its unexpected and splendid origin in *Luncheon on the Grass* of 1865. We can now confirm that a new concept of space and relationship between the observer and painting had begun to bud in *Luncheon*. The consistency of Monet's work lay in his having continued to follow the path right through to the greatness of his decorative panels, and his genius in having understood that it was only made possible by painting every day *en plein air*, however dangerous it may have seemed. In this *plein air*, the sense of involvement—tested and transmitted—is implicit; and, in turn, instantaneousness and the notion of time are both inherent in the involvement of the observer.

Monet's work can be interpreted in another and more abstruse way. During his impressionist years, Monet had taken the poetry of transience and fleetingness to its zenith; he had fixed the "intuition of the instant," the suddenly extinguished splendor of the moment, in painting after painting; having entered the flux of nature with all the strength of his body and spirit, he understood that this flow was unstoppable and saw the supreme but short-lived beauty that is derived from living beings, things, and pleasures. But perhaps he also suffered melancholy and anguish from the recognition that this transience is accompanied by an obscure and hidden death, and that this death is already a part of those beings at the moment of their greatest splendor. The invention of the "series" seems to suggest the sadness of the ephemeral. Monet attempted to defeat transience with duration but, at the same time, he tried to give it new emphasis. With the instantaneousness of impressionism and the duration of his "series," and using the profundities of nature as his inspiration, Monet continued to paint, like Proust, the beauty and anguish of time.

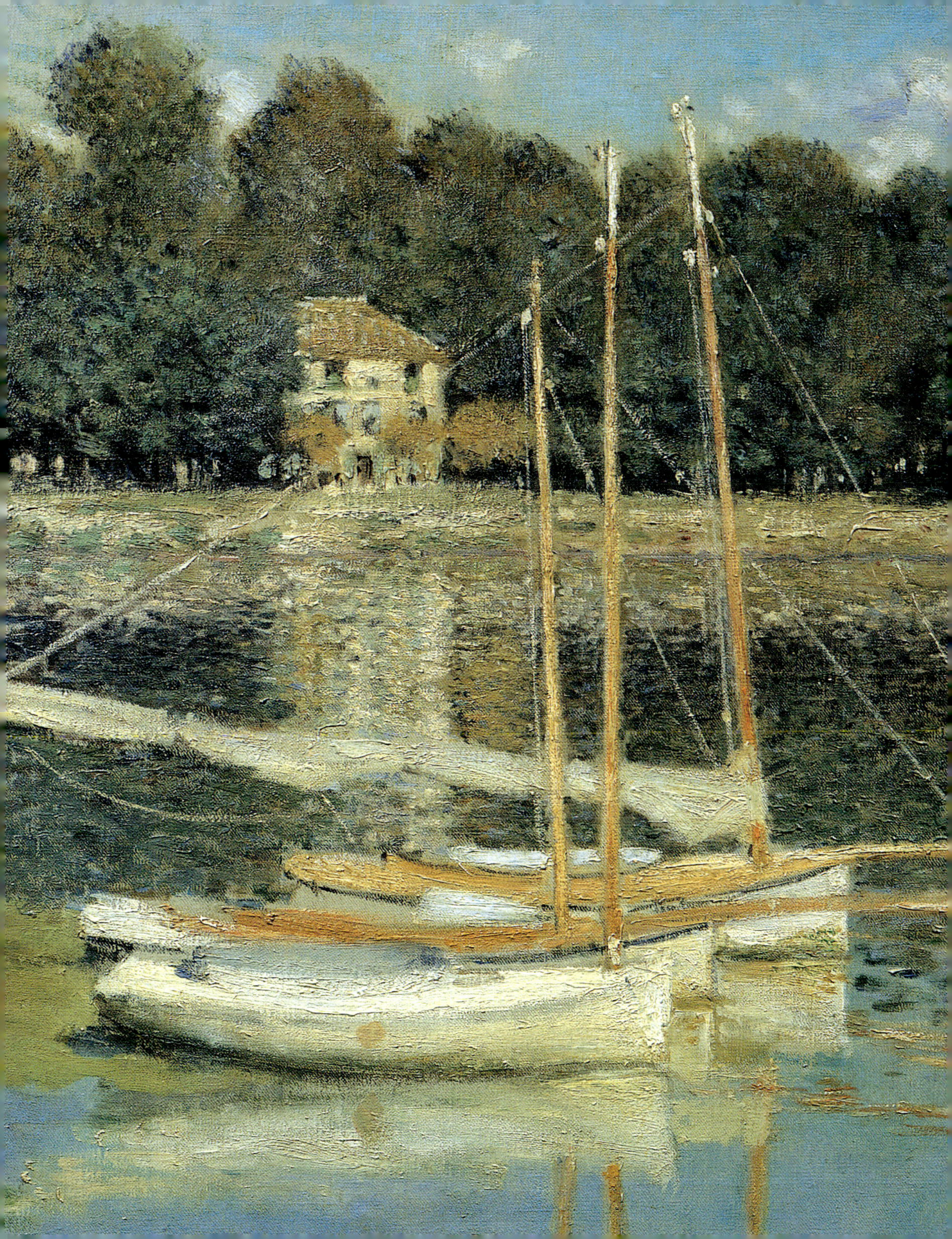

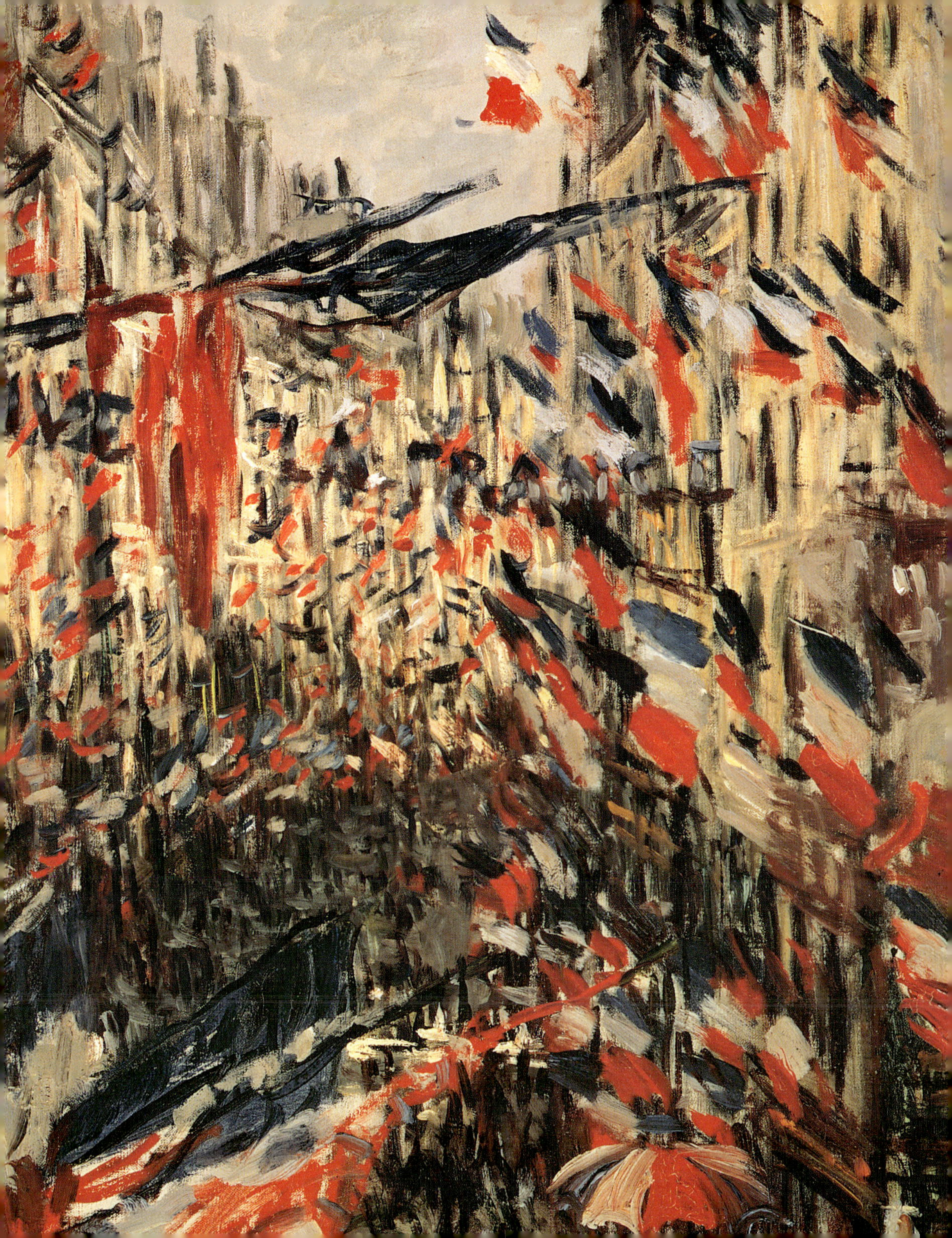

His Life and Art

Cézanne's comment "Claude Monet is nothing but an eye, but […] what an eye!" showed approval of his method of painting on the one hand and, on the other, awareness that the act of seeing—a miraculous process for all human beings—was for an artist the fundamental moment of cognition. For a reader with no knowledge of the history of art, this may seem a somewhat banal fact, however, the history of western art, which is filled with examples in which nature is taken as the starting point for an artistic creation, was never so closely tied to the process of vision as it was with impressionism. And more than any other impressionist artist, Monet made this human faculty the basis of an undertaking to which he applied himself unceasingly throughout his life. In the many written references and accounts he left, we find that he was almost always involved in research and experimentation. Yet, though it may seem obvious for a painter, Monet did not just search out places that inspired him, what he was looking for was a full understanding, through pictorial transcription, of what the process of vision suggested to him: in other words, he tried to decode reality. Initially attracted and then permanently swept away by the vocation of painter, he dedicated his entire existence to it without doubting, even during times of difficulty, the validity of his aims. He did, however, doubt the value of his paintings, with which he was never satisfied, but this continual starting over allowed him to believe that the possibilities offered by his palette were inexhaustible. He almost always painted natural scenery, constantly varying the infinite possibilities that the theme—altered by his chosen method of viewing it—offered. He only rarely allowed himself to depict the human figure, and when he did, he tackled it like an instance of reality, simply as one of the many aspects of the variety of nature. The many people with whom he surrounded himself over the years often belonged to his artistic sphere, however, there is no trace of enmity or rivalry

on page 22
The Rue Saint Denis.
Celebration of June 30, 1878
(detail), 1872
Rouen, Musée des Beaux-Arts

in his biography and this attitude of correctness in his human relationships resulted in long-lasting and solid friendships. Monet was offered support and help by his friends at times of need and these instances he never forgot, always claiming, even when his fame had amply rewarded him, that the harmony that had bound the group of impressionists together had been necessary to give life to his artistic studies and to nourish his creativity.

Claude Monet was born in Paris on November 14, 1840 to Adolphe Monet, the owner of a grocery store, and Louise-Justine Aubry. He spent his childhood in Le Havre where his family moved when he was five years old. Their house was near the sea in the suburb of Sainte-Adresse where Monet learned to explore the countryside and seaside, to which he was to remain intimately bound throughout his long artistic career. His first paintings were charcoal and pencil caricatures of the inhabitants of Le Havre that he made at age fifteen.

Monet's spiritual father was the painter Eugène Boudin, who introduced him to painting *en plein air* (outdoors) in 1856. At this time, Boudin, who was Monet's first painting master, was also the person who explained the artistic facts that the young man observed when he went to Paris to visit the Salon. The Salon was the exhibition put on by the École des Beaux-Arts as the official window on contemporary artistic thought. Of the many painters who exhibited there, the ones he preferred were named enthusiastically in the letter he sent to Boudin from the city on February 20, 1856: "You will not believe the interest you will find if you come to Paris. There is an exhibition of modern paintings that includes the works of the school of 1830 and which proves that we are not in such a decline as is said. There are eighteen splendid Delacroixs [...]. There are as many Decamps, a dozen Rousseaus, Duprés, there are also seven or eight Marilhats [...] and know that the only good painter of seascapes that we have, Jongkind,

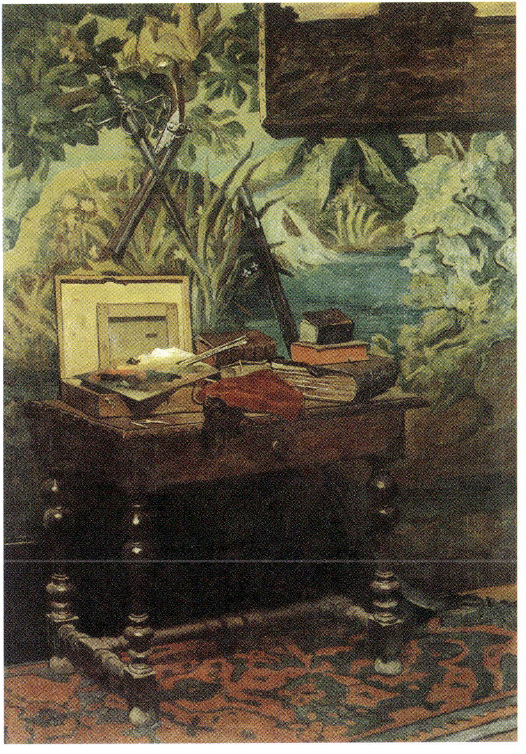

died for art; it is utterly crazy. [...] I forgot to tell you that Courbet and Corot also stand out in this exhibition, like Millet." In these few lines Monet showed himself to have been an up-to-date and thoughtful connoisseur of the painting of his time. The painters that he referred to as "of 1830" were those who, with the not so young Corot, worked *en plein air* in the forest of Fontainebleau to the south of Paris and who profoundly renewed French landscape painting. To Monet these painters of nature must have seemed prophetic, applying in their paintings teachings that were consistent with what he was learning from Boudin: that of painting outdoors, immersed in nature and experiencing its influence directly. The painters of the Barbizon school—Théodore Rousseau, Charles-François Daubigny, Jean-François Millet, Constant Troyon, Jules Dupré and Diaz de La Peña—had interpreted the natural landscape by implicitly exalting the mythical value of nature where the hand of man had not yet made its mark, and had

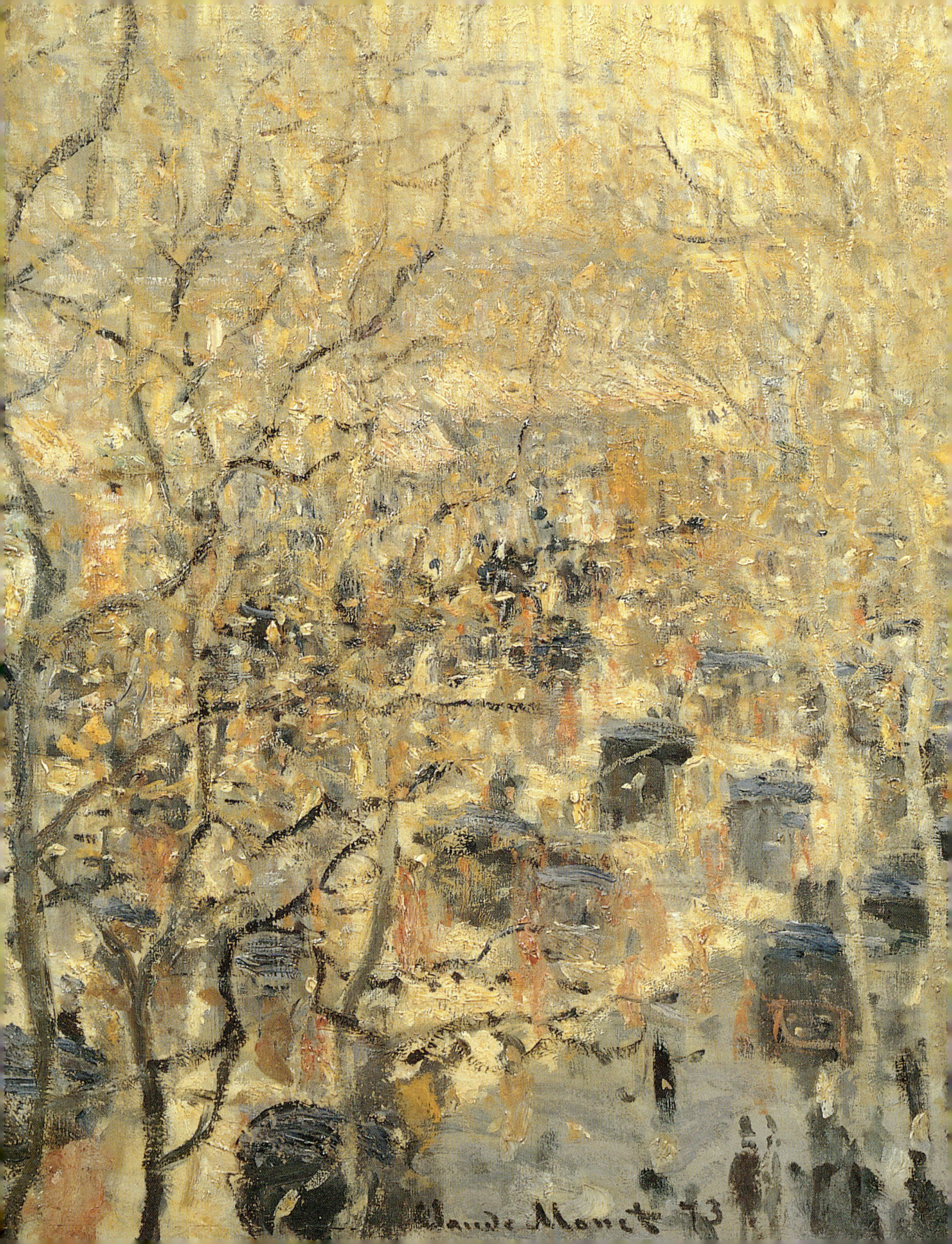

Claude Monet 73

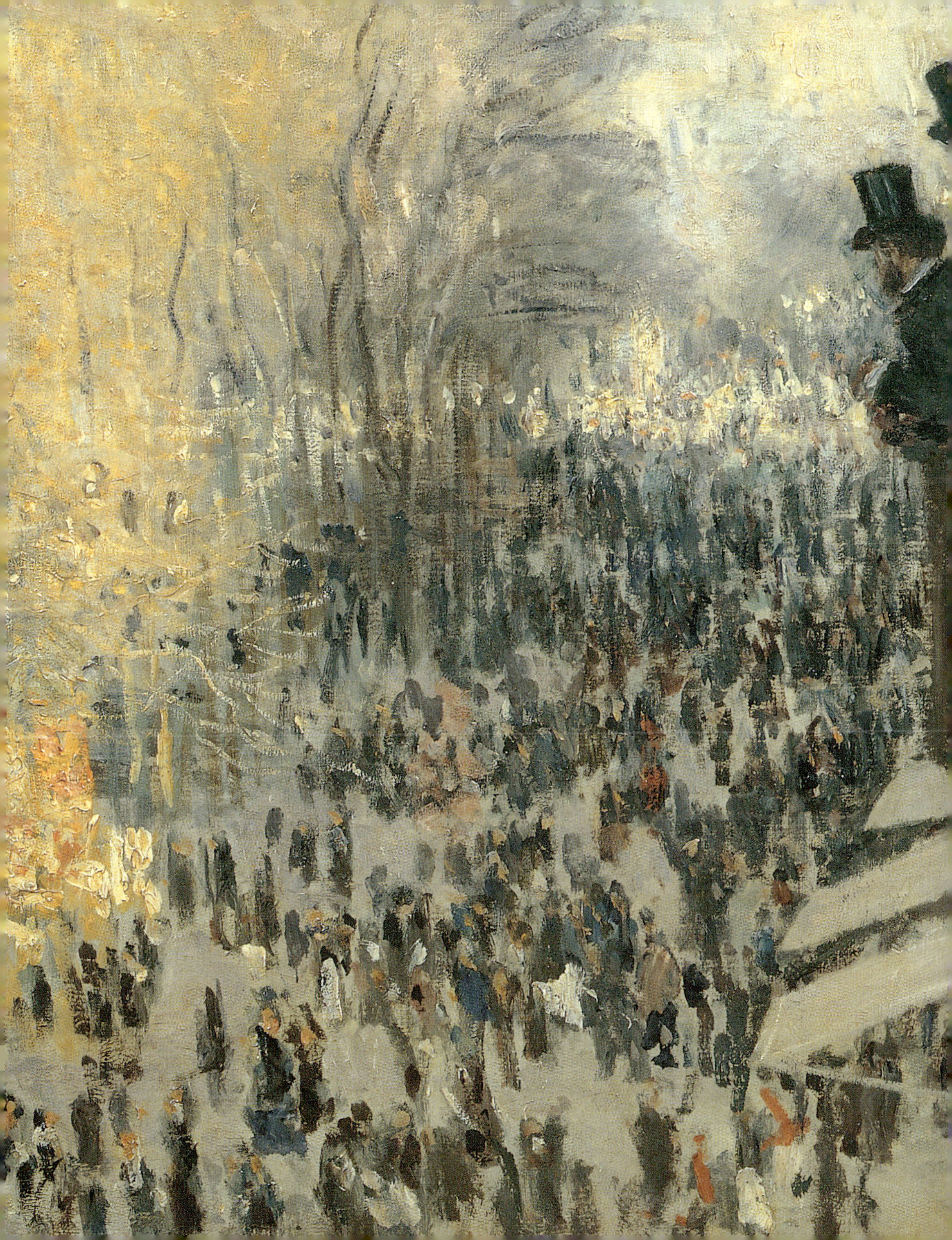

eschewed the conventional rhetoric of land-scape painting through the desire to represent nature directly. In other words they had not painted following the academic, conventional models of theme or composition but really immersed themselves in the country-side with their canvas, easel, and paints. They had substituted cultural subjects with simple sentiments that made a strong impression on Parisian society: the large woods and forests and the cultivated fields of the countryside appeared like the happy remnants of a terrestrial paradise where it was possible to take refuge from urban life.

The painter's early years were fundamental to the formation of a series of acquaintanceships that were to become long-lasting friendships and nourish both his art—through reciprocated encouragement and aid—and his personal life. In advanced age he was to show real attachment to his impressionist companions, who recognized Monet as being an authentic point of reference in the group. The artistic choices he made when young compared to the painting of his time acquired emotive and ideological values, and these were perpetuated when, having returned to Paris from Le Havre, he decided not to study at the École des Beaux-Arts but at a "free academy" with youngsters who shared his ideas. He frequented the private studios of artists, the "Libre académie Suisse" (where he met painters who had already become established, like Eugène Delacroix, Gustave Courbet, and the young Camille Pissarro); he also visited the Brasserie des Martyrs, which was the meeting place for the realist school headed by Courbet, and where Monet met Charles Baudelaire and Edmond Duranty. Duranty was later to become a great supporter of impressionism in the pages of the *Gazette des Beaux-Arts*. During this period Monet often returned to Le Havre to paint by the sea with Boudin and, one day, during one of the many days spent attempting to depict the effect of the water on canvas, by chance he met Johann-Barthold Jongkind, a marine painter of

Dutch origin who could teach Monet about the great masters of seventeenth-century Dutch painting.

With several paintings he had produced during the summer, the young artist was accepted at the Salon where he received discreet recognition from the critic Mantz for two marine paintings. Mantz described him as a young painter worthy of praise as he was able to catch the attention of the observer with his bold manner of seeing things. The critic hoped that Monet would dedicate himself to studies that would allow him to reach that degree of subtlety only achieved through a long apprenticeship.

On his return to Paris, for a short while Monet used to visit the studio of Charles Gleyre where he met the young Auguste Renoir, Frédéric Bazille, and Alfred Sisley, with whom he went painting in the forest of Fontainebleau. In spite of his continual escapes from the city, he remained attentive to what was happening in the principal art scene and, probably prompted by Édouard Manet's complex painting *Le Déjeuner sur l'Herbe* (Luncheon on the Grass), which he had seen in the Salon des Refusés in 1863, he decided to paint a work on the same subject. Manet's version, which today seems to us refined and cultivated, was received with mockery by a public scandalized that a nude woman was sitting in the middle of a garden chatting with two fully dressed men. Monet's version of *Luncheon on the Grass* took Manet's picture as a starting point but he altered its intention and in some way criticized its intellectualism. The unfinished canvas was begun at Chailly, for which his wife Camille posed with the painter Bazille and perhaps also Courbet. It was a very ambitious project because it was supposed to be of enormous size (10 x 20 feet). Stylistically it was close to the work of Courbet in its manner of depicting the natural context in great detail while injecting a note of caricature in the faces of the figures, in the way that resem-

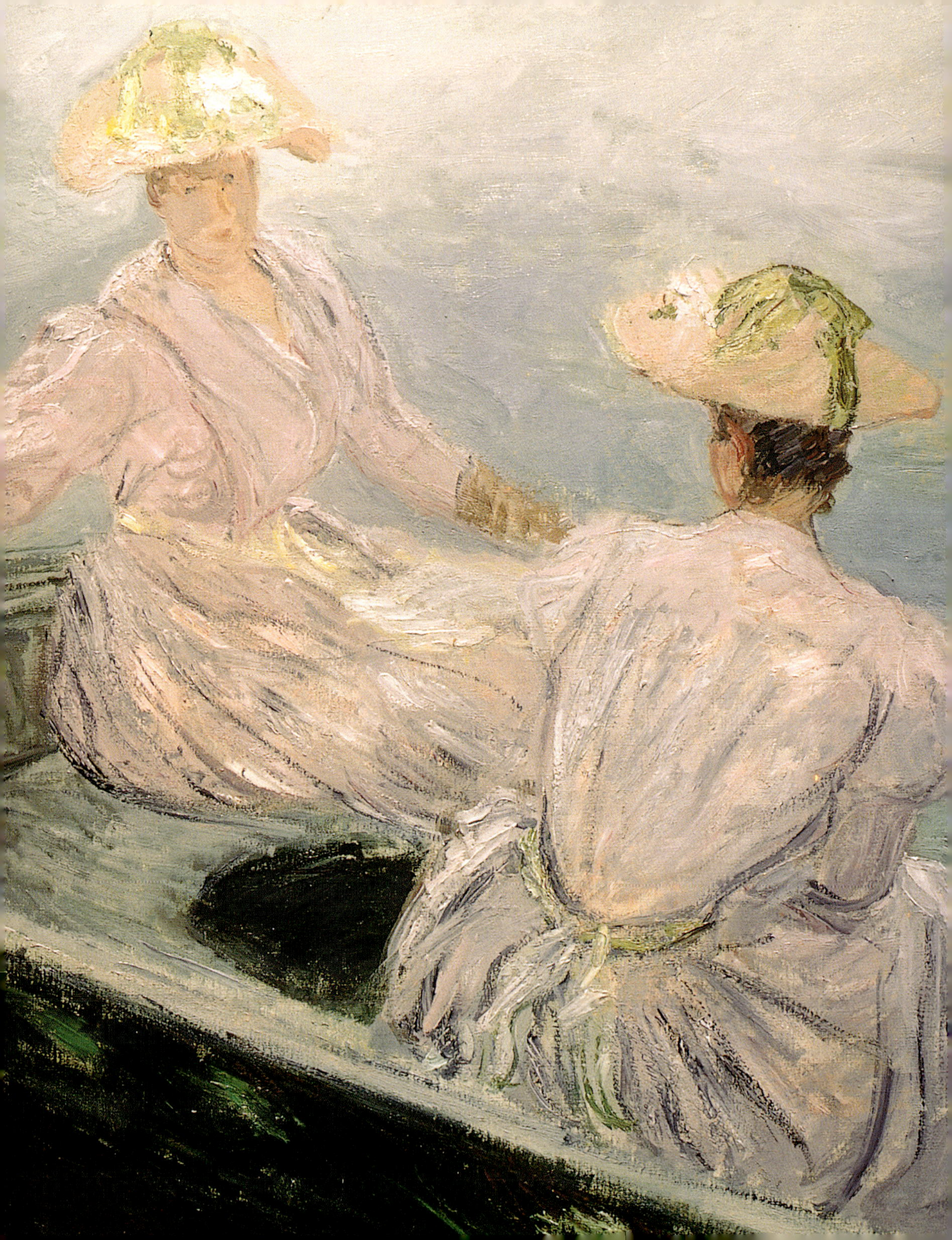

bled the dissatisfaction with bourgeois idleness that Courbet conveyed in *Young Ladies on the Banks of the Seine*. An instance of this important moment in Monet's development was *Women in the Garden* of 1867, a painting of which it seems pertinent to mention the genesis. Monet was at Ville d'Avray when he prepared to begin the work with Camille as the only model. To be able to paint a canvas of such a size he thought he would have to dig a trench in the ground in which he could stand the painting.

Of the various influences on his painting during this happy phase in the 1860s, one was Japanese woodblock painting that affected many painters in Paris. In 1866 Monet painted *Jeanne-Marguerite Lecadre in the Garden at Sainte-Adresse*, today in the Metropolitan Museum in New York, which Monet defined as "a Chinese painting with flags." It can be compared to a Japanese print by the painter Hokusai of which Monet had a copy. He learned from the Japanese to be more daring in the use of foreshortening and views from above, something he often employed to magnify the emotional effect of nature. Théodore Duret later said that "It was necessary for us to see Japanese albums for someone to dare [...] to put together on a canvas a brilliant red roof, a white wall, a green poplar, a yellow road and blue water, before it would have been impossible. Painters were always lying. They were blinded by nature and its violent colors; the only colors on their canvases were delicate and immersed in a series of mellow shades."

The spread of the orientalist style had a strong effect on Parisian taste and received its greatest recognition at the Exposition Universelle of 1867 at which numerous graphical works by contemporary Japanese artists were exhibited. The phenomenon was also reflected in the works of writers: Baudelaire mentioned the diffusion of oriental prints amongst collectors, and the brothers Jules and Edmond de Goncourt (who owned approximately 1,500 Japanese objects) dedicated an entire chapter of the novel *Manette Salomon* to the impression made on the hero of the book by Japanese art. In 1862 the Desoye, a married couple who had lived in the East, opened a shop in Rue de Rivoli called La Porte Chinoise that was visited by intellectuals who loved to collect exotics objects. Monet—who later confirmed he had bought his first Japanese prints in a shop in Le Havre as early as 1857—certainly purchased prints of this type during his trip to Holland in 1871–1872.

In 1870 Claude married Camille and together they moved to Trouville on the Normandy coast where he painted the *Hotel des Roches Noires à Trouville* in which he made use of the same foreshortening seen in the *Garden at Saint-Adresse*. Affected by the Franco-Prussian war, the couple took refuge that same year in London where Monet met up once more with Daubigny (who had been there since 1868) and Pissarro. He also met the Parisian art dealer Paul Durand-Ruel who had opened a gallery in New Bond Street in London due to the political problems in France. On Monet's return to France the following year, he stopped off in Holland where he bought some Japanese prints in Amsterdam. Unfortunately, his return to his homeland was greeted with upsetting news: he learned of the death in combat of his friend Bazille and the imprisonment of Courbet. He therefore decided to retire to Argenteuil where he experienced one of the most creative periods of his painting career. In 1874 Renoir, Sisley, Caillebotte, and Monet painted together, stimulating one another in their search for their individual styles. Monet seems to have found his natural vocation by abandoning himself to the painting of the sky and water, the vibrations and movement of the atmosphere, and the effects and reflections produced by light. He devoted a series of canvases to Argenteuil where he investigated the effects of light in relation to the changing position of his *bateau-atelier* (boat-studio) which, following the example of Daubigny, he had had made so that he might be properly immersed in the natural world and therefore find viewpoints that would otherwise be impossible. Comparison of two paintings of the boat races at Argenteuil, painted respectively in 1872 and 1874, shows that Monet produced two very different results from the same scene (and therefore from the same vision): one is very busy, with a use of strong colors applied with broad horizontal brushstrokes; the other is diaphanous and based on a harmony of whites, grays, and light blues in which the touches of the brush suggest the movement of the wind and the slight rippling of the water by the breeze.

The painting *Impression, Sunrise* (1872, Le Havre) was charged with the same emotional temperament. The painting appeared at the first exhibition of the group Société Anonyme des Peintres, Sculpteurs et Graveurs, etc. that opened in the studio of the photographer Nadar on the Boulevard des Capucines on April 25, 1874. The idea of organizing an exhibition independent of the Salon had been put forward by Monet back in 1867, but due to a lack of funds it was put off year after year until a group of thirty artists was finally formed on January 17, 1874. Among those who exhibited were Boudin, Cézanne, Pissarro, Berthe Morisot, Renoir, and Sisley. The reactions of the critics were immediate and harsh, and labeled the group of painters "impressionists" in the sense that they were amateurs incapable of using a brush. The term was used by the critic Louis Leroy in a review of the exhibition in *Le Charivari*. In it Leroy invented a dialogue between two visitors to the exhibition, one an art critic, the other a pupil of a famous master at the École des Beaux-Arts. Both visitors are already stunned by the paintings they have seen when they find themselves in front of *Impression, Sunrise* by Monet and exclaim: "Ah, look at that, look at that! What does this canvas represent? Look in the catalogue." "*Impression, Sunrise.*" "*Impression,* of that I was sure. There must an impression somewhere in there. What freedom, what ease of workmanship! A preliminary drawing for a wallpaper pattern is more highly finished than this seascape! [...]." Then the painter, as though possessed by the absurdity of the canvases exhibited, begins to show signs of madness and becomes agitated; he performs a crazy dance before the municipal guard, whom he then looks in the face and exclaims, "Goodness, how ugly he is! [...], from the front he has two eyes, a nose and a mouth. Impressionists wouldn't have thus sacrificed to detail. With what the painter has expended in the way of useless things, Monet would have done twenty municipal guards."

The first impressionist exhibition was followed by seven others during the period between 1874 and 1886. At the last show, held at 1, Rue Laffitte, in addition to the impressionists, Seurat and Signac also exhibited for the first time.

Due to the lack of success the group met with at the first exhibition, it broke up for a while and Monet decided to withdraw once more to Argenteuil where every so often he would welcome his painter friends. There are some very interesting pictures from this period which demonstrate that they were painting the same subject together: while Manet was working on *The Monet Family in Their Garden at Argenteuil* in which Claude also appears, Renoir was portraying the same scene but only of Madame Monet and their little boy Jean. The same private, family setting is the context in Monet's *The Luncheon* in which he reworked the theme he had painted some years earlier in the painting of the same name. In the later version he showed he had moved on from Courbet's realism, whereas in the first version (1865) he had depicted everything with great attention to detail and given the figures particular emphasis: in other words, he had portrayed a bourgeois group of people engaged in friendly conversation at a luncheon in the countryside. In his more mature version, the most important aspect of the same scene is a still life in the foreground

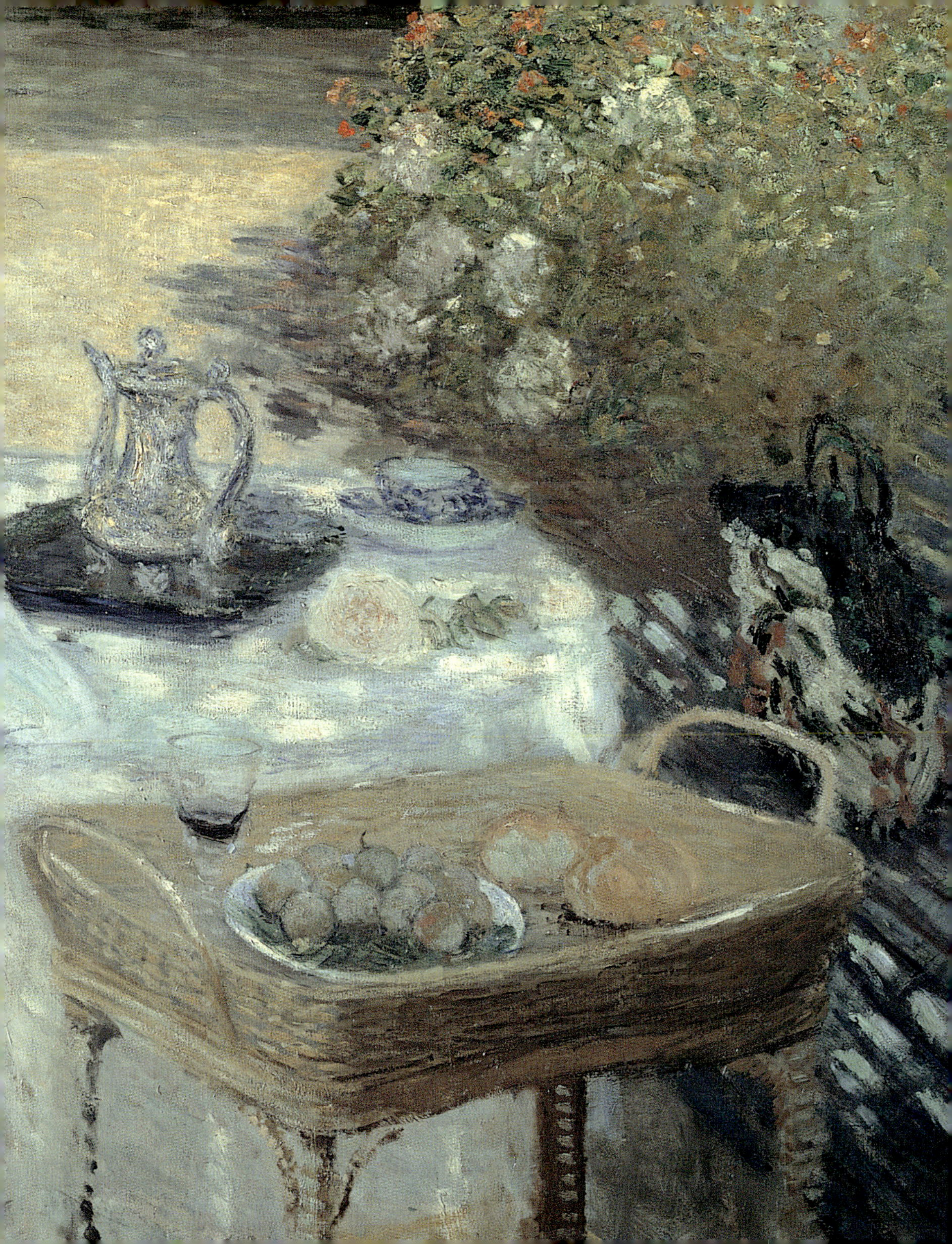

composed of a wicker trolley and the set table. His method of applying oil paint had also changed: the brushwork was denser and heavier in the lighter zones while it became dramatically longer in the detail of the bench in the foreground on the right, which provides the point from which the perspective view carries the eye toward the luminous center of the painting. Stylistically the painting is similar to Renoir, with whom he seemed to be in perfect harmony during this phase at Argenteuil. Monet experimented with a frothy and joyous rendition of nature and made use of long, threadlike brushstrokes that simulate the soft pastel effect that was so dear to his colleague. Renoir, on the other hand, for a while abandoned his figurative painting to try landscapes.

Monet's years in Argenteuil were difficult ones for two reasons: severe financial problems that did not allow him to look after his family properly, and the illness of his wife Camille, which at this time became serious. In the correspondence that has survived from this period, many letters to his friends contain passages of deep worry in which Monet confides his frustration at his inability to provide for his loved ones through his work as a painter. What is most surprising is that in spite of these difficulties, he never questioned the value of his work. Aware of its artistic value though never personally presumptuous or proud, he restricted himself to stating sadly that the public was not yet ready for his painting. On June 28, 1875 he wrote to Manet: "Though I have faith in the future, the present is truly difficult to deal with." In 1877, when he was obliged to leave Argenteuil, he wrote to his doctor friend De Bellio, "Once again I have been struck by misfortune; as if having no money were not bad enough, my wife is ill again." Before leaving Argenteuil Monet had formed a close friendship with the painter and collector Gustave Caillebotte and his dealer Ernest Hoschedé who both helped him and provided moral support during the worst moments. Both also became his sincere admirers and clients. Ernest Hoschedé, for example, commissioned Monet to decorate his castle in Rothenburg in Montgeron, following which their respective families became close friends. Unfortunately, financial difficulties also hit the Hoschedés with the result that, having been legally forced to sell their property, they decided to move into a single house in Vétheuil with the Monets where, by combining their forces, the two families could more easily deal with their financial problems.

Throughout the 1870s Monet returned often to Paris to portray the city. He was particularly enamored of the large boulevards, public gardens, and railway stations, which he treated in his paintings like great monuments to modernity. His choice of subjects fell once again on painting outdoors, so that his paintings describe and document the face of the city transformed by industrial progress and the city development plans of Baron Georges-Eugène Haussmann in the city fabric that demolished, reorganized, and reconstructed the center of Paris. Like the other intellectuals of his era, Monet interpreted this metamorphosis as the sign of impending modernity and proposed to illustrate it using a form of painting that had qualities of mobility and transitoriness, together with a fluid and changing perspective. The paintings *Rue Montorgueil* and the views of the Boulevard des Capucines are a clear example of the Paris of the era described by Zola in *La Bête Humaine* and later by Proust in his *In Search of Lost Time*. One of Monet's last pictorial experiences in the city was the series of views of *The Saint-Lazare Station* at the end of the 1870s. He wrote to his friend Renoir of his decision to paint the station with the words, "When the trains pull out, the smoke of the locomotives is so dense that you can hardly see anything. It is like magic, a real phantasmagoria." He painted the station from different viewpoints and at different times of

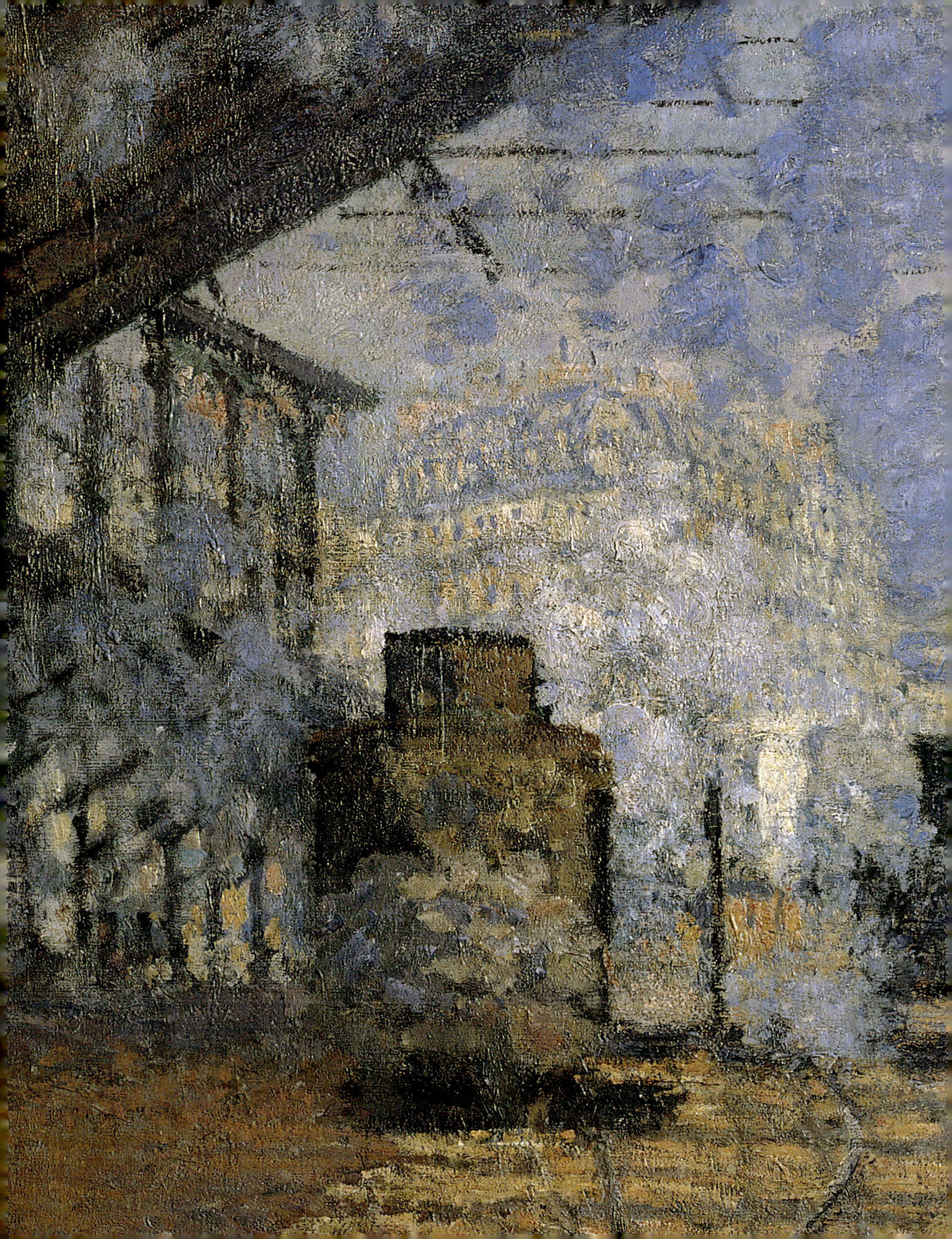

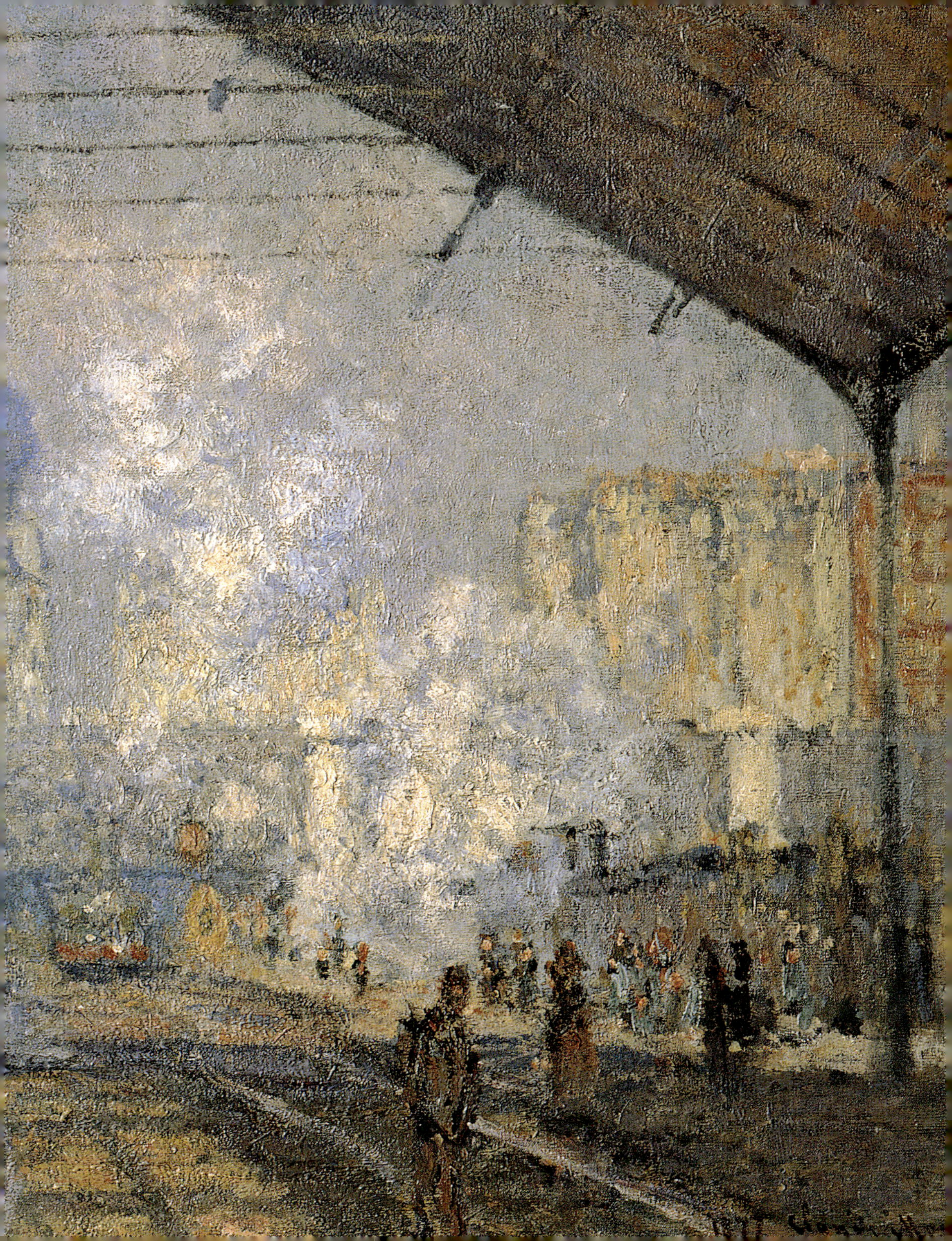

the day, so producing his first series, all variants of a single theme. The views he chose were unusual and undoubtedly influenced by the possibilities that photography suggested in those years. His paintings seems as though an immense eye is looking out at the vast sloping iron roof from the interior of the station, but which, because the eye is too open, is unable to focus properly with the result that all that is visible is a cloud of steam swirling upwards and outwards. Baudelaire too sang the praises of Paris deformed by the fantastic power of the imagination: "Babel of endless stairs, arcades, / It was a palace multifold / Replete with pools and bright cascades / Falling in dull or burnished gold; / And the more weighty waterfalls / Like crystal screens resplendent there / Along the metal rampart walls / Seemed to suspend themselves in air."

The experience of painting a subject in which the forms almost completely dissolve was to be retried with even more extreme results in the cycle of the *Haystacks*, the views

of *Rouen Cathedral*, and the huge undertaking that occupied Monet's last thirty years of life: the *Water Lilies*. The *Saint-Lazare* series was a first step on this path which reveals the value of Monet's continuous experimentation: though the subjects were apparently monotonously repetitive, the main aim was to test out the possibilities of pictorial vocabulary. When looking at the *Saint-Lazare* paintings Émile Zola wrote in 1877, "Our painters of today have been obliged to discover the poetry of railway stations in the same way that their predecessors discovered that of the woods and rivieras." What Zola appreciated most in Monet was his total adhesion to the contemporary world, which was in harmony with the ideas of the realist current that had considered mythological and historical painting irrelevant—in this context, the term "historical painting" meant subjects from past history which, according to the realists, were painted by pompous masters imagining things they had never seen. In this sense Monet remained faithful to one of his friends and masters from his youth—Courbet—even if the older master was interested only in the themes and did not have the ideological commitment.

Regardless of Zola's praise, Monet's financial position certainly did not improve and in his correspondence of March 30, 1878, we read, "My wife has just had another child and I am worried because I am unable to cover the expenses for the medical cures that both of them require." Friends once more came to Monet's aid but Camille's conditions did not improve. Monet abandoned the brilliant colors that he had been using in previous years and took up instead the refined but sad painting of the Vétheuil period, the place on the banks of the Seine where he had moved in 1878. Here he painted the winter landscapes of the Seine that were infused with the sorrow he felt following the death of his wife and the disappointment caused by the break-up of the impressionist group. Winter 1879–1880 was extremely cold and the desolate, haughty landscapes became

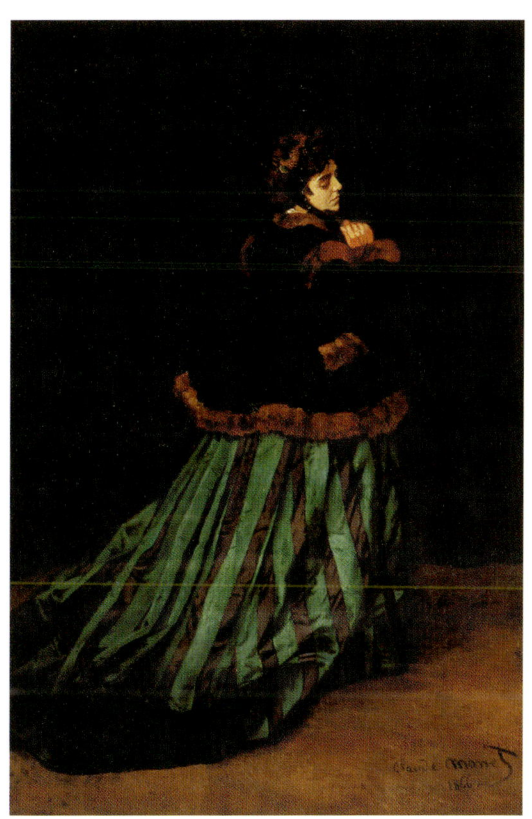

his favored subject, as though the artist's private afflictions had materialized in the surrounding countryside. Camille died in 1879 at the age of just thirty-two. She had been his companion since their youth and her loss represented the end of a phase of his life. From a personal point of view, he had already begun to feel a special affection for Alice Hoschedé, perhaps even during Camille's illness. Moreover, after Camille's death, Ernest Hoschedé was often in Paris on business, which further allowed his wife Alice to become close to Monet. The Vétheuil period was important to Monet for more than one reason but in particular because Monet isolated himself from the group of impressionists and set about developing his art alone. From this moment, landscape painting dominated his art, and figures, when they appeared, were treated as no more than "objects," the equal of a tree, bush or stream. This cognitive value, as opposed to the value of reality, entailed a subjectivism that the impressionists did

not fail to claim responsibility for. Vincent van Gogh, for example, confided to his brother Theo that he saw the colors that he would paint on the canvas, therefore, even if his vision was different from that of others, it was still legitimate. The explanation Van Gogh used to justify his painting was the same one used by Monet though the latter certainly did not suffer from schizophrenia. The landscape aroused feelings in him and the representation of it that resulted was the outcome of this interior process. Writers adopted the same mechanism: Marcel Proust was a master in allowing the thread of the novel to stray between the interior and exterior, memory and reality, evocation and reason. There was no longer the possibility of being objective, as the naturalists had supposed was possible, and in French culture the ego came to represent the division between the internal and external worlds and received attention. In some way this consideration might also explain the enormous stylistic

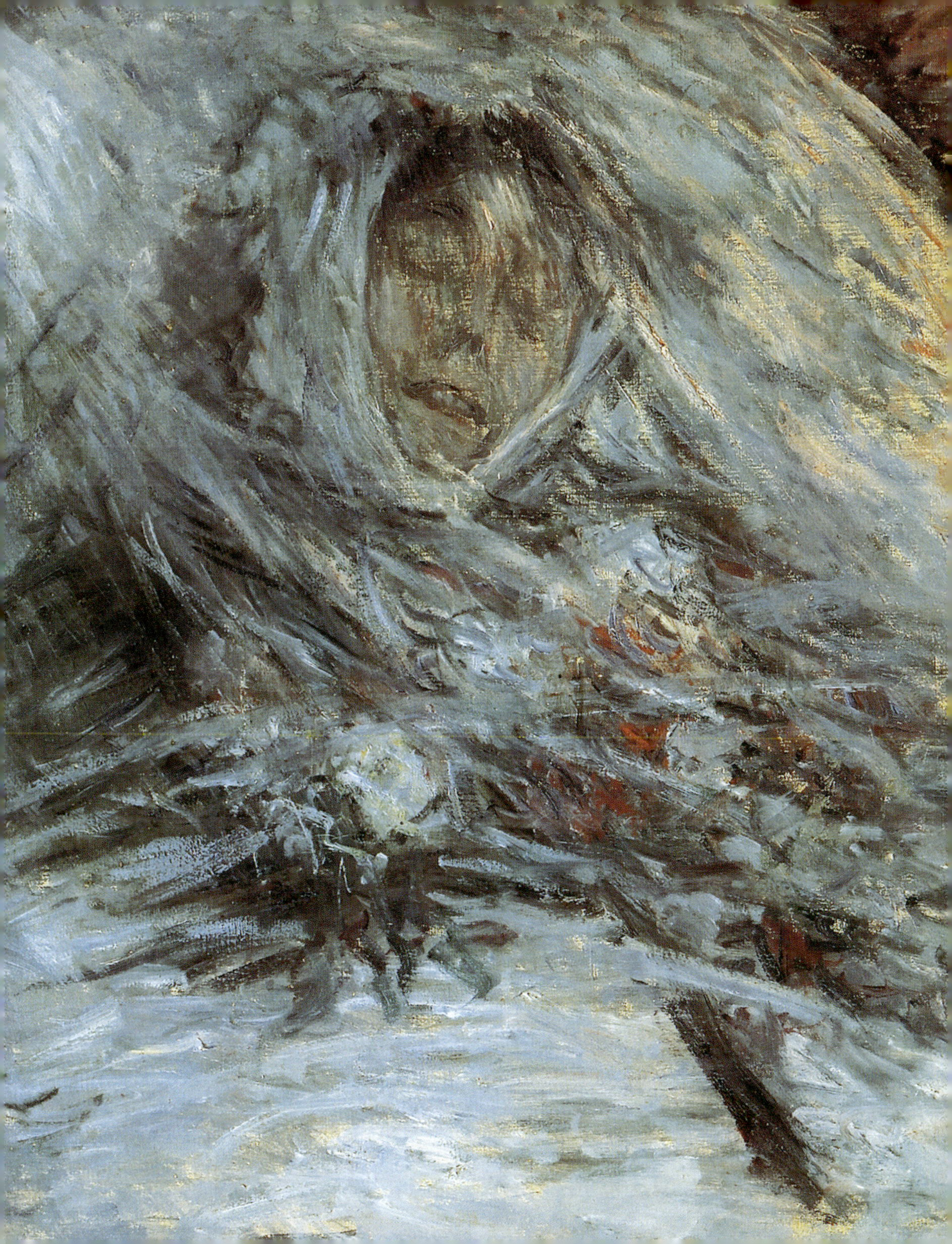

differences that existed between the impressionists who, though sharing an approach, produced very different results; consider, for example, Manet's work compared to that of Cézanne or Gauguin.

Proust was dazzled by Monet's winter landscapes: "Everything is glittering […] this thaw is like a mirage: it isn't possible to tell the difference between the ice and the sunlight; all these floating fragments break into the clamor of the sky, sweeping it away; the splendor of the trees is such that you wouldn't know if it comes from the autumnal red or some essence inherent in their species; in the end you no longer know what you are looking at, whether the bed of a river or a clearing in a forest."

The time that Monet spent alone in Vétheuil was fundamental to successive developments. Vétheuil represented a stage between Argenteuil and Giverny, the country village near Paris where he settled in 1883 and where he found the ideal place to nourish his artist's imagination. Monet

wrote that Giverny was a splendid place and that it would not be possible to find a house and countryside so beautiful elsewhere.

Monet settled down in Giverny with Alice Hoschedé (who had by then become his partner) and their respective children. In December Monet left on a trip with Renoir to explore the Mediterranean coast of France but, stimulated by the extraordinary colors they saw, the two friends continued as far as Genoa. In January of the following year Monet decided to return to the coast to spend time in the Italian town of Bordighera.

He wrote to his friend and gallery-owner Durand-Ruel about this plan from Giverny: "I want to spend a month at Bordighera, one of the loveliest places I saw on our trip. From there I hope to bring you a series of new things. So I ask you please not to talk to anyone about this, not because I wish to make a mystery of it, but because I am set on doing it alone: in the same way that it was enjoyable to do the trip as a tourist with Renoir, I would find it embarrassing to do it for work purposes with another: I have always worked better in solitude and following my own impressions." In Bordighera Monet was caught up once again with enthusiasm, something he had lost during the period of his difficulties. He sent many letters to Alice in which his astonishment at the colors of the Italian coast is evident. He attempted to paint the landscape, but the thick vegetation was unusual for him and difficult to reproduce, as were the colors of the sea and sky, which he called "impossible." In a letter to Alice he wrote, "I work like a madman on six canvases a day. I am finding it heavy going because I am still unable to catch the tone of the village; at times I am frightened by the colors that I have to use and I am scared of doing badly [...]; the light is atrocious. I already have studies that took six sittings, but everything is so new to me that I am unable to finish." It is interesting to note

these thoughts on the judgment that his work might have brought once he returned to France. He imagined that his paintings might have been accused of a lack of verisimilitude by those who had never seen Italy or, he added, were unable to look at paintings. As far as Monet was concerned, the public's excessive interest in over-polished, refined painting was something he could never agree with.

This period of Monet's painting was characterized by continual enthusiasm, which is manifest in his canvases of nature and his diligence, which led him to produce a great number of works. Referring once again to his letters, we learn how much strength Monet derived from his work and how many different lines of experimentation he already had in mind in those early years. "Every day I find more beautiful motifs. I want to do everything so much that it would drive me crazy—my head is exploding." Monet's visual voracity and the perseverance with which he studied the same view or item in nature was recorded by Guy de Maupassant in his *Vie d'un paysagiste*: "I often followed Claude Monet in search of impressions. He was no longer a painter but a hunter. He walked followed by several children who carried his canvases [...]. He took [the canvases] or left them, following every change in the sky, he waited, watching the sun and the shadows, captured with a few brushstrokes the perpendicular rays or a wandering cloud and, when he had dealt with every delay, he transferred them rapidly onto the canvas. In this way I saw him catch a dazzling cascade of light on the white rocks and fix it with a flood of yellows that reproduced in a strange manner the surprising and fleeting effect of that elusive, blinding reflection. On another occasion he grabbed a storm out at sea and threw it down on the canvas. It was really the rain that he painted, nothing else than the rain penetrating the waves, rocks, and sky, which were hardly identifiable beneath the downpour." Maupassant wrote these words at Étretat in September 1886. Both he and Monet took holidays in this village on the Normandy coast. Following in the footsteps of Courbet, Monet set out to depict the cliffs there that rise directly out of the waves. In confluence with the landscape, the colors are dark or bright depending on the weather. At Belle-Île Monet met the famous journalist Gustave Geffroy—who in the years to followwould become Monet's great admirer—whom he asked to visit his house in Giverny. Geffroy's detailed description of the house tells us that the walls were completely covered with paintings by Corot, Jongkind, Pissarro, Manet, Degas, Renoir, and Cézanne, sketches by Boudin and Fantin-Latour, watercolors by Delacroix and Signac, and that there were two bronzes by Rodin. This refined collection is now mostly housed in the Musée Marmottan Monet in Paris where the artist's private collection of Japanese prints and the caricatures he had drawn during his apprenticeship in Le Havre are also held.

The Japanese prints were almost all bought during Monet's various journeys to Holland, and in Giverny he used to line the walls of the dining room with the panels. Besides bearing witness to Monet's appreciation of japonisme, which had spread rapidly through Paris, his collection of prints indicates an interest in the arrangement of space by such artists as Ogata Korin, Horunobu, Hokusai, and Hiroshige, which contrasted with that seen in the West. However, the interest in this composition style was common to many painters at that time; among the various paintings on this subject that might be mentioned, most significant for Monet was the almost philological interpretation of James Abbott McNeil Whistler in his landscape *Variation in Violet and Green*, today in the Musée d'Orsay in Paris.

The second half of the 1880s was of fundamental importance to the sale of Monet's works. He began to exhibit them in the gallery belonging to Georges Petit who, with Durand-Ruel, represented his commer-

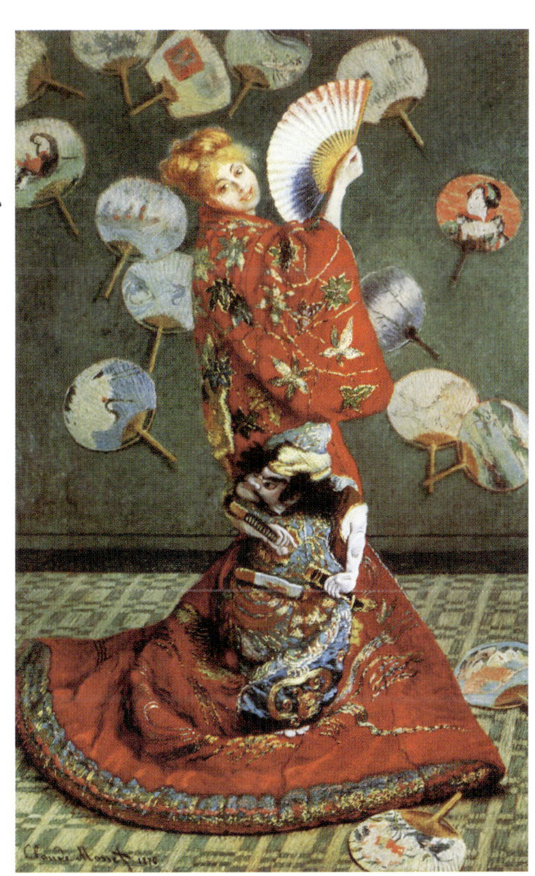

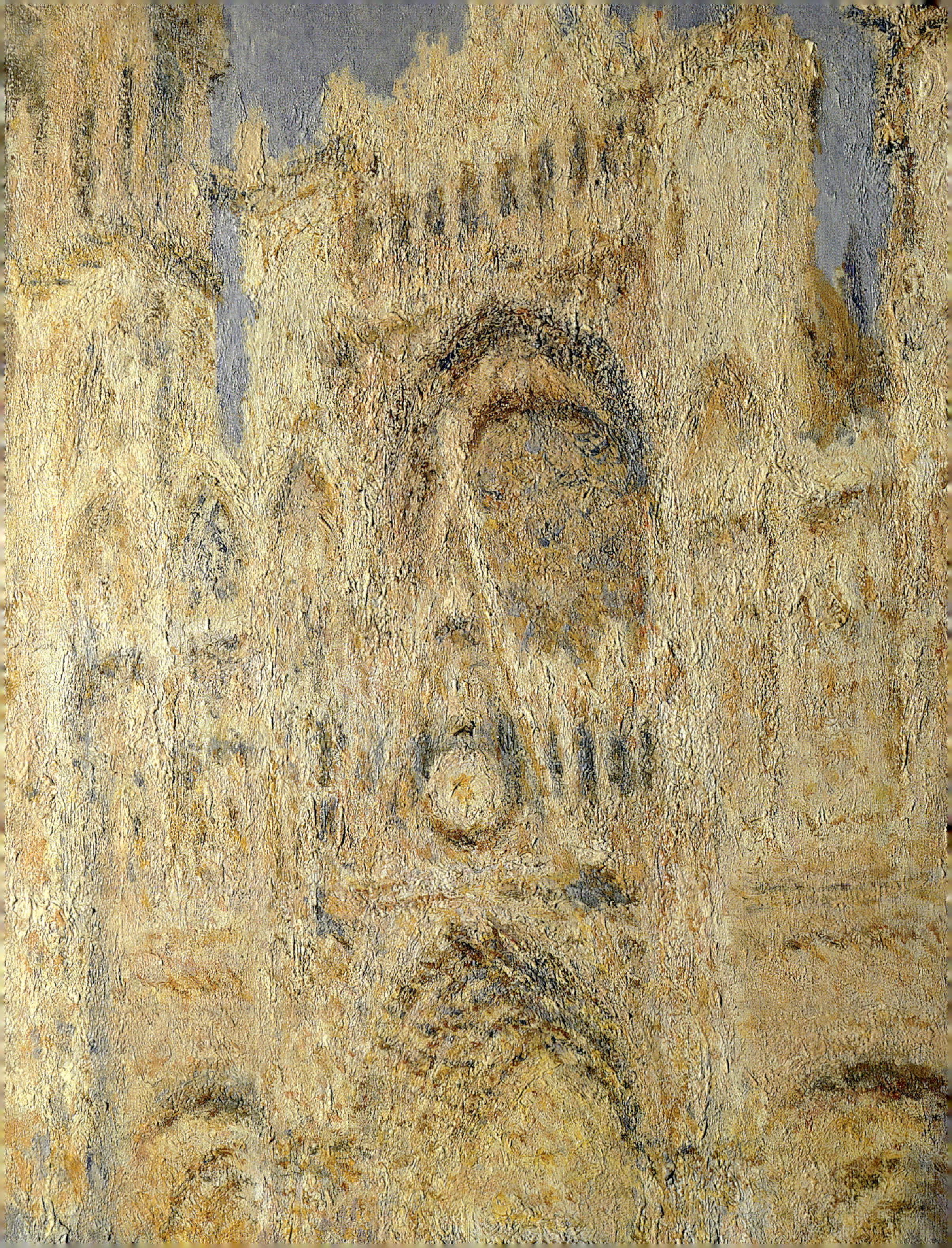

cial outlet. Moreover, Durand-Ruel expanded his business in the United States and found excellent contacts for Monet with the result that on the financial front things seemed to smooth out for the painter. In fact, by the end of the decade, Monet was in a position to buy the house at Giverny and begin work on building the lily-pond that he was later to paint over and over again.

The two pictorial cycles that led up to the poetry of the *Water Lilies* were those of the *Haystacks* and *Rouen Cathedral*. As a prelude to these studies of light were the two well-known full-length paintings of Suzanne Hoschedé (Alice's daughter) in a field holding a parasol. The titles of the two paintings, commonly known as *Woman with Umbrella Turned toward the Left* and *Study of a Figure Outdoors (Facing Right)* clearly indicates the direction the artist was taking and determined the development of the evocative, emotional and therefore symbolist values of his painting.

The paintings of his mature period surprised some of his admirers. The poet Stéphane Mallarmé wrote to Monet that the sight of his *Haystacks* had affected him so much that he had been induced to look at the countryside through the "prisms" of Monet's paintings. The transition from a realistic observation of reality to a perception that lay outside of the real influenced, during these years, a movement in french poetry begun by Baudelaire, continued by Verlaine and Rimbaud, and taken to its extreme consequences by Mallarmé. This process represented a gradual dematerialization of reality in poetry with the aim of disengaging it from the impositions placed upon it by realist vocabulary. According to the above poets, poetry should be more than the mere definition of the object placed before us: it should be capable of suggesting that object to us, and evoking it because, if it does not, our imagination will be disengaged. This refusal of the traditional poetic formulas was begun by Baudelaire and resulted in a broadening of the limits within which poetry operated. It also found correspondences between disciplines, not least the musical component of poetry, as investigated by Verlaine.

There was an analogous evolution in impressionist painting. The studies that had taken their cue from scientific conjectures based on modern optical theories developed into (not only by Monet, but also Cézanne and Van Gogh) a broadening of perceptive possibilities to the point that made possible the symphonies of color in the *Water Lilies* during the last twenty years of Monet's life. In addition, the peremptory introduction by decadentism of the binomial art knowledge, which led art to broaden its field of investigation, appears fundamental. For example, poetry and painting absorbed characteristics from music and were increasingly transformed into activities for initiates. Nor can we ignore the influence exerted on his contemporaries by Richard Wagner who, in his opera *The Ring of the Nibelung,* successfully engaged the arts in a higher reality in

the field of music: verse, sound, and dance—by dance I mean the action on stage—were supremely combined to evoke a lost ancient unity.

Sometime between February and April 1892 Monet began to paint the *Rouen Cathedral* series, which he was to work on until 1894. The cycle covered more than fifty paintings in which Monet systematically investigated the alteration in the colors depending on the time of day and the angle from which he viewed at the cathedral. The results of his studies are different despite having the same subject, demonstrating the mutability and relativity of the observer's vision: reality loses its consistency at different times, though all of them are equally valid. The technique Monet used to put the color on the canvas created a spongy effect which, when seen from close up, appears as though the paint was trickled onto the surface. From a short way away the volumes seem mixed together but, when viewed from a distance, they take on an extraordinary and vibrant

50

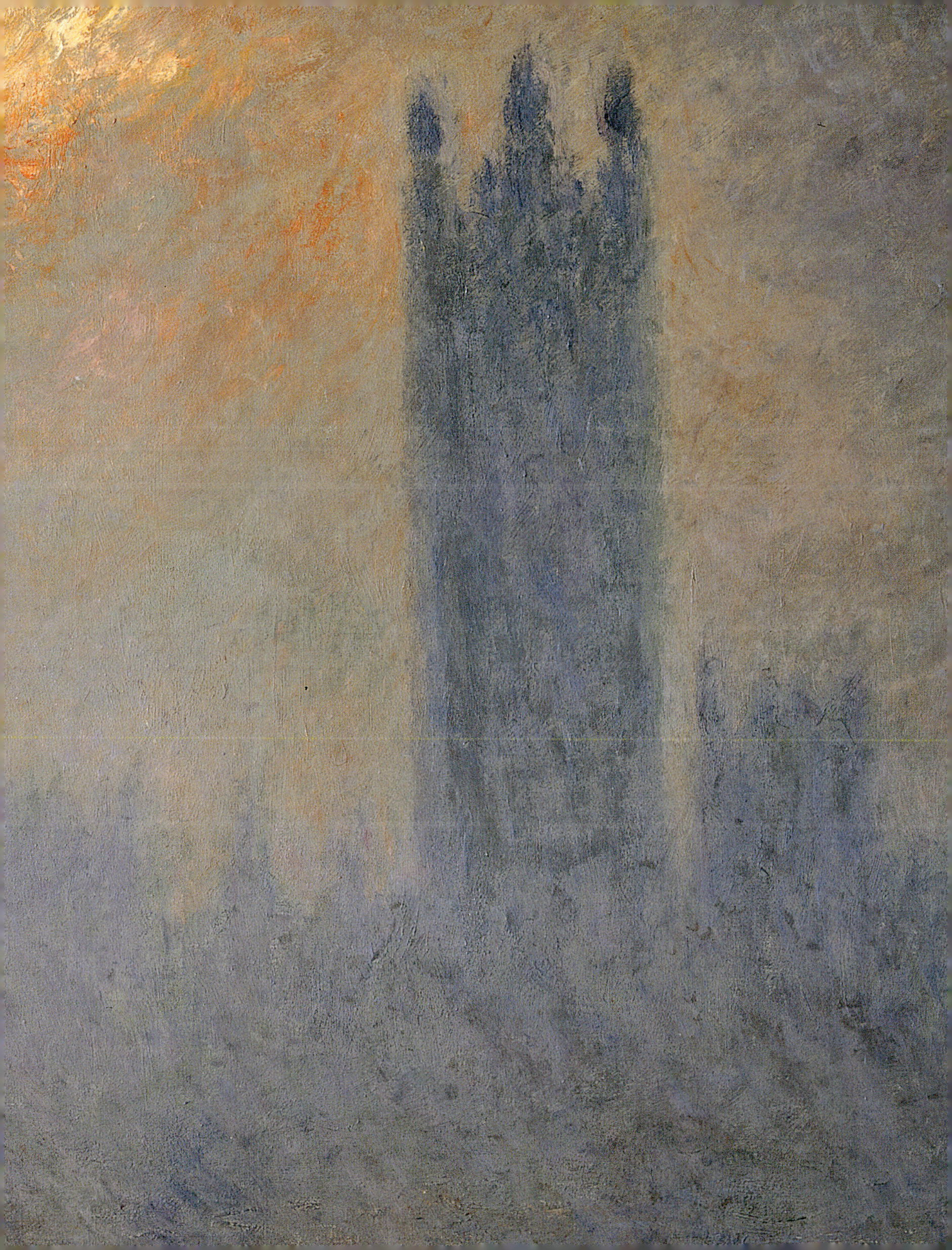

definition. However, what to us appears lyrically perfect in his series of cathedrals was for Monet a source of creative torment. His letters give the impression of an artist eager and anxious to see and represent what he considered far-off and elusive. "My stay here is going ahead: that does not mean that I am close to finishing my cathedrals. [...]. The more I see, the worse I succeed in rendering what I feel; and I tell myself that anyone who says he has finished a canvas is an arrogant so-and-so. [...] I work quickly but without making progress, searching and groping but without achieving very much though I am on the point of exhaustion." Once he had discovered the possibility of intellectually developing the actual signals received through his sense of vision it was impossible for him to turn back. He searched for special motifs, launched into impossible undertakings and performed miracles of technical ability. During the *Rouen Cathedral* cycle he made a leap beyond his time toward the informal and

built a bridge between impressionism and the future of art.

The series of views of London dates to a stay in England in 1901 in which Monet returned to representing the themes of a city but recoiled from illustrating a chaotic, teeming metropolis. He substituted Paris with a foggy London in which the haze was interpreted as silence and the metaphysical graveyard of modernity. His observation of London's cityscape seems affected by the melancholic style of Whistler, whose work was highly regarded by the impressionists for its delicate use of color and suffused atmospheres.

Monet no longer put off his desire to paint series and began on the *Water Lilies* in the 1890s, specifically in the garden he had laid out on his property in Giverny; here he had a pond dug specially to grow this particular species of aquatic plant. Many years later, in 1908, he wrote to his friend, the writer Gustave Geffroy, "These views of water and reflections have become an obsession." In the first versions of the *Water Lilies*, the impasto is similar to that in the versions of *Rouen Cathedral*, which had been painted only a short while before. The scenes are again conceived using the compositional framing of landscape painting: the viewpoint is very close and spatial construction reiterates the influence of the Japanese art of previous years. However, as time passed, Monet's vision became increasingly broader until it reproduced details of the lilies on a large scale, making the flowers themselves the subjects of the painting. Structured space was abolished and replaced by a symphony of forms and colors without the use of traditional expedients like perspective, planes that signify depth and chromatic variations to signify distances. The process was analogous for color: the first paintings of the *Water Lilies* were based on harmonizing different pigments with a dominant tone occasionally prevailing. In the late versions, Monet's use of color varied around a single tonality to almost give the impression of monochrome. When placed beside one another, we see that the variations in the many canvases are necessary for a full expression of the single theme. The magnified vision of the subject means that the result is close to abstraction. The phantasmagoria generated by the brushstrokes in *Blue Water Lilies* in the Musée d'Orsay creates a whirlwind of color so that the observer is no longer able to perceive the difference between the actual lilies and their reflections in the water due to the mingling of cobalt blues, the greens of the plant leaves, and the whites blended with the lighter blues of the flowers.

The years of the *Water Lilies* were particularly important for general recognition of Monet's artistic prowess. In 1909 in Durand-Ruel's gallery he exhibited the *Water Lilies* he had completed at that point. The exhibition was a great success and the painter—who was by then old—finally achieved fame, but he did not allow himself to be affected by this newfound renown as his fixed idea remained that of being able to paint uninfluenced by the opinions of others. This is revealed in his written words of 1913: "The public can talk and discuss my work but my life will be no-one's business but my own."

In October 1920 Monet contemplated offering the State twelve canvases, each at least seventeen feet long, to be installed in a pavilion that was to be built in the garden of the Hôtel de Brion (the future Musée Rodin). The project never came to fruition and the canvases were hung in the Orangerie in the Tuileries, the park in front of the Louvre. Nearly blinded by cataracts, Monet continued to work on the last *Water Lilies*. For approximately twenty years he had painted the flowers in his sanctuary in Giverny and they then became the theme of a large decoration. He painted immense canvases that were housed in two oval rooms; there the large lily-pond is studied and portrayed at all hours of the day, morning, afternoon, evening and night. The painter concentrated on the surface of the water and studied its emotional qualities, intonations, and the reflections of the light. The result is a dreamlike spectacle that reflects our thoughts and desires. The canvases in the Orangerie are placed beside one another and form a single painting that rings the entire room. Visitors are held spellbound by the colors that emerge from the depths of the water and blend with the reflected sky.

Soon after Monet's death on December 6, 1926, art critics and the early-twentieth-century masters of the avant-garde became interested in his work. The last *Water Lilies* are powerful, noble paintings that fueled the minds of many painters who later studied them. André Masson wrote of these last canvases, "We would have rejoiced at seeing Claude Monet begin to make use of width in his paintings—clear and extended like Veronese and Tiepolo. But let's leave that aside for a moment to consider his supreme work, the *Water Lilies*. In spite of their monumental dimensions, they have nothing in common with great Flemish or Venetian decorative painting. Monet's mental attitude seems to me that of a great master of easel painting who decided to expand his vision to the width of the world. The sheet of water becomes, by analogy, the entire universe. A cosmic vision. Michelangelo, the sublime creator of solitary figures, had to wait to be called by the Vatican to be able to demonstrate his greatness. For this reason it gives me deep satisfaction and pleasure to refer to the Orangerie as the 'Sistine Chapel of impressionism.'"

In 1883 the critic Jules Laforgue wrote that "the eye of impressionism is the most advanced in human evolution" and, with those words, a decade after the group's first exhibition, the critic fully recognized the revolutionary importance of their way of interpreting reality. At that time Laforgue's positive opinion was only shared by an elite of "admirers" who were able to appreciate, right from the start, the innovation brought by the impressionists to the standard way of painting.

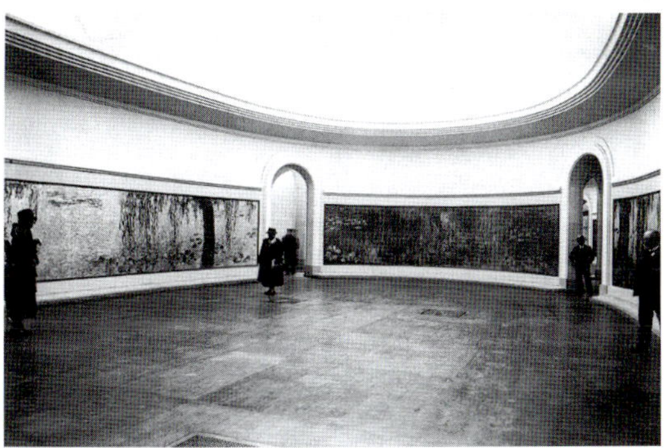

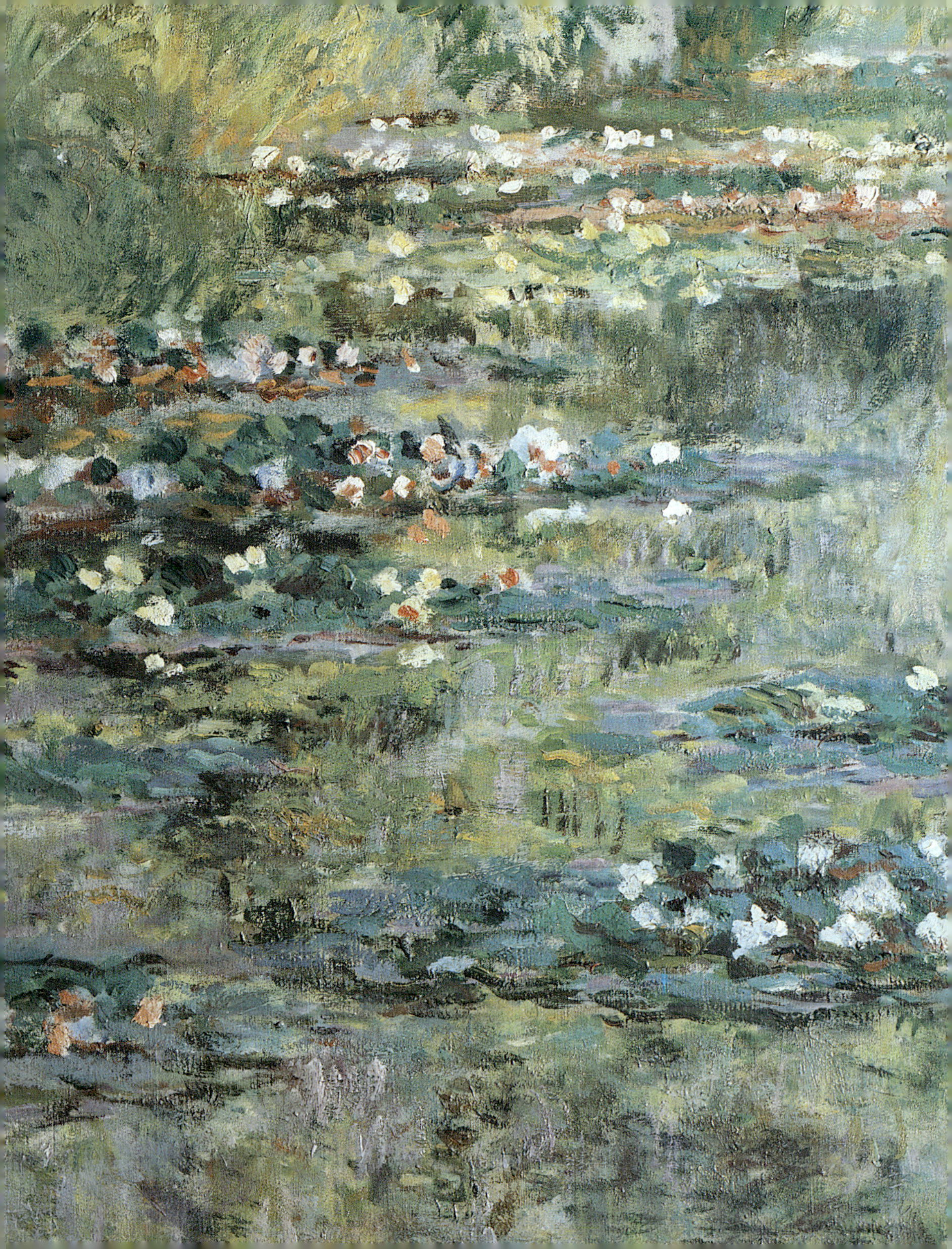

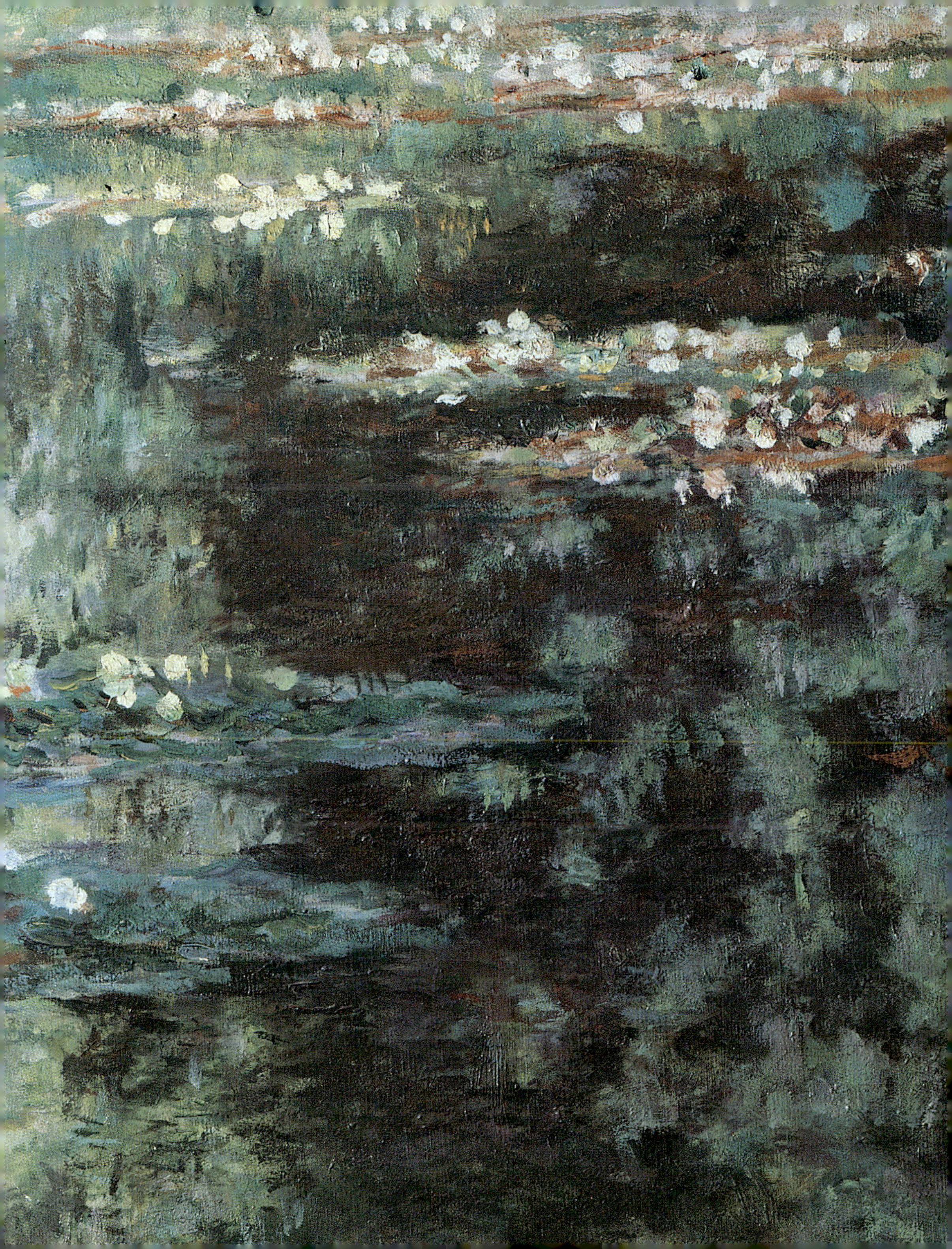

previous pages
Water Lilies
(detail), 1904
Paris, private collection

Today the situation has been completely overturned and no one in the Western world has not heard talk of, even in passing, the impressionists. Due to the enormous success—including financial—the movement enjoyed during the twentieth century, the way in which we think about landscape and figure painting can no longer be disassociated with the disordered vision of small touches and great emotional impact that the impressionists brought into being in the 1870s. It may even be said that our figurative background, through which the events in the history of art are filtered, is undeniably derived from that vision. In light of these facts, if today it seems easy for observers to share the aesthetic vision of the impressionists, it becomes more difficult to understand how they were considered by their contemporaries and what type of reaction their painting aroused. An important fact when pondering this question is that the term "revolutionary" (which is often used when assessing the movement) must be taken with a grain of salt. Impressionism should not be thought of as an avant-garde movement in the twentieth-century meaning of the term. It is undoubtedly true that these painters were pioneers who broke out of the perceptive and representative system, but it is equally clear that none of them, after entering the artistic debate, had achieved a mature vision. The impressionists took up and developed a figurative, cultural, and scientific legacy developed during the nineteenth century that was rich in possibilities. The speed at which the impressionists actually painted their works, require different techniques to those taught in the fine art academies, and this was attacked by those art critics who were accustomed to evaluating a work of art by the care taken in its execution. The canvases of the impressionists, particularly those of Monet, did not respect the traditional canons of art and seemed to have been left in the preliminary stages.

Writing in 1936, when impressionism was universally recognized, Paul Valéry explained how the concept of the "refinement" of the work was gradually superseded by the modern canon of "subjective representation of reality." He continued, "Taking a work of art to completion means erasing everything that reveals or suggests the procedure of production. According to this antiquated conception, the artist should only be revealed through his style and must continue until his physical work has cancelled all traces of itself. But gradually the person and the attention to the moment prevailed over the artwork itself and the duration of execution, and perfection seemed not only useless and annoying but also contrary to *truth, sensibility*, and the manifestation of *genius*. Personality seemed essential, even to the public. A sketch is the equal of a painting." As happens in all eras, this spiritual movement was subject to the criticism of those who did not accept the progress of thought, and even the idea that a profound change was taking place in the way the external world was being represented was abhorrent to some.

The process of assimilation was neither simple nor free of consequences. The impressionists convinced the artists of future generations that the limitations imposed by the nature of paint could be overcome. They taught their contemporaries that what a painter investigates is not the nature of the physical world but the nature of our reactions to it. This notion can, however, mean everything or nothing: who can argue with certainty that painters like Turner and Constable—who were active earlier than the impressionists—did not have an equally "subjective" vision of the world?

There is another question to be considered. Around the 1950s—following the rise in Europe of informal art and of another current in America, action painting, whose major exponent was Jackson Pollock—some extreme art critics reevaluated Monet's painting at the end of his life, defining it a precursor of the abstract work of future generations. Today this fascinating argument seems a slightly strained interpretation of Monet's

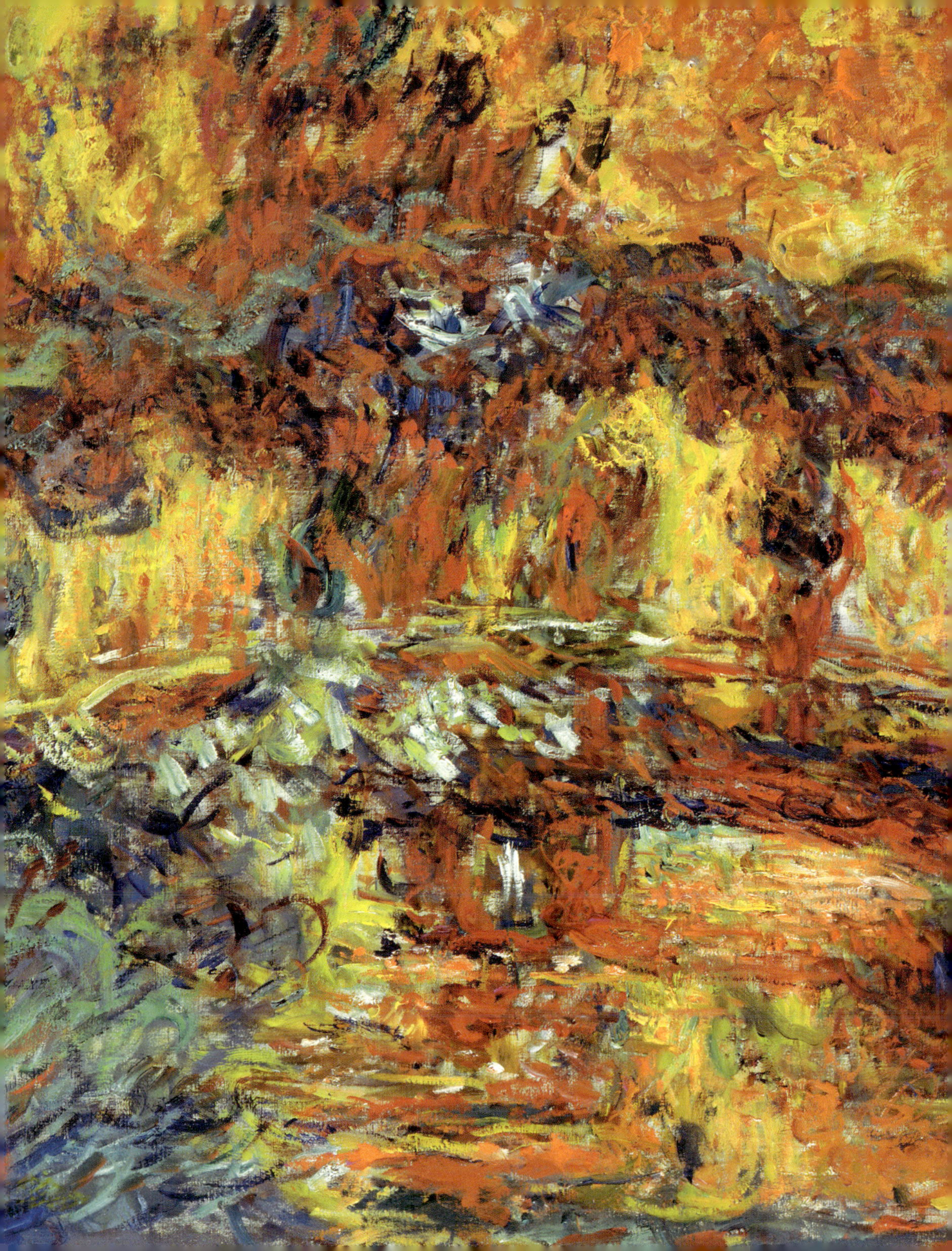

personality, who would certainly have been unable to imagine the fruits of the seeds he sowed. An unexceptionable assessment of the impressionist phenomenon was made by the great art historian Ernst Gombrich, basing his reflection on the attempt to understand in what terms the public approached impressionist painting.

"Whatever the initial resistance to the painting of the impressionists was once the first shock had worn off, the people learned to understand them. Having learned this language, they began to explore fields and woods or simply to look out of the windows onto the boulevards of Paris: and they discovered, with great pleasure, that the visible world could, after all, be seen as bright patches or flecks of color. The transposition worked. The impressionists had taught them not to look at nature with an innocent eye but to explore an unexpected alternative, something that was able to correspond to certain experiences better than all previous paintings. The artists convinced art lovers so overwhelmingly that the phrase 'nature imitates art' became common. As Oscar Wilde said, there was no fog in London before Whistler painted it."

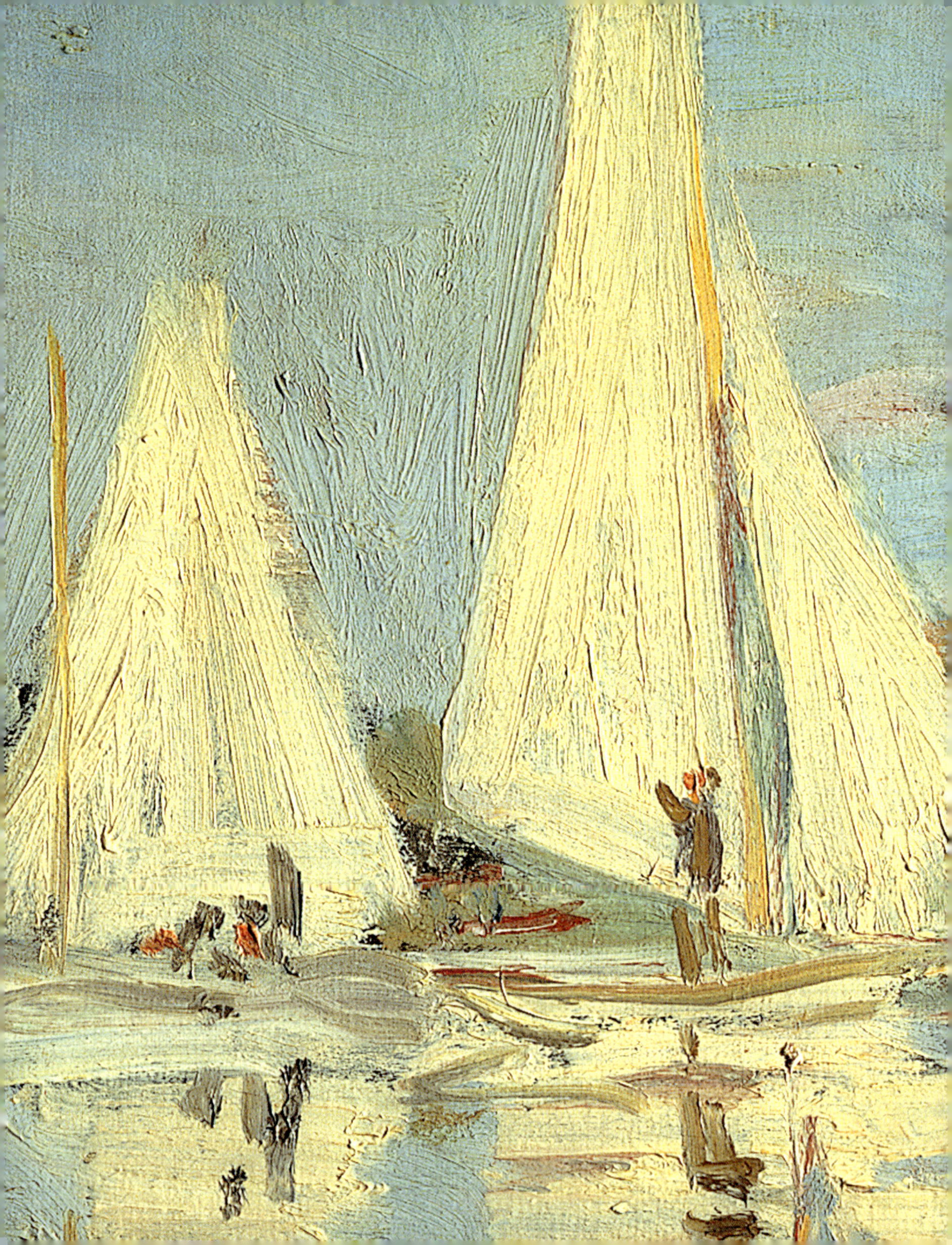

The Masterpieces

Regatta at Argenteuil
(detail), 1872
Paris, Musée d'Orsay

Still Life with Meat

1864
Oil on canvas, 24 × 33 cm
Paris, Musée d'Orsay

Some time before painting this picture, Monet had visited the studio of Charles Gleyre where he had met Renoir, Bazille, and Sisley. Still lifes were very much in vogue in the private schools as an alternative to the more traditional instruction given at the École des Beaux-Arts. In addition to painting still lifes, pupils painted models from life.

Monet was not satisfied with Gleyre as he did not approve of the latter's teaching method or his ideas on art. He later said, "It was with a heavy heart that I set up my easel among the pupils in the studio run by the famous artist. I worked conscientiously for a week and diligently worked on a study of a nude model [...]. When Gleyre passed in front of me [...] I heard him say, smiling, 'Not bad, but it is too much like the model. You have before you a small, thickset man with enormous feet and you have rendered them as just that. That's unattractive. Remember young man that when you portray a figure you must always think of antiquity. Nature, my friend, is fine for when you make studies but it is of no interest to anyone'."

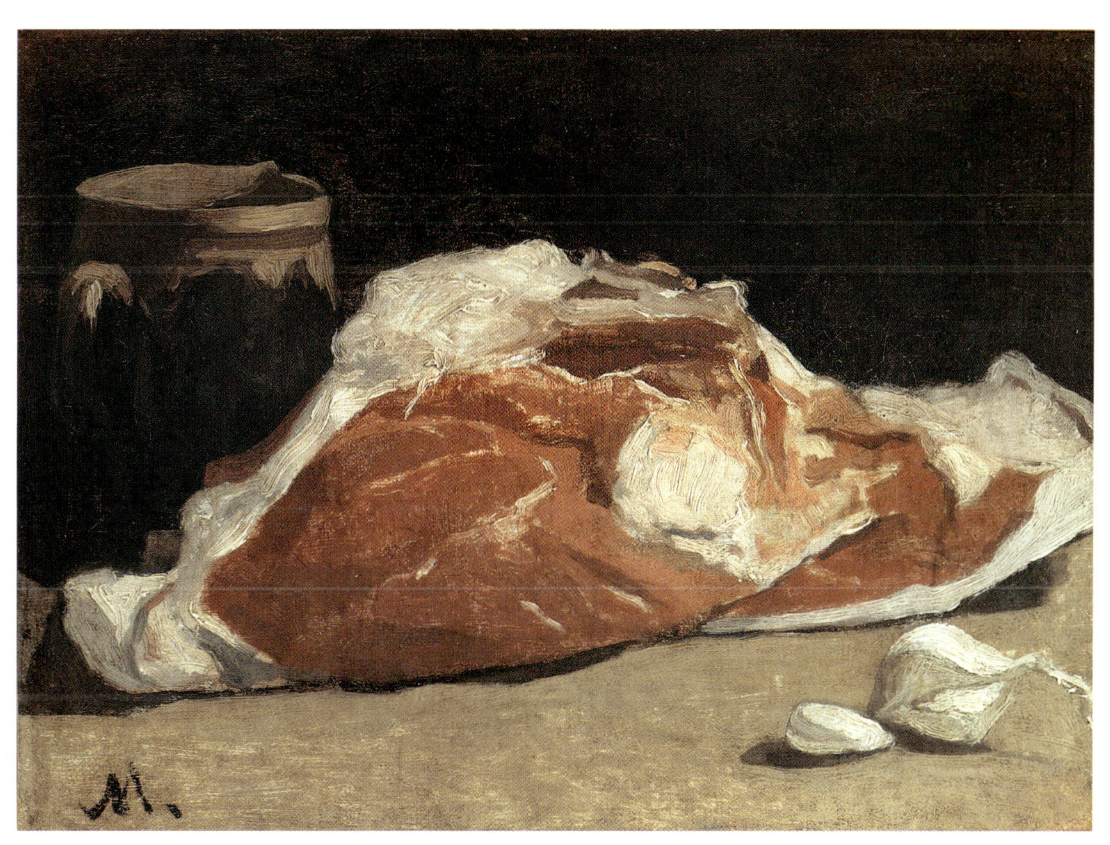

Luncheon on the Grass
(Déjeuner sur l'Herbe)

1866
Oil on canvas, 124 × 181 cm
Moscow, The Pushkin State
Museum of Fine Arts

This painting is a replica or a study for the well-known composition entitled *Luncheon on the Grass*, on which Monet worked in 1865 and 1866 in Chailly. The painter produced an ordinary bourgeois scene of daily life and planned to turn it into a painting in which the figures were life-size. At the start of May 1865 he told his friends of his plan to paint an immense composition (400 x 600 cm) called *Luncheon on the Grass*. The inspiration for the work was undoubtedly Manet's painting *Déjeuner sur l'Herbe* exhibited in 1863 at the Salon des Refusés. During August, Camille, Monet's future wife, and the painter Bazille posed for almost all the figures.

The initial plan to produce a huge painting more realistic than Manet's and which was closer to the style of the head of the Realist school, Gustave Courbet, was never completed. The work remained unfinished because Monet decided to subject it to the judgment of Courbet himself, who criticized it heavily. Probably shaken by the critique, Claude decided to leave the painting unfinished and to cede it as security for a missed payment of rent for the guesthouse where he was staying. A few years later he retook possession of it and, finding it in very poor condition, he managed to save only a section of the canvas (418 × 150 cm), which is today in The Pushkin State Museum of Fine Arts in Moscow.

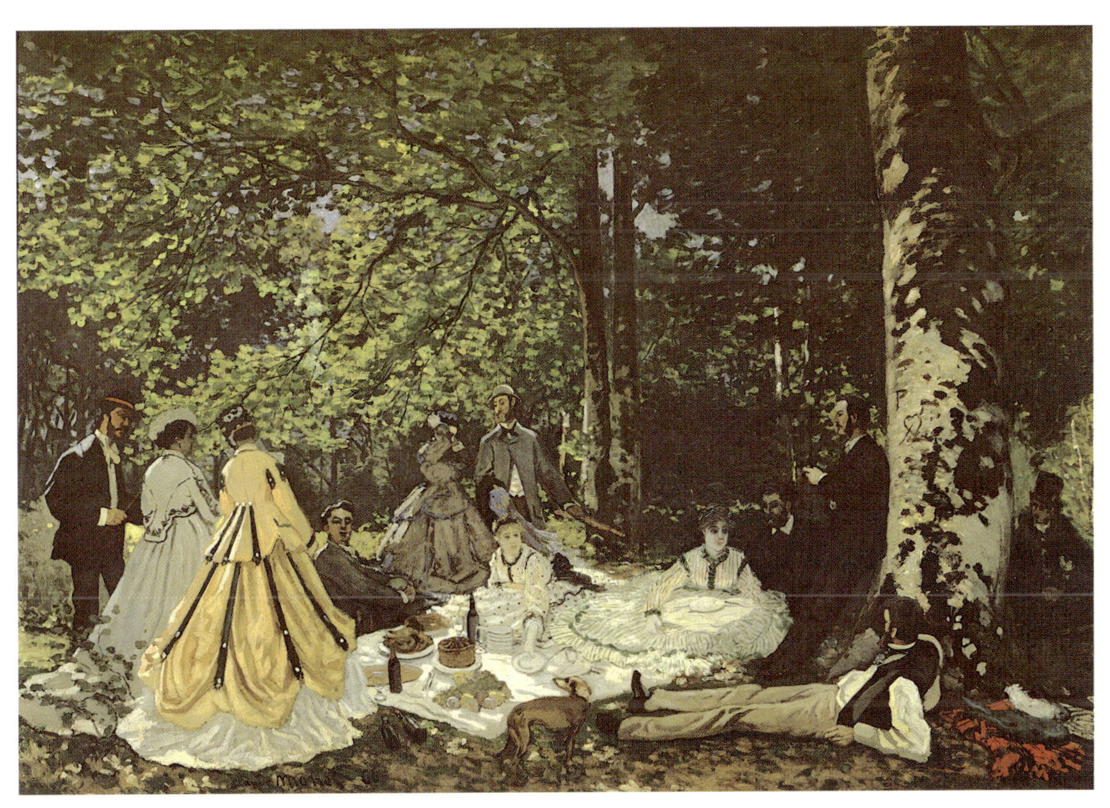

Jeanne-Marguerite Lecadre
in the Garden at Sainte-Adresse

1867
Oil on canvas, 82.3 × 101.5 cm
St. Petersburg, The State
Hermitage Museum

Monet was attracted by seaside views from an early age. In 1866 he moved to Sainte-Adresse where he stayed with an aunt. In June he wrote to Bazille, "I am working very hard. I have about twenty canvases on the go, views of the sea, figures and gardens." At that time Monet was working with wide brushes and quick movements. He applied thick coats of paint to create a rough effect on the surface. He concentrated on the forms and interpreted them mostly as flat surfaces contrasted by deep shadows. Opaque colors portray the light without making it penetrate, while the luminous, pure blues, reds, and yellows provide dazzling tonalities.

The technical and compositional ideas he used in this painting are very close to those in other works painted at Sainte-Adresse. With masterly use of color and a less sentimental interpretation, Monet went beyond the influence of Courbet in his experimentation with landscapes.

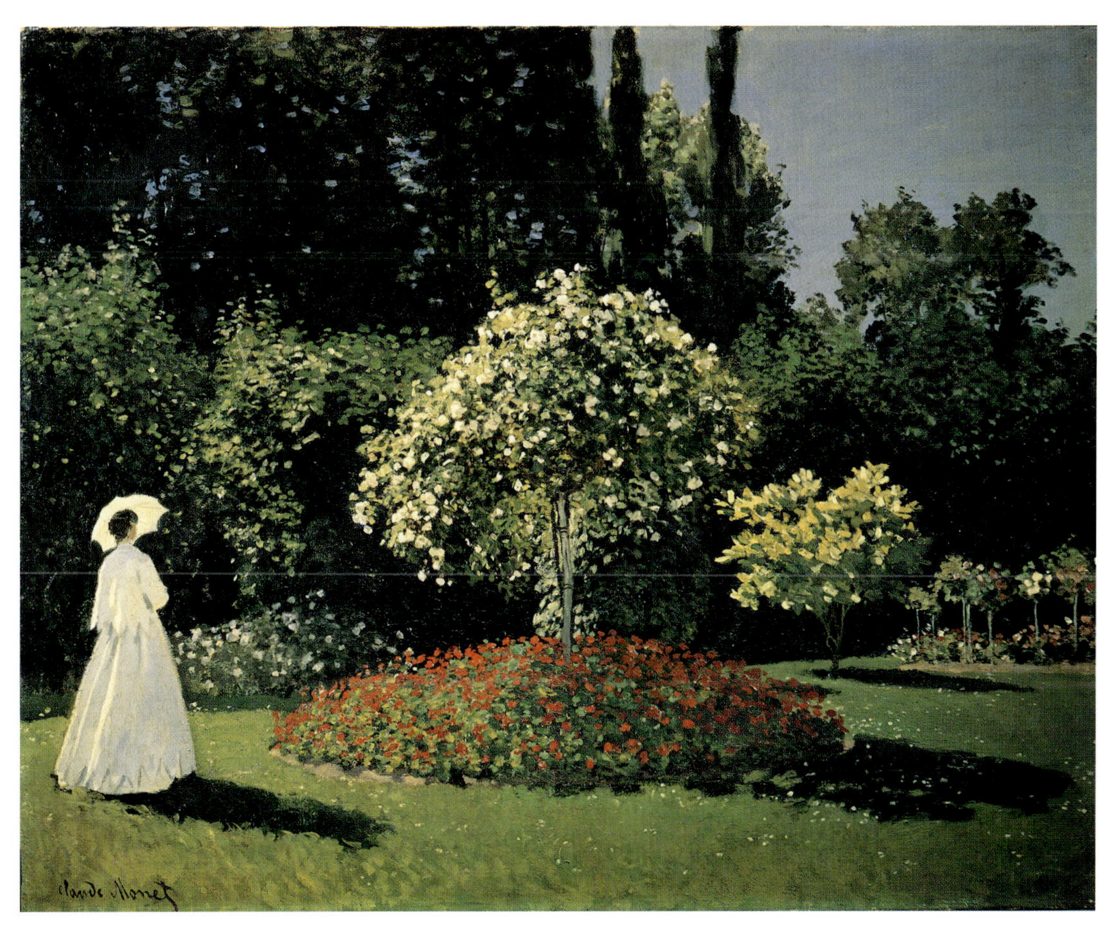

Women in the Garden

1867
Oil on canvas, 255 × 205 cm
Paris, Musée d'Orsay

The picture was painted directly in the open at Ville d'Avray and completed in Honfleur. The painting was made famous by the *en plein air* method Monet adopted, which was completely new in contemporary art. During preparations for the painting, for which Monet's wife, Camille, was the only model, the artist thought of digging a trench in which to place the enormous canvas while he painted. The painter Alèxandre-Louis Dubourg reported the matter in a letter to Boudin: "Monet is still here [in Honfleur] and he is still working on an enormous painting [...] about three meters high. The figures are just smaller than life-size and several women, wearing summer dresses, are picking flowers in a garden. It is a painting that he began to paint directly outdoors."

The canvas was refused by the jury of the Salon to Monet's great disappointment. Bazille bought it for 2,500 francs, partly to help his friend as he was in financial distress. It later came back into Monet's possession and was purchased by the French government for 200,000 francs. Today the painting is considered one of the most important in the Musée d'Orsay.

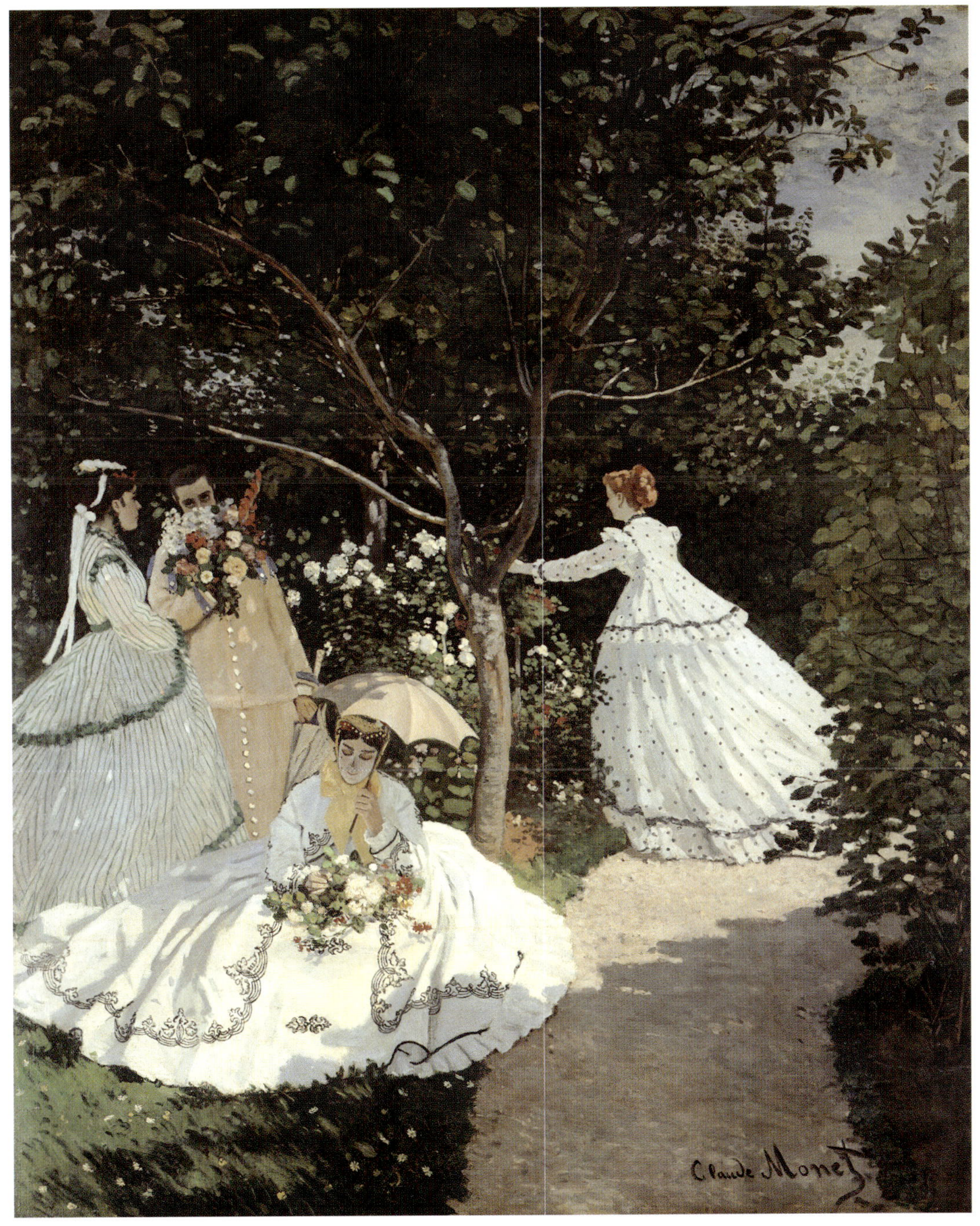

The Beach at Sainte-Adresse

1867

Oil on canvas, 75 × 101 cm
Chicago, The Art Institute
of Chicago

Monet moved to Sainte-Adresse in autumn 1866 as he was obliged to leave Ville d'Avray due to the debts he had run up. On Sainte-Adresse beach he painted several marine views inspired by the manner of his master Boudin. Boudin had taught him the technique of tracing sketches directly from the subject and then developing them in the studio. Compared to the views painted by his first master, Monet's are fresher and more spontaneous. He did not employ, as Boudin often did, eighteenth-century landscape canons such as the use of faded, yellowish tones and static frontal viewpoints. Monet began to "see" and use colors that resembled as much as possible those of the subject he was painting, and he employed them with small, soft, almost palpable touches.

This painting is an example of the technique that he used during those years. The line that distinguishes the beach from the sea is slightly foreshortened. Two boats rest on the shingle out of the water and three small male figures stand around two more boats that have been drawn right up onto the beach. A few sailboats are seen in the distance. On the other side of the inlet there is a village in which a church spire stands out. The sky is entirely covered with bluish-white clouds and fills half of the entire painting. In general the seascape has been described in visual detail but this manner was soon to be abandoned by Monet.

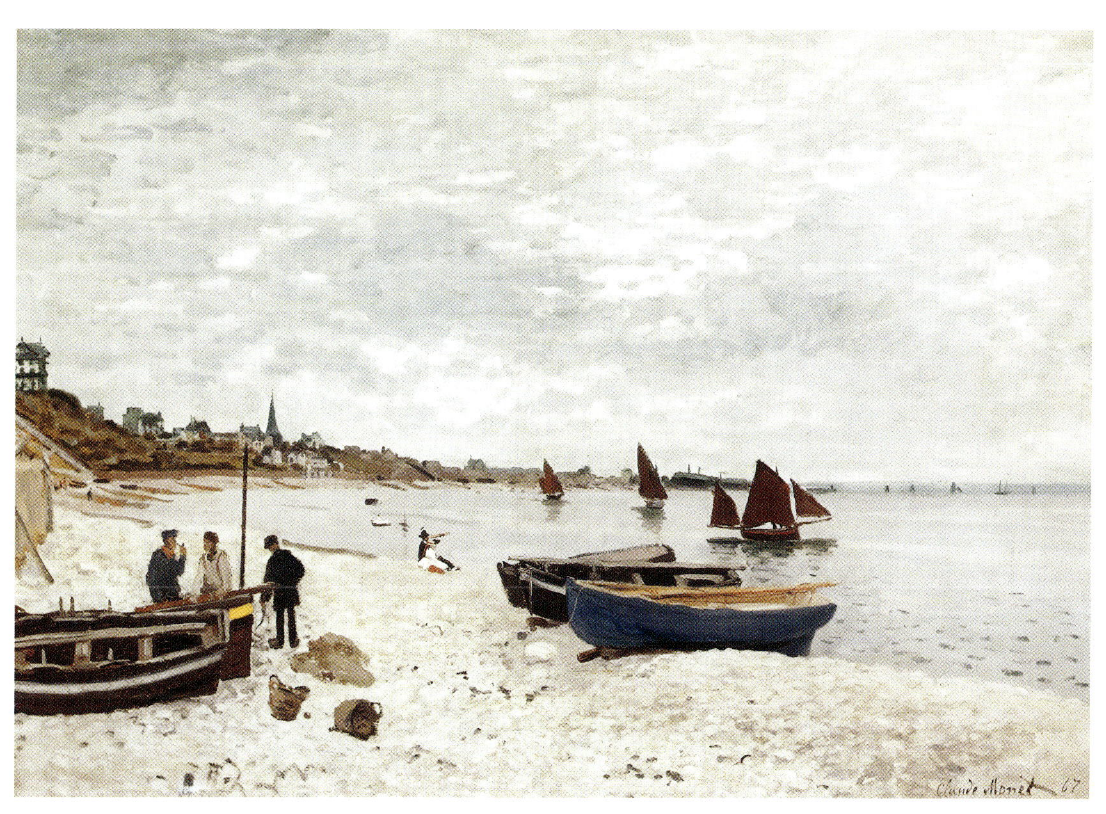

L'Hôtel des Roches Noires à Trouville

1870
Oil on canvas, 81 × 58.5 cm
Paris, Musée d'Orsay

Soon after his marriage to Camille, Monet and his wife settled in Trouville on the Normandy coast, a resort that was much visited by the French well-to-do bourgeoisie. Here he produced a set of marine views and a series of town views. This painting depicts a section of the promenade that overlooks the sea and was executed using the fresh, clear tones characterizing this period. The building after which the painting is named is strongly foreshortened with perspective lines that carry the eye to the center of the painting and the promenade where figures in summer dress are dashed in.

From this moment Monet's intention was no longer to give a detailed depiction of the view but to provide the impression of a sunny summer's day using general intonation; consequently, the painter's attention was mostly concentrated on the zones of light and shade. The boldness of the fluttering flag in the foreground at the top of the painting harks back to the *Garden at Sainte-Adresse*, which Monet had referred to as a "Chinese painting with flags" to emphasize the influence that the compositional method of Japanese painting was having on the way he created a perspective construction of a view.

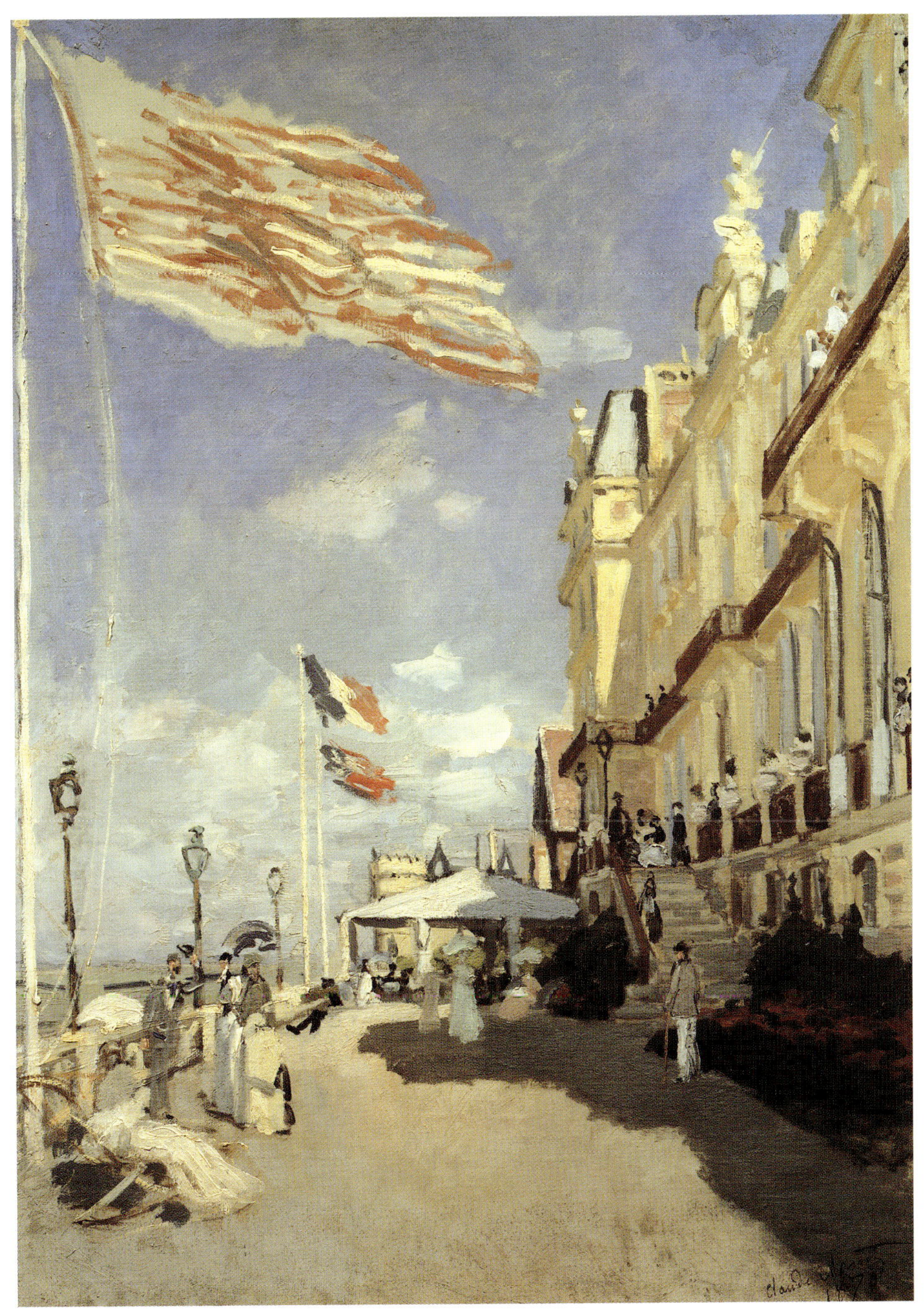

Impression, Sunrise

1872
Oil on canvas, 48 × 63 cm
Paris, Musée Marmottan
Monet

Impression, Sunrise was executed in 1872 at Le Havre and became famous because it was hung in the first exhibition of the impressionists held in 1874 in the studio of the photographer Nadar. Its fame rests on a review written by the art critic Louis Leroy who used the painting's title to coin the name "impressionists" for the painters who displayed their works in that year's show. According to Leroy, their paintings were approximate and unfinished. Monet painted his picture ignoring the conventional criteria for a view of this type. The entire scene is immersed in a bluish haze in which we can only just make out the shapes of the boats in the background. With extraordinary innovative power, he invites us to view nature through the emotions aroused by the harmonies of colors, consciously ignoring the traditional rules of "fabrication" of painted surfaces.

Leroy's obtuse judgment is unsurprising, therefore, as such a "new" approach as the one taken by Monet on the subject of the visual process undoubtedly required a period of assimilation for it to become familiar and then accepted. This painting, held in the Musée Marmottan Monet, is one of the most famous works and greatest attractions in the Paris collection.

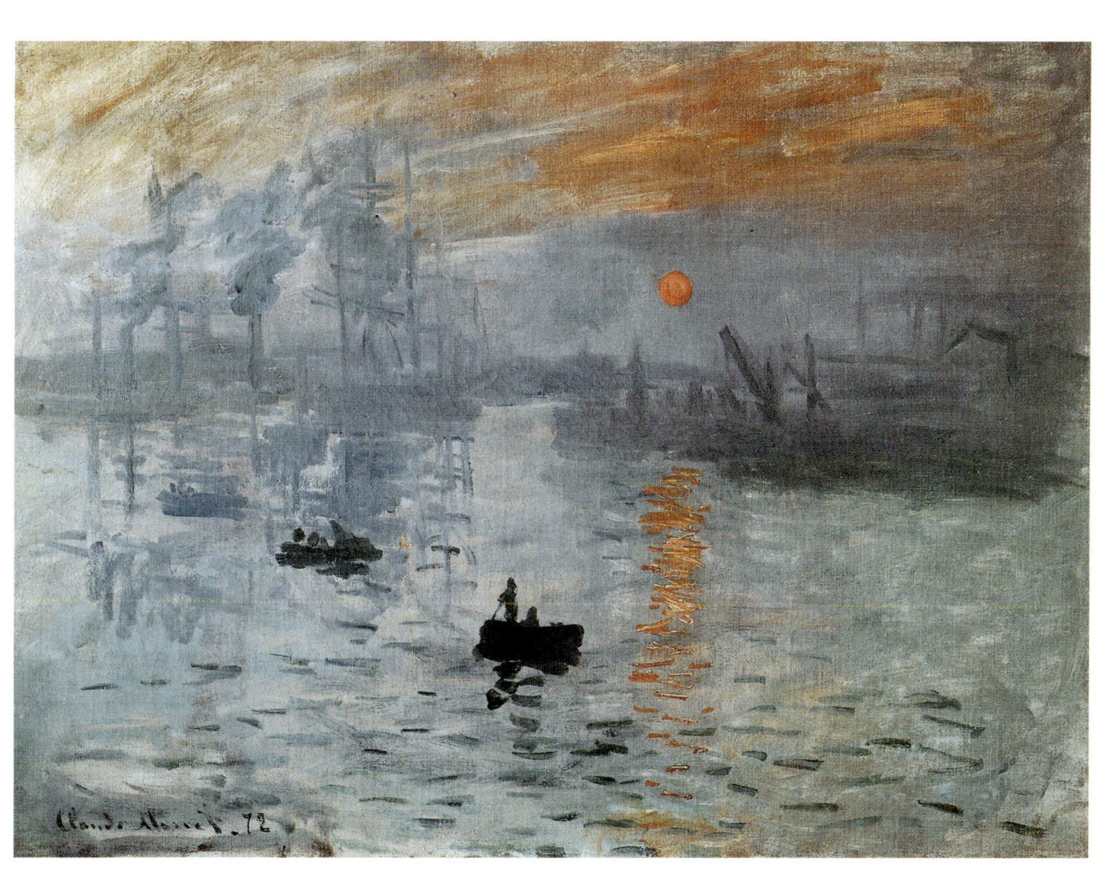

Regatta at Argenteuil

1872
Oil on canvas, 48 × 75 cm
Paris, Musée d'Orsay

This painting was one of the first that Monet produced at Argenteuil, where he moved in 1871 with the financial help of Manet. His time at Argenteuil was one of the most fertile and productive of the artist's life. He painted next to the other Impressionists Renoir, Sisley, Pissarro, and Manet, who often liked to fix on a particular theme and revisit it several times. Monet produced various versions of the *Regatta* with the clear intention of studying in detail the variation in forms and colors depending on the different lighting conditions.

Painted in 1872, this version shows the joyous view in full light and was executed with just a few colors. Monet used a spatula to apply the whites, oranges, blues, and greens with speed and energy so that the composition emphasized contrasting and well-defined zones of color rather than detail. Details are completely lacking in this scene which, being a favorite aspect of conventional painting, are sacrificed in favor of an overall vision with a strong and striking emotional power. The touches and colors on the water surface are fragmented to give an effect of mobility to the reflections. The orange tones of the houses are the brightest in the picture and once again hark back to Japanese art. Théodore Duret said some years later, "It was necessary for us to see Japanese albums for someone to dare […] to put together on a canvas a brilliant red roof, a white wall, a green poplar, a yellow road and blue water; before it would have been impossible."

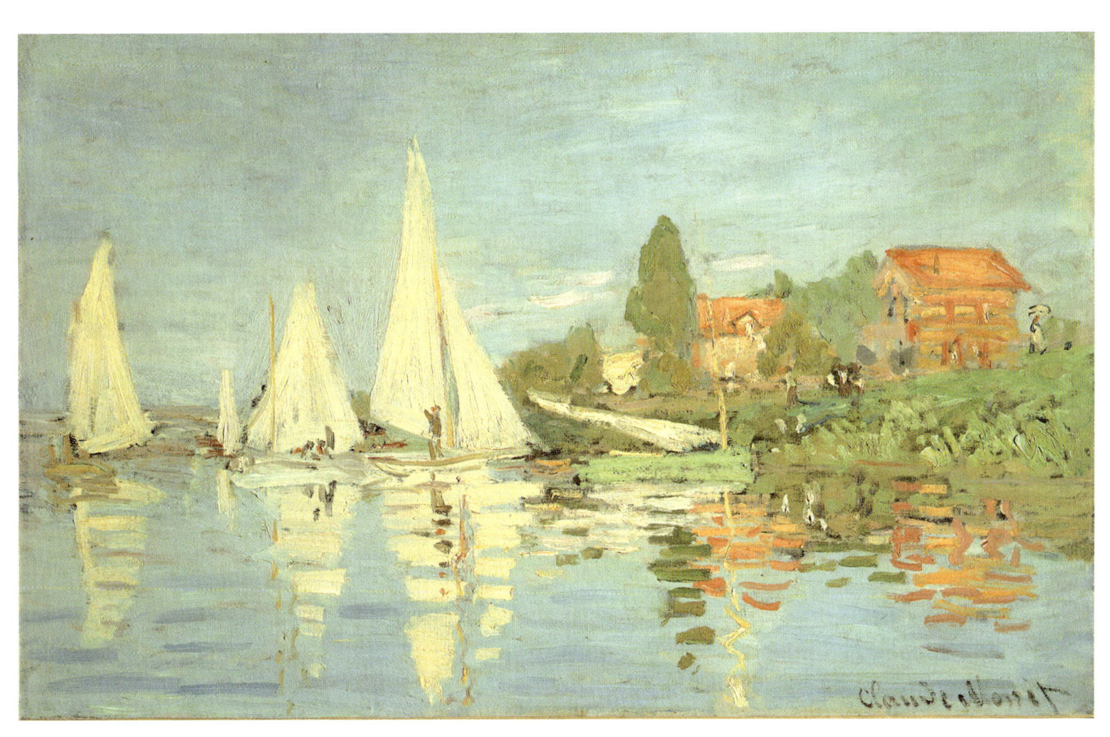

The Port at Argenteuil

c. 1872
Oil on canvas, 60 × 80.5 cm
Paris, Musée d'Orsay

This painting was produced during Monet's early period in Argenteuil. The view is composed in a manner that brings to mind the landscapes of Sisley and Pissarro, with whom Monet painted during this period.

The motif of the shadows of the trees that offer a perspective view of the path was to become popular in landscape painting of the later nineteenth century, and not only in France. The sky is flecked with clouds and painted using different tones of blue, gray, and pale violet that overall create an impression of movement. In short, the sunny view appears dynamic as opposed to the immobility long suggested by traditionally classical landscapes that evoked mythological scenes. Here nature is in evolution: wind, sky, grass, and people are all vital elements. Turning his back on the traditional poetical evocation of nature, Monet chose to depict a single instant in its vibrant process, capturing it on canvas using the new technique of instantaneous vision.

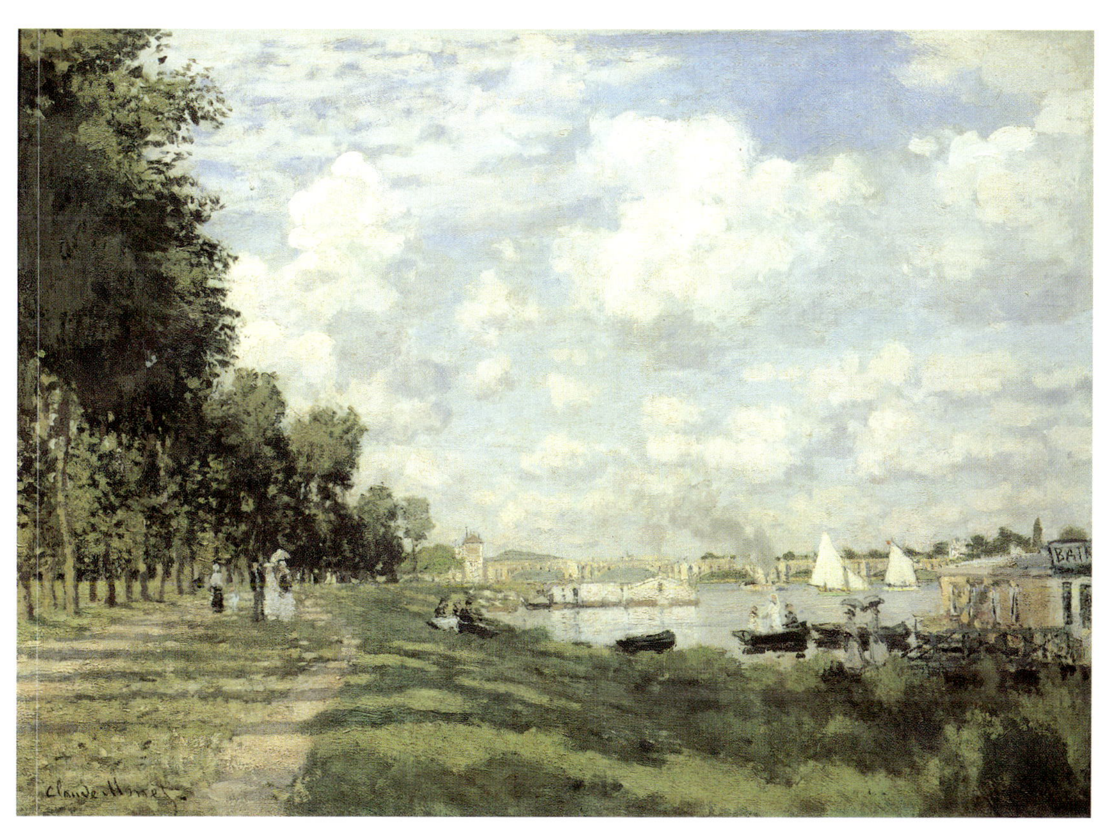

Poppies at Argenteuil

1873
Oil on canvas, 50 × 65 cm
Paris, Musée d'Orsay

Monet painted this scene in the countryside of Argenteuil, and the woman in the foreground is Camille, the painter's wife. She is set in the scenery as though she were an "impression" that blends into the landscape at a perceptual level. The outlines are indefinite and Monet concentrates on the patches of color that he used to describe the objects at an emotional level. Even the sense of depth is simulated because, if we look closely, the scene has been painted using flat zones of different tones. The composition has been constructed around the horizon that cuts the view into two parts: the sky and poppy field respectively, which, in terms of size, are almost the same. The luminosity of the scene is concentrated in the sky while the field, speckled with poppies, carries chromatic weight. The colors are overall very delicate and oil paints have been used to convey a soft pastel effect.

The artist's emphasis here is decided by lyrical and subjective in the sense that he has chosen, out of the vast range of possibilities open to him, his personal interpretation of the countryside.

Monet tackled the theme of walks and relaxation in pastoral settings on many occasions during this relatively happy period of his life when he felt free to choose the themes he wished to paint. This aspect of his continual and extenuating artistic experimentation on what should be represented was a part of the experiences that later led him to concentrate on a single subject for increasingly long periods.

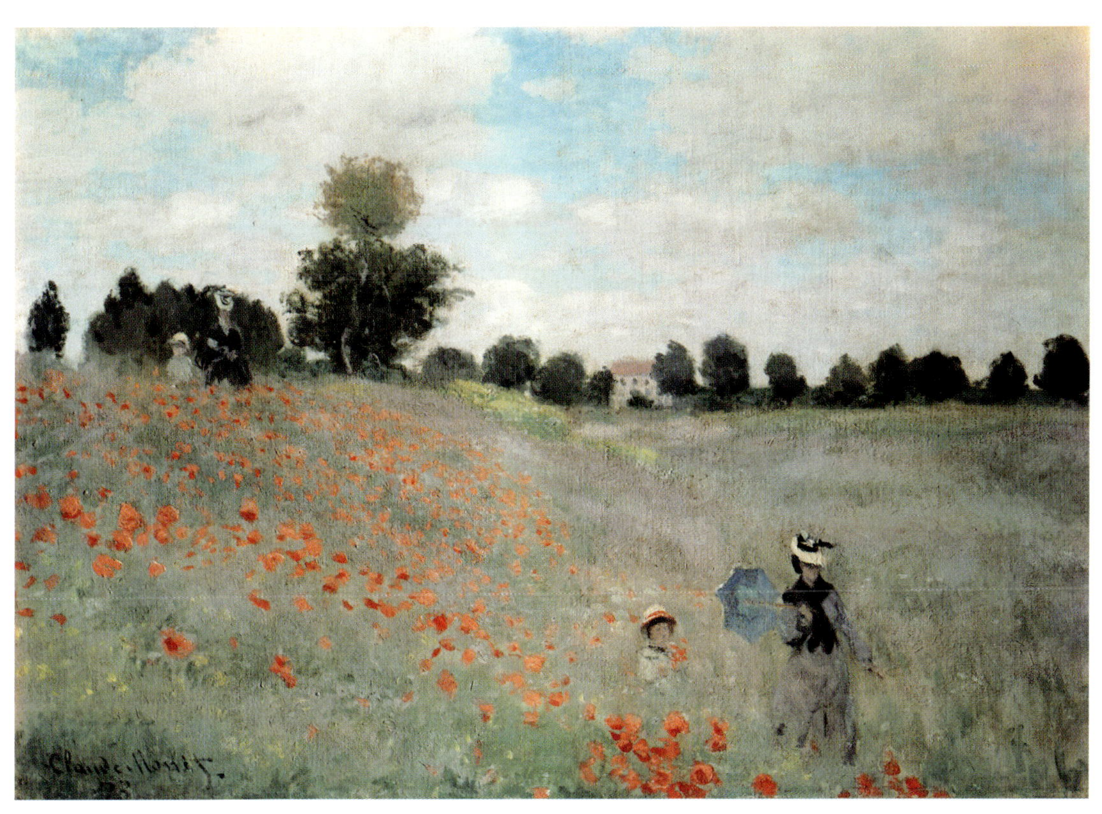

Lilacs. Gray Weather

1873

Oil on canvas, 50 × 65 cm
Paris, Musée d'Orsay

In this painting Monet experimented with variations of light and shade. The picture has a very wide luminous range: from zones that are almost completely obscure and where it is difficult to make out the forms, to light-filled zones in which the outlines are at times overwhelmed by brightness. It is a painting of great refinement though this is not immediately perceptible to the observer and requires careful consideration of the variation in tonal values. The lilacs that bloom on the bushes in a rather frothy manner are where the chromatic emphasis of the painting is placed, whereas the figures resting beneath are almost swallowed up by the shade.

The experimentation that Monet carried out on light was later theorized by the art critics who supported the impressionist movement. Edmond Duranty exhaustively explained the theoretical assumptions of the group in his essay of 1876 entitled *La Nouvelle Peinture. À propos du Groupe d'Artistes qui expose dans le Galeries Durand-Ruel* ("The New Painting: Apropos of the Group of Artists Exhibiting in the Durand-Ruel Art Gallery"). Émile Zola took up the argument once more in 1880 in an article published in *Le Voltaire* with the title *Le naturalisme au Salon* ("Naturalism in this year's Salon"): "Today our young painters have taken another step towards truthfulness by immersing their subjects in real sunlight—not the false light of the studio, like the chemist or physicist who returns to the sources—and by placing themselves in the same phenomenal conditions [they are painting]. Since it is life that they wish to create, it is necessary to catch that life in the completeness of its mechanism. Thus, in painting, there follows the requirement for plein air and light studied in its causes and effects."

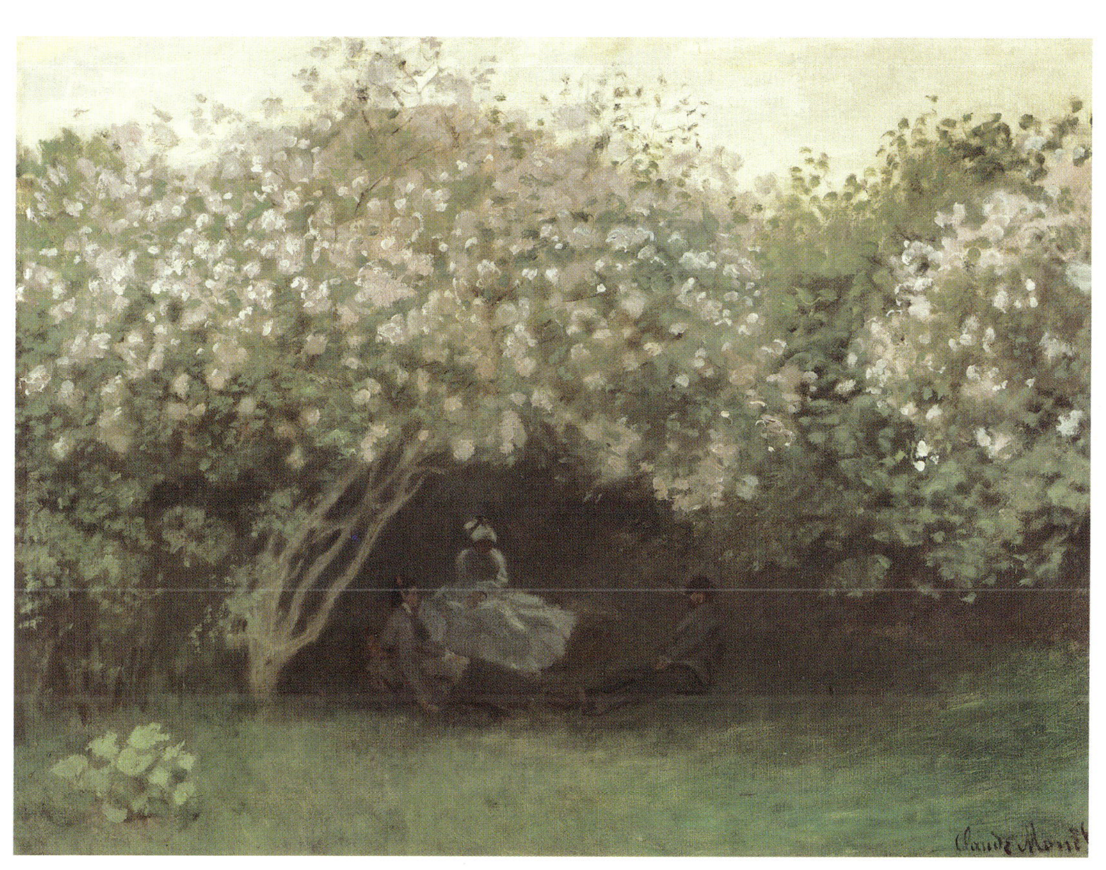

Lilacs in the Sun

1873

Oil on canvas, 50 × 65 cm
Moscow, The Pushkin State
Museum of Fine Arts

This painting in The Pushkin State Museum of Fine Arts in Moscow is the pendant to *Lilacs. Gray Weather* in the Musée d'Orsay. Both are identical in size and it is logical to suppose that they were conceived together to study the impressionist theory that color becomes paler in direct sunlight. The Moscow painting was the first of Monet's works to enter Russia, having been bought from Durand-Ruel by the collector Sergei Schukin. The scene shows a moment of relaxation beneath a flowering bush. It is probable that the woman was Monet's wife, Camille, who in this period was his favorite model. The artistic choices made by the artist means that this painting is one of a set of works he produced in the country-side around Argenteuil, including *Poppies at Argenteuil* and *Lilacs. Gray Weather*; *Monet's Garden at Argenteuil* and *Woman with Umbrella Turned toward the Left.*

Monet alternated these subjects with views of the river, which were also characteristic of his Argenteuil period. In those paintings in which the countryside is shown, the sensation suggested by the use of color is of muffled softness, while in those representing the Seine Monet creates more crystalline effects by concentrating on the brightness of objects reflected in the water of the river.

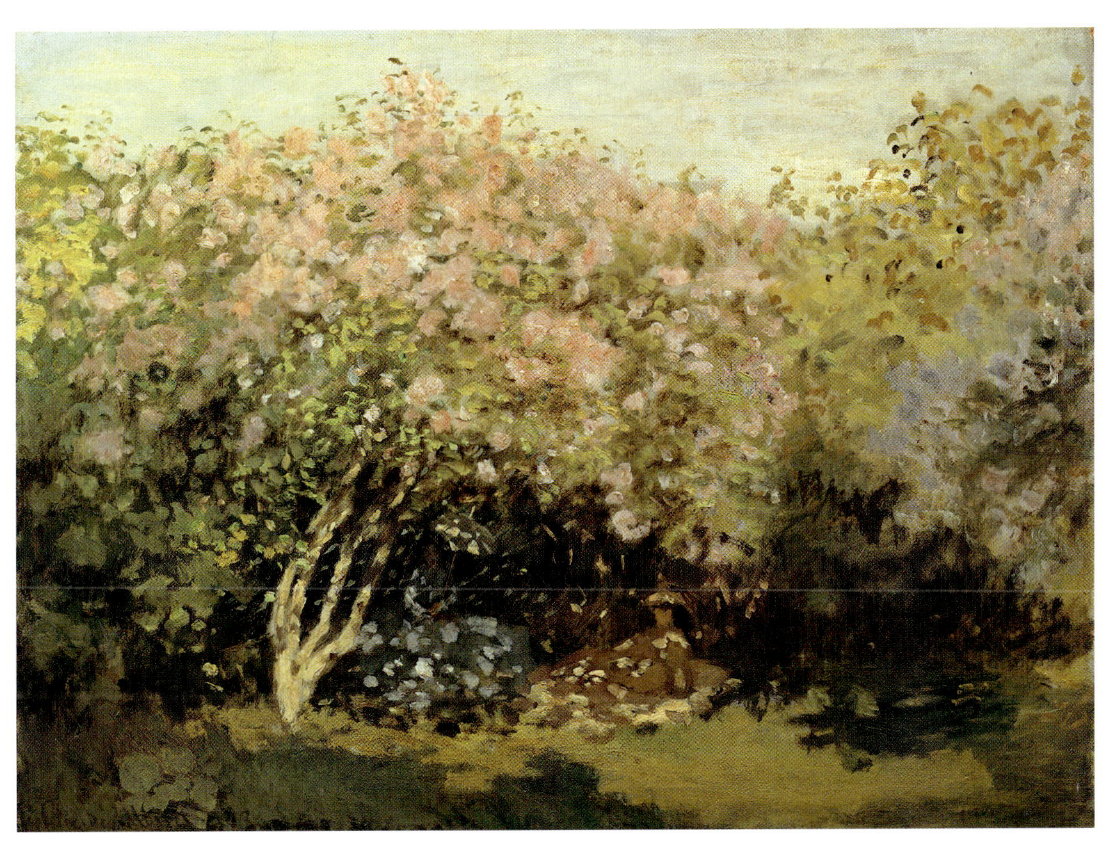

The Boulevard des Capucines

1873

Oil on canvas, 60 × 80 cm
Moscow, The Pushkin State
Museum of Fine Arts

The painting is of the *Boulevard des Capucines* in Paris where Nadar had his studio. Nadar was the photographer who lent his studio to house the first impressionist exhibition. Some experts think that this painting was displayed in the exhibition of 1874, while others consider it was another version of the same subject today in New York.

A pink glow illuminates the crowd, carriages, and trees that line the boulevard. The painting was probably made from a balcony similar to the one from which the two men look out on the right edge of the picture. The feeling of movement is created with great skill by Monet who, rather than depicting the figures with accuracy, prefers to sketch them using the tip of the brush.

Monet's contemporaries were amazed by so much "approximation" in the way the forms were handled. Alluding to the "black tongues in the lower part of the canvas" in the review written by Louis Leroy for *Le Charivari*, the critic wondered, "Do I look like that when I walk down the Boulevard des Capucines?"

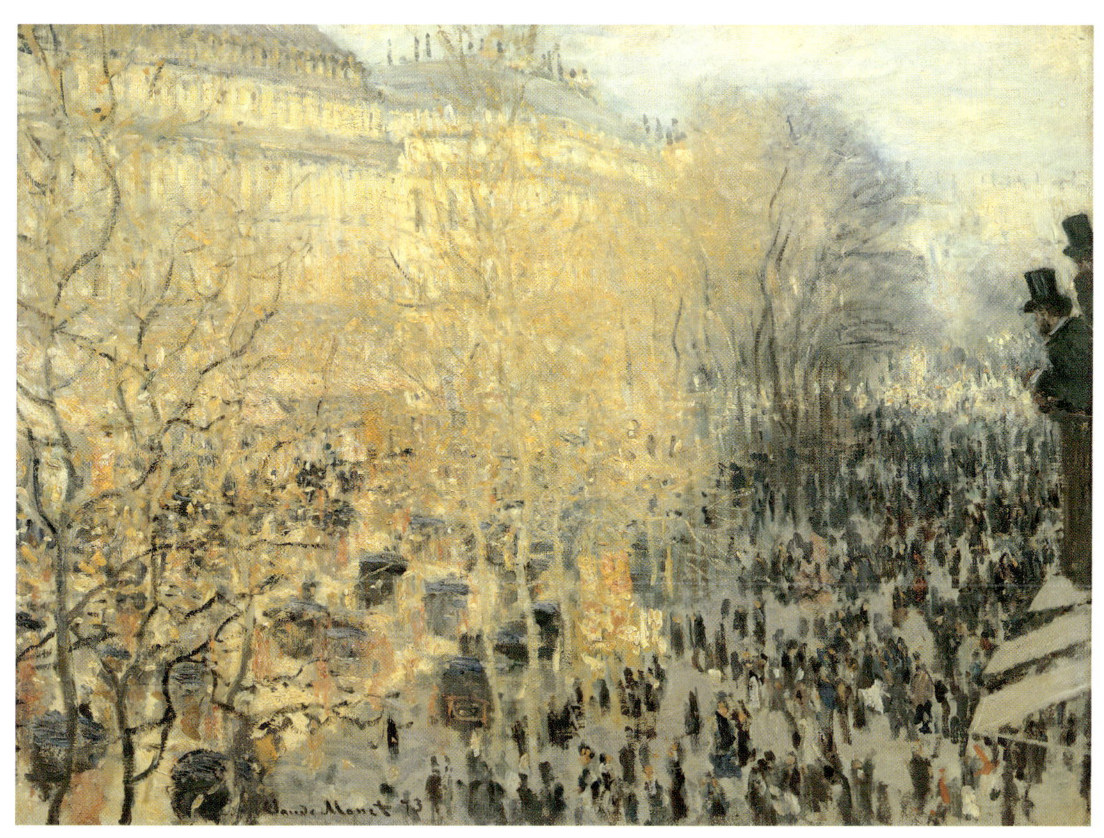

The Luncheon
(decorative panel)

c. 1873

Oil on canvas, 160 × 201 cm
Paris, Musée d'Orsay

Here Monet gave a new treatment to a theme he had already tackled a year earlier with *Luncheon on the Grass*, demonstrating that he had by then risen above the realist painting of Courbet. In the earlier version Monet depicted everything with great particularity and the figures were given strong emphasis. In this version of the same subject, the protagonist of the scene is the still-life composed of a table laid with a tablecloth, cup, glass, and jug, and a wicker trolley. There are figures in the picture but they have no more importance than the objects. Manet's young son, Jean, sits on the ground next to the table playing, and in the background there are two women walking, partially hidden by the flowers and tree. The elements in the painting offer an enchanting picture of the outdoor life: the composition of fruit and the crockery on the table, the white tablecloth and the bushy plants in bloom; the parasol and bag left on the bench tell us that the luncheon has just ended and that the diners have just left the table.

This large painting was presented at the second impressionist exhibition (1876) with the title *Decorative panel*, which is a direct indication of the bourgeois custom of decorating interiors with paintings of the countryside to remind the occupants of the happy, sunny rural life. The successful blend of colors and use of long, thin brushstrokes in some ways resemble the work of Renoir, in whose paintings the surface was very smooth and luminous, almost mother-of-pearl. Monet, on the other hand, used a denser brushstroke that is particularly visible in the white tablecloth, the most luminous section of the painting. The motif of sunlight filtering through the branches onto the table and bench was later used by Renoir to create the dizzying effect in his *Dance at the Moulin de la Galette*.

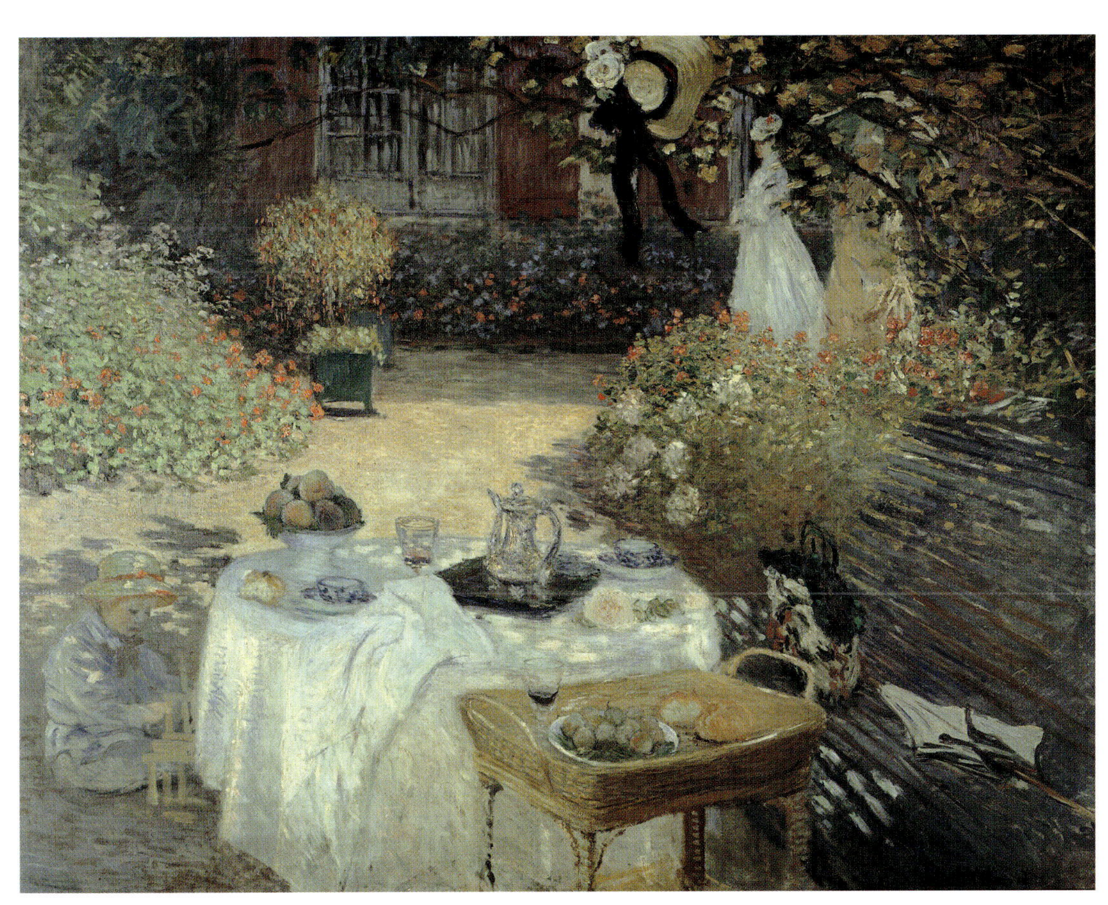

The Railway Bridge at Argenteuil

1873–1874
Oil on canvas, 55 × 72 cm
Paris, Musée d'Orsay

In his paintings of this period Monet made use of strongly fore-shortened and unusual composition, as is evident in this picture where the viewpoint is slightly raised and conditions the acute perspective angle of the massive metal bridge. This cast-iron structure of columns and deck dominates the landscape like a monument to modernity. A fundamental aspect of impressionism was its interest in the contemporary and Monet's painting gives us a view of humankind's domination of nature and progress at the expense of the countryside that was at that time still considered in a positive light.

Painting of this nature acts as a record of contemporary history and as a visual document of the "effective state of things;" even the technique Monet used follows this intent. The strong, almost arrogant impact generated by the metal bridge is produced in masterly fashion. The contrast between the clear and dark zones generates a backlit effect that immediately attracts the attention. The ripples on the water, which grow denser closer to the bridge, increase the emotional tension aroused by the passing of the train in a place that would otherwise be calm and silent.

Cast iron, steel, and zinc—the materials of modernity—also took on a leading role in many intense pages written by Émile Zola in his descriptions of the bustling center of Paris and the crowded fruit and flower market of Les Halles, of which "the enormous cast-iron skeleton was gradually tinged with blue," then reduced to just a dark outline "against the sudden burst of light from the rising sun."

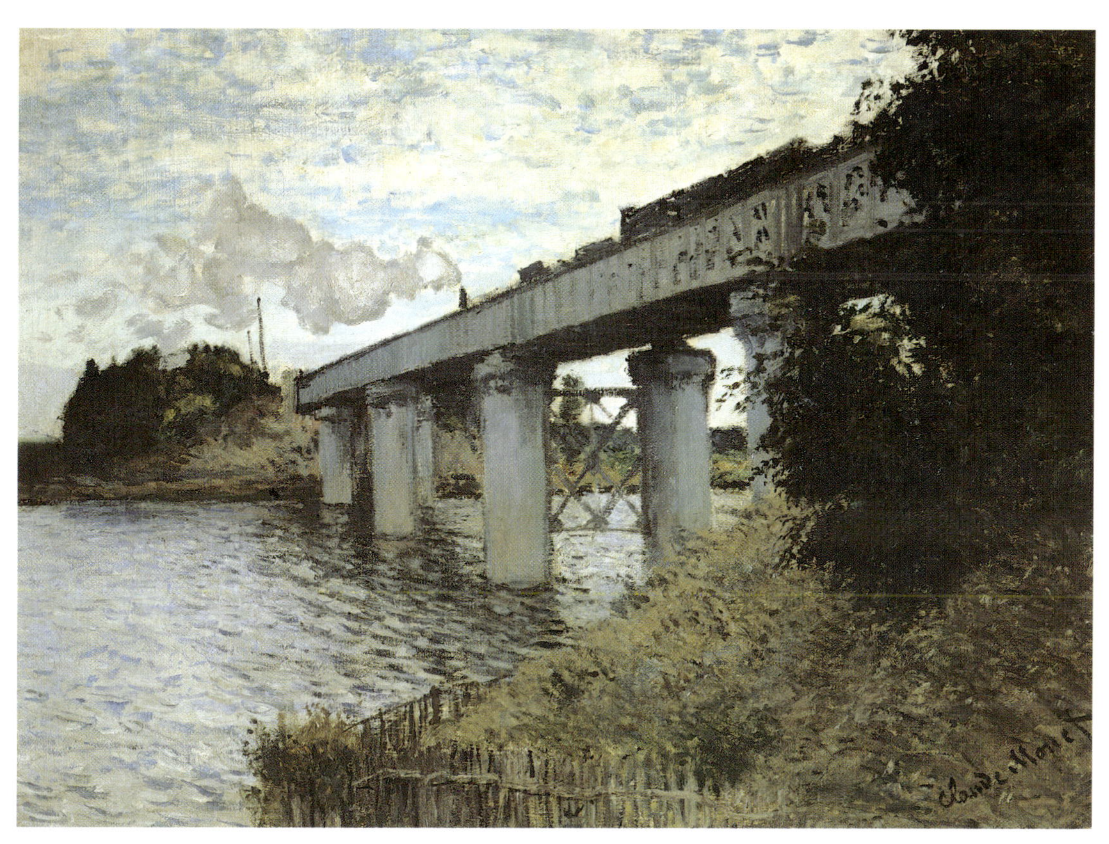

The Bridge at Argenteuil

1874
Oil on canvas, 60.5 × 80 cm
Paris, Musée d'Orsay

The year in which *The Bridge at Argenteuil* was painted was a moment of fundamental importance to the painters in the impressionist group, who exhibited together that year for the first time. Monet achieved results of extraordinary clarity in his experimentation into the representation of light. Some of the landscapes painted at this time are illuminated by a special aura that rightly aroused astonishment in several admirers of his work. *The Bridge at Argenteuil* is one of these masterpieces. It is a fragment of reality rendered in a strongly analytic key that successfully recreates the poetics of the original view. The merging of the different luminous elements has been done with great delicacy, but the painter has concentrated above all on the representation of the transparency of the water and sky. The brushwork was executed in hundreds of tiny touches in order to illustrate the sparkle of the light on the surface of objects and the reflection of the boats, bridge, trees, and house in the water.

Renoir, Sisley, Caillebotte, Manet, and Berthe Morisot were also working on the same subject at the same time. The goal of their common activity was undoubtedly cognitive and based on the methodological assumptions closely connected to the contemporary theory that vision is a moment of awareness and internalization of data arriving from reality. Vision depends on external impulses that come into contact with the retina and are subsequently processed by the brain. The result is a perception that must perforce be subjective even if two people are looking at the same object. Comparison and debate between the artists exploring the same theme took on seminal importance as this too became a moment of understanding.

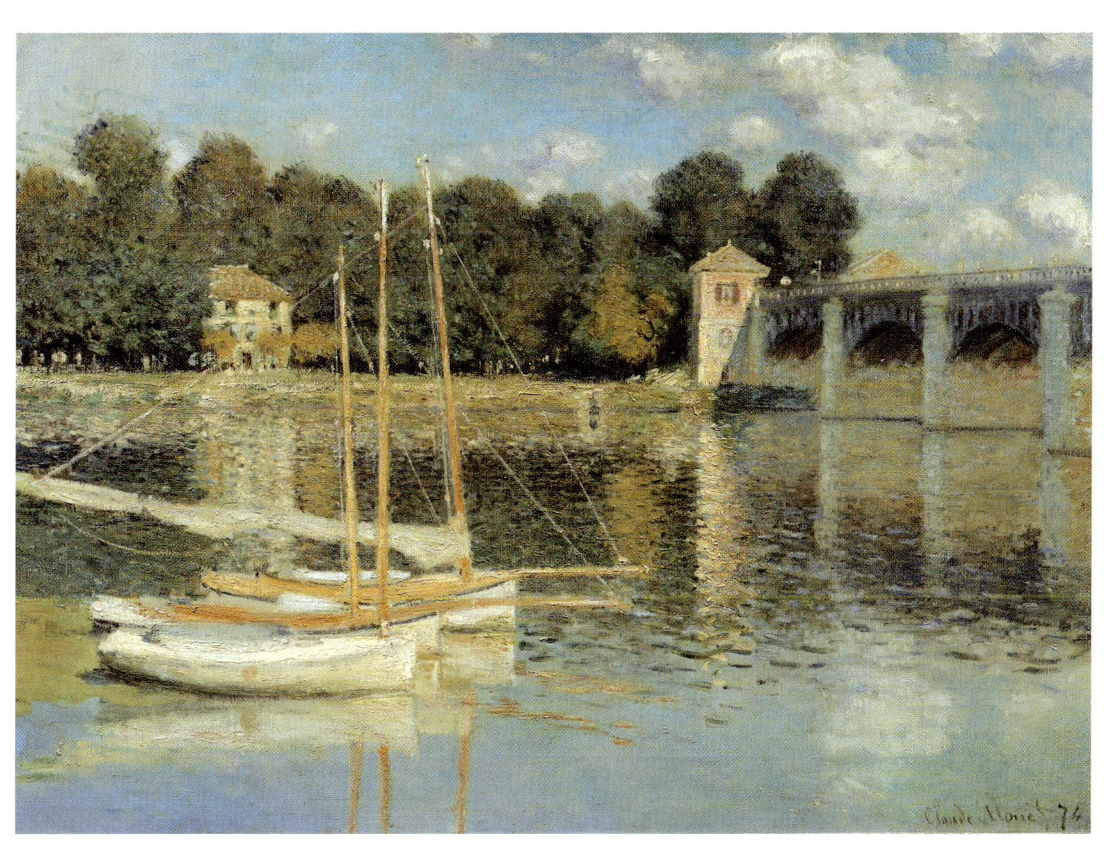

Regatta at Argenteuil

This version of *Regatta at Argenteuil* was two years later than the 1872 picture painted at the start of the artist's stay in the hamlet on the bank of the Seine. Following Daubigny's example, Monet had a *"bateau-atelier"* (boat-cum-studio) built which he could maneuver on the navigable sections of the river to reach points from which to paint that would otherwise have been unattainable. The view in this painting seems to be from the water itself. We see a windy day and the sky dotted with clouds that Monet succeeded in portraying in masterly fashion. The dynamism of the scene is suggested by the swelling of the sails as the boats appear to skim across the water from left to right.

The harmony of the colors is based on the blending of the whites and pale blues, in the water with light touches of the brush to create the ripples, and in the sky with a heavier application to generate the changing state of the clouds. Compared to other interpretations of the landscape during Monet's period in Argenteuil, this work has greater emotional power. It is probable that the start of the stormy season prevented the painter from adopting an analytical, studied approach as he had done, for example, in the *Bridge at Argenteuil* and the first version of the *Regatta*.

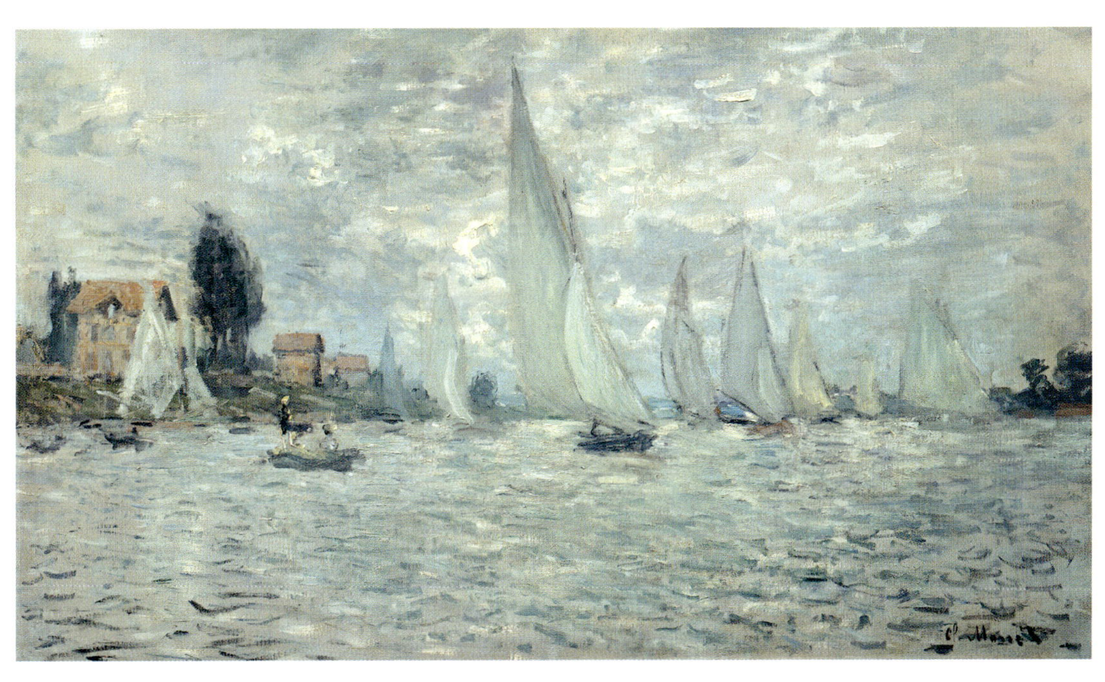

The Garden at Montgeron

1877
Oil on canvas, 172 × 192 cm
St. Petersburg, The State
Hermitage Museum

While in Argenteuil, Monet went from time to time to Paris to intersperse his countryside views with urban landscapes. It was probably during one of these journeys, in spring 1876, that he met Ernest Hoschedé who, fascinated by Monet's painting, invited him to his residence in Montgeron where he commissioned him to decorate his castle in Rothenburg. Monet accepted the work and produced four paintings that illustrate the two seasons he stayed in Montgeron. Two canvases were of the garden, another of the pond, and a large one of turkeys pecking at the ground.

The Garden at Montgeron was a part of this decorative cycle. In it he permanently turned his back on traditional perspective of space and organized depth through surface values from bottom to top rather than structuring it through different planes. The colors he used were bright and vivid, and perfectly render the luxuriant vegetation through the prevalent use of yellows, greens, and reds.

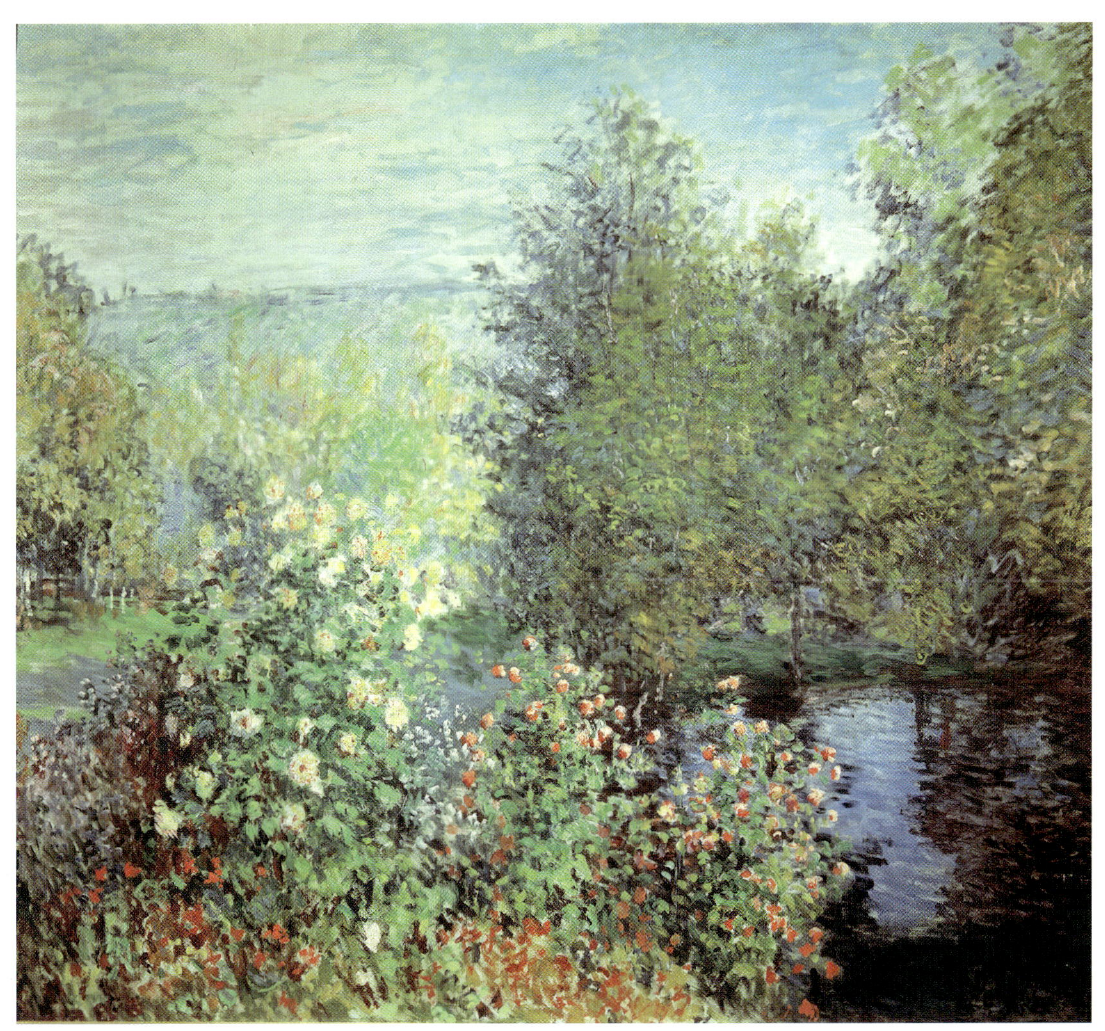

The Pond at Montgeron

1877
Oil on canvas, 172 × 193 cm
St. Petersburg, The State
Hermitage Museum

This painting was executed as part of the decorative commission from the Hoschedé family for their residence in Montgeron. It shows a pond where Monet was able once more to concentrate on his favorite theme: water. The trees reflected on the surface hang down at either side like curtains. The general tone of the painting is luminous and it emanates a sense of peace and silence that is underlined by the green and gold tonality.

During this period Monet was still concentrating on rendering the complexity offered to his eyes by the great "book of nature." He tried to decode what he saw through a process of close analysis, however, in later years, as a result of his great natural versatility, he was prompted to search inside himself for the key to interpret what he saw. Paul Valéry offered an excellent summary of the process of "internalization" that some artists engage in when painting landscapes, as opposed to others who spend their entire lives illustrating but without interpreting. "Every artist has his own reactions to the visible. Some make efforts to render as faithfully as possible what they perceive. […] Others, […], though they begin like the first, and generally always maintain their intention to produce an accurate study of objects, to which they every now and then return to test their patience and the extent of their acceptance of nature for what it is, they yet desire to make us feel what they feel when they look at nature and to paint themselves while painting it."

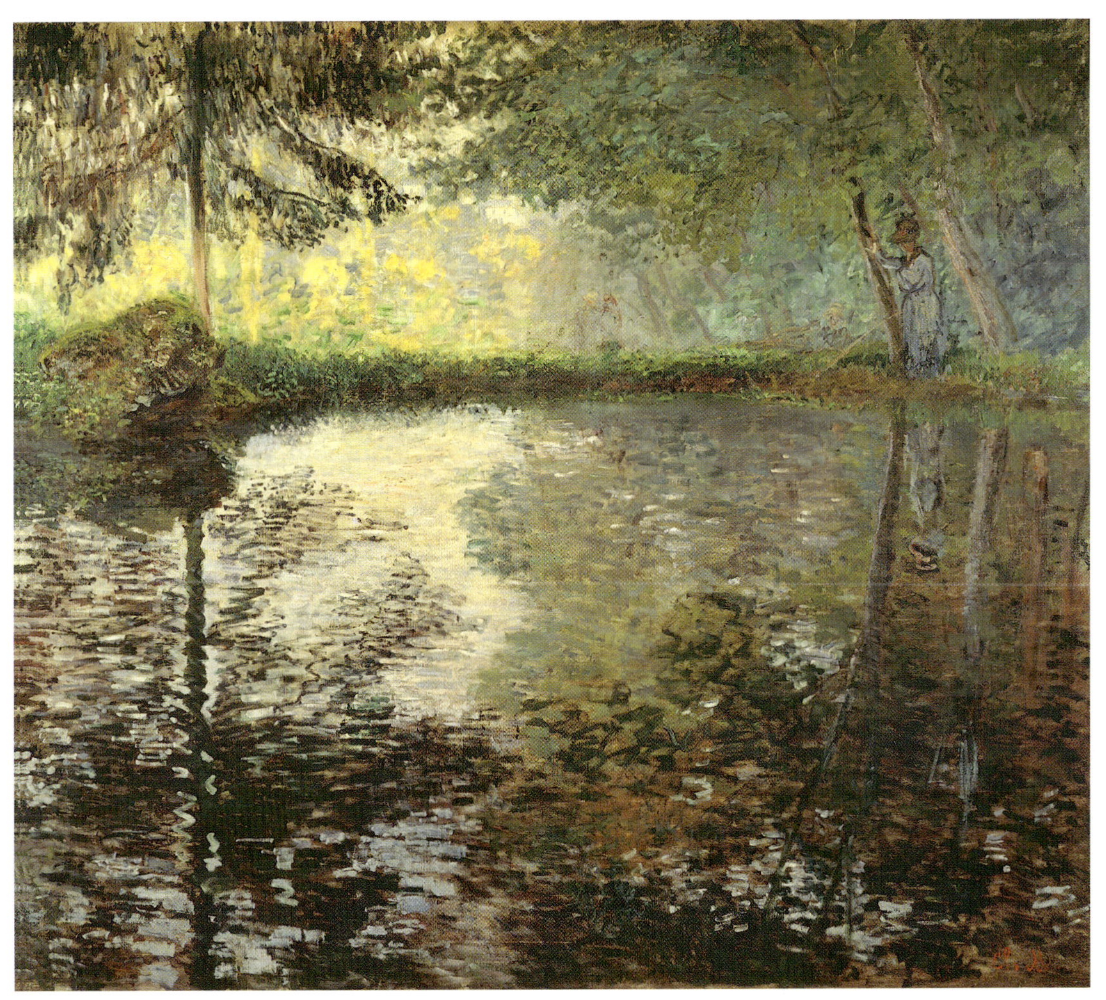

Turkeys
(Les dindons)

1877
Oil on canvas, 174.5 × 172.5 cm
Paris, Musée d'Orsay

Painted for the Hoschedés, this large work depicts a group of turkeys pecking on a grassy slope. The brushstrokes are much broader and separate from one another. The green of the grass is obtained by combining many different hues mixed with tones of blue and dark blue. The thick grassy surface is broken up chromatically by the white masses of the enormous turkeys, whose pale feathers have been created using a mix of whites, pinks, blues, and greens.

Toward the end of the 1870s Monet began to study the reciprocal effect of colors on one another. He used large bristle brushes that allowed him to keep the broad brushstrokes separate so that when seen from a distance the painting appears to have a very clear definition, but this is lost when viewed from close up. The emotional power of the painting is very strong and its unusual subject surprising. It is not at all a picture of a garden with poultry but a very close-up view of a section of a garden dominated by turkeys that seem to be moving forward from the foreground to outside of the picture.

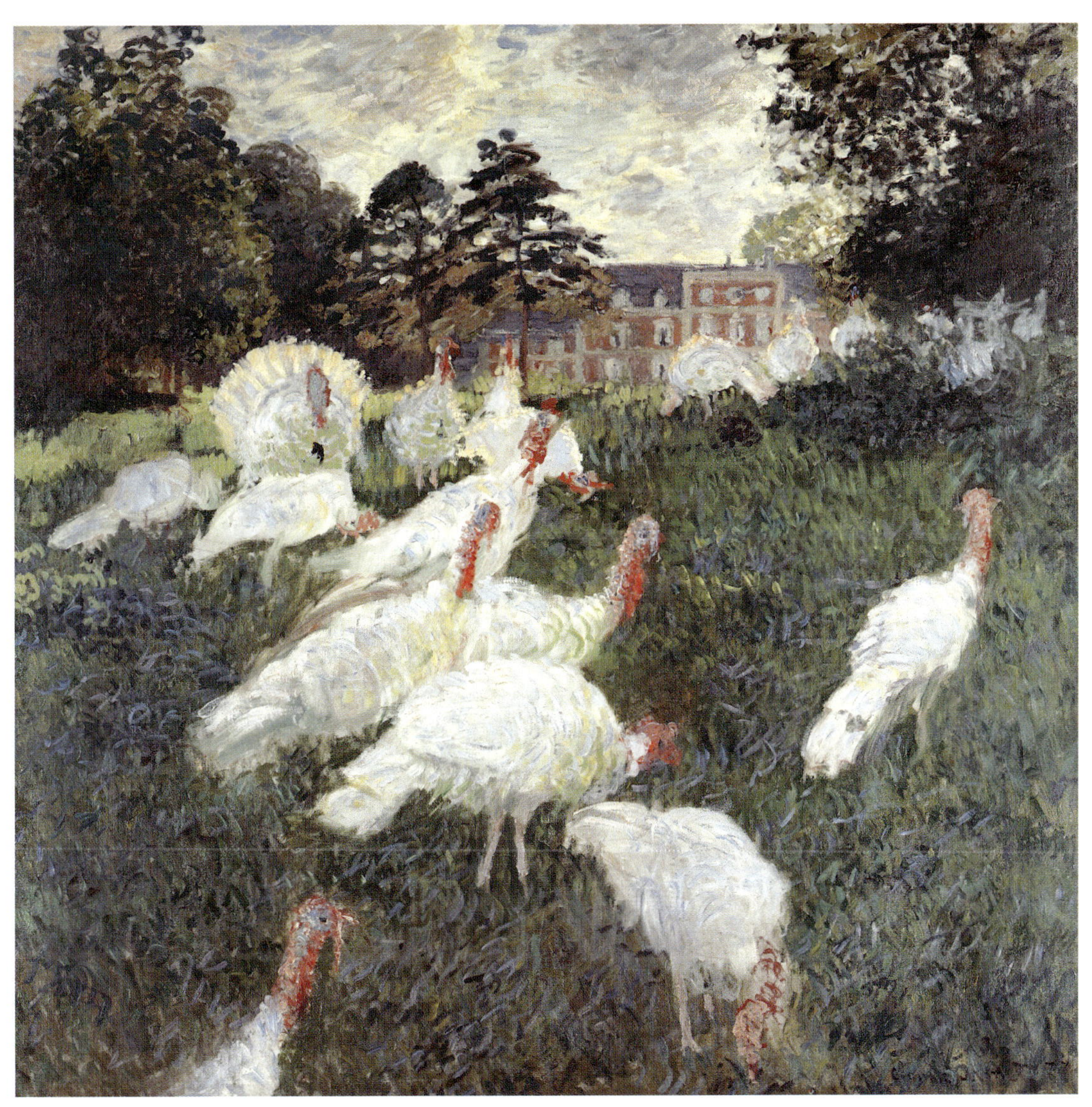

The Saint-Lazare Station

1877
Oil on canvas, 75.5 × 104 cm
Paris, Musée d'Orsay

"When the trains pull out, the smoke of the locomotives is so dense that you can hardly see anything," wrote Monet to Renoir describing his idea of painting Saint-Lazare station. As sources record, he was to paint half a dozen or so canvases of the subject, his first series of works on a single subject, each painted from a different viewpoint and with a different color tonality. The views he produced were unusual and certainly influenced by the kind of results photography was producing at that time. The views are painted as though seen by a large eye looking out from within the large sloping metal structure, but which is unable to focus clearly on the objects as it is open too wide; the upshot is that what is being viewed is blurred by an immense phantasmagoria of steam that curls upwards.

The different views in the series are today spread between different collections: some have remained in Europe while others are in the United States. The Musée d'Orsay in Paris has only one. Since the paintings were conceived as a series, they are difficult to appreciate separately. The one in the Musée d'Orsay is constructed around a symmetry that increases the sensation of mystical verticality produced by this modern cathedral. The glass roof allows us to see the sky of Paris, the billowing blue steam renders the architectural space evanescent and majestic, and those figures that we see are tiny and almost imperceptible.

The visionary appearance of modern Paris was also referred to in prose in Émile Zola's description of the market of Les Halles in *The Belly of Paris*: "A huge beam of sunlight entered from the end of the covered road, slashing through the mass of the pavilions with a portico of light, while incandescent rain drummed down on the expanse of roofs. The enormous cast-iron skeleton was gradually tinged with blue. It was now just a dark outline against the sudden burst of light from the rising sun."

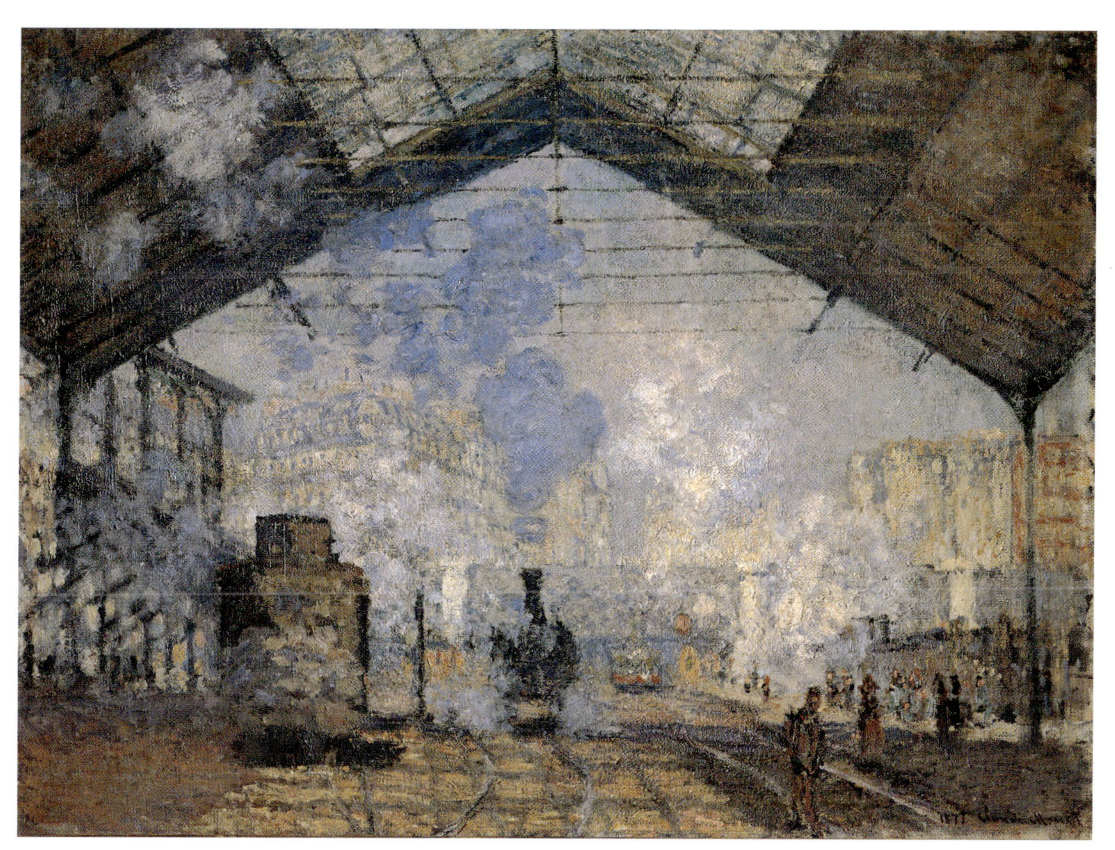

The Rue Saint Denis
Celebration of June 30, 1878

1878

Oil on canvas, 81 × 50.5 cm

Rouen, Musée des Beaux-Arts

From his early apprenticeship Monet had been attracted to Paris as it was the center of the art world in France and the place where one studied and met interesting people, but more importantly he liked it for what the city represented overall visually. To Monet, Paris was rich with subjects to paint and he returned there many times over the years to alternate his paintings of the countryside, sea, and the Seine with views of the city. Monet lived in the area of Paris that Baron Georges-Eugène Haussmann had rebuilt between 1853 and 1870 in a marvelous pattern of wide, tree-lined boulevards of elegant apartment blocks, restaurants, cafés, and shops.

Rue Montorgeuil lies between Rue de Rivoli and Boulevard de Sébastopol right in the heart of Paris just north of the Île de la Cité. Monet painted it on a national holiday, thronged by crowds and lined with French flags fluttering from the windows. The composition is a whirl of moving colors: the red, white, and blue of the flags fill the entire painting with their colorful display.

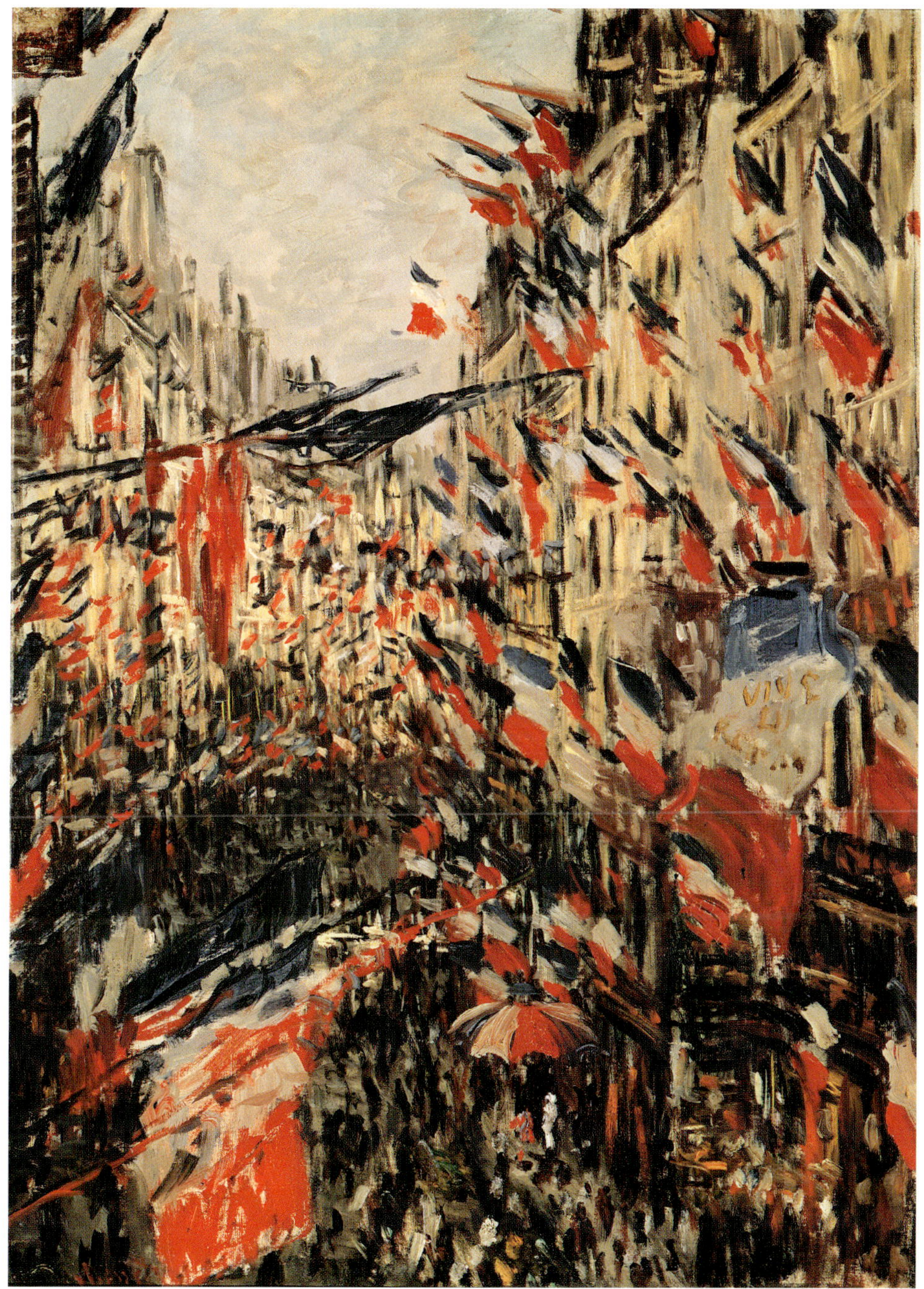

Cliffs at Étretat

1886
Oil on canvas, 65 × 81 cm
Moscow, The Pushkin State
Museum of Fine Arts

In September 1886 Monet returned to Étretat where he had stayed and painted three years earlier. Courbet had already painted here and, like his predecessor, Monet tackled the magnificent landscapes and seascapes of the area. He returned to paint the sea and, in particular, the most spectacular natural feature of the town, the one that had convinced him to take up painting during his youth. Guy de Maupassant, who met him in Étretat during this period, described Monet's method of painting. "I often followed Claude Monet in search of impressions. He was no longer a painter but a hunter. He walked followed by several children who carried his canvases […]. He took [the canvases] or left them, following every change in the sky, he waited, watching the sun and the shadows, captured with a few brushstrokes the perpendicular rays or a wandering cloud and, when he had dealt with every delay, he transferred them rapidly onto the canvas. In this way I saw him catch a dazzling cascade of light on the white rocks and fix it with a flood of yellows that reproduced in a strange manner the surprising and fleeting effect of that elusive, blinding reflection. On another occasion he grabbed a storm out at sea and threw it down on the canvas. It was really the rain that he painted, nothing else than the rain penetrating the waves, rocks and sky, which were hardly identifiable beneath the downpour."

The view is foreshortened from above so that the size of the rocky coast seems magnified. Most of the canvas is filled by the bay, the sea is apparently calm and gives the impression that a storm is imminent.

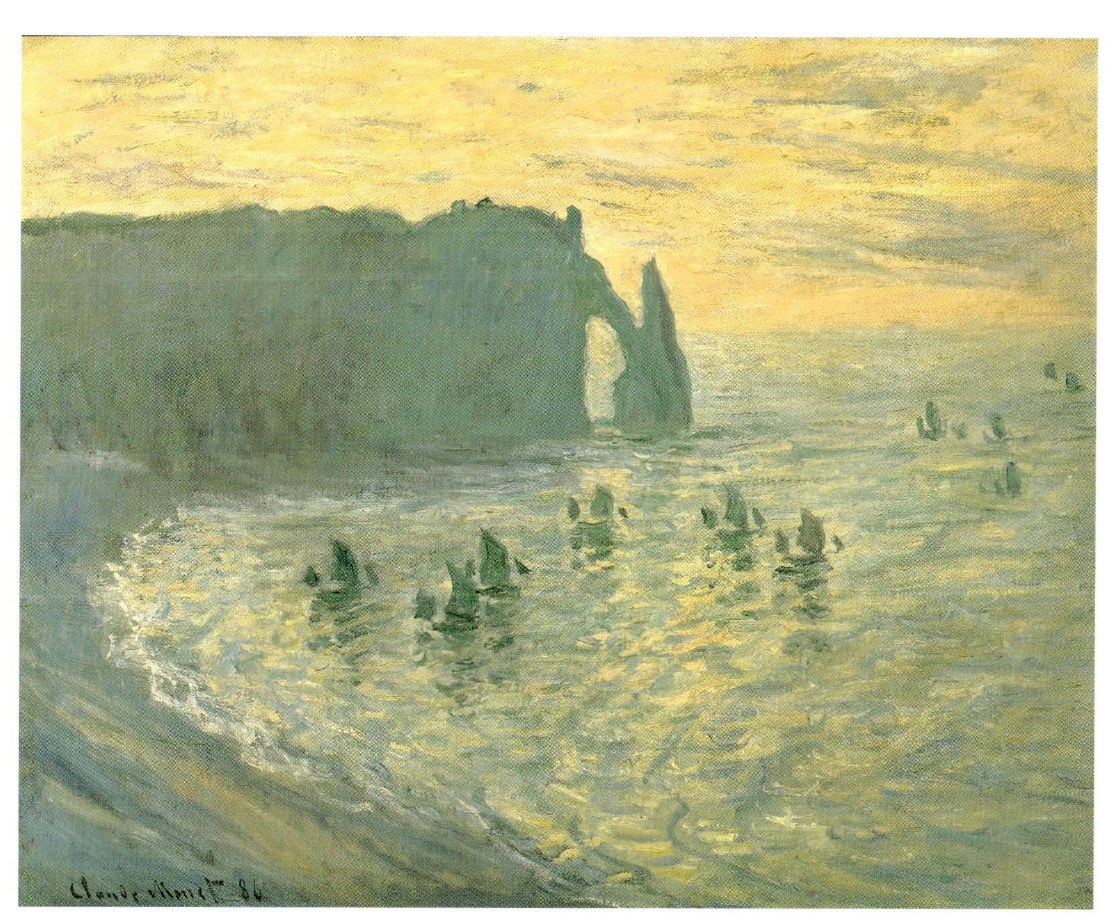

Pyramids at Belle-Île. Rough Sea

1886
Oil on canvas, 65 × 80 cm
Moscow, The Pushkin State
Museum of Fine Arts

In a letter from Octave Mirbeau, one of the most spirited defenders of Monet's art, to the sculptor Auguste Rodin, we read, "I spent a weekend with Monet on his island of Belle-Île. [...] he painted really beautiful pictures that show him to have a renewed talent. [He is] an extraordinary, tremendous Monet [...]. He is a courageous and heroic man. If there is anyone who deserves to be recognized, it is most certainly him." Monet himself stated in a letter to Berthe Morisot that he was exploring the jagged, wind-lashed coastline of a somber but very beautiful area. Monet used deep blues flecked with white to create a dense, restless sea that broke against the dark cliffs, the crumbly rock walls of which hardly resisted the foaming sea.

The scene is painted from above and the artist chose to depict only a small strip of sky on the horizon. The tips of the scattered rocks seem to rise above the waves with difficulty.

In this period Monet's paintings bear a strong resemblance to those of Van Gogh though it was not for another two years that he would see any. The opportunity came in 1888 at Theo van Gogh's, Vincent's brother, who was looking after Monet's interests at that time. The color is dense and full-bodied, the brushstrokes are distinguishable on the surface, and the use of contrasting colors is deliberately chosen to create the desired emotional impact.

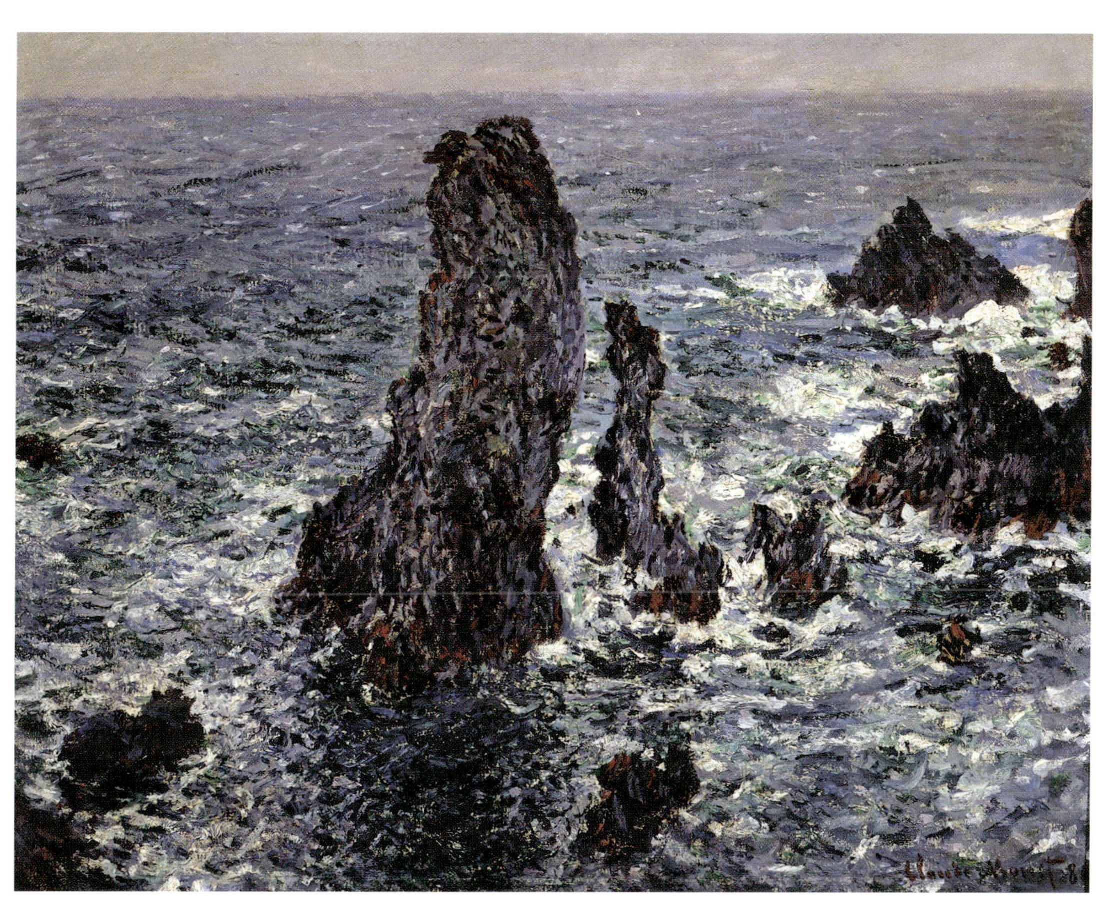

Storm off the Belle-Île Coast

1886
Oil on canvas, 65 × 81.5 cm
Paris, Musée d'Orsay

This is one of the group of paintings Monet made in 1886 at Belle-Île, where he stayed for some time with the aim of taking back home views of the majestic but forbidding place. He moved to the coast of Brittany to experiment with the wild, primitive landscape that was so in contrast with the exotic gentleness of the Mediterranean coast at Bordighera. The bad weather began in October and Monet enthusiastically studied the nature of storms. He decided to prolong his stay and wrote on October 30, 1886, to explain why to Alice Hoschedé, his partner, who was dissatisfied at his absence. "You know my passion for the sea, and this one, in particular, is so beautiful. Accustomed as I am to painting, I believe that by studying it patiently I could produce something excellent in just a few months. I know that I will feel its essence more each day […] in short, I love the sea and know that, to paint it properly, it has to be watched every day, at all hours, and from the same spot in order to understand its life."

The sea is shown in a range of whites with pink and blue shading. The rocks are beaten violently by the foamy waves and almost entirely submerged. The small section dedicated to the sky is blurred with the white of the sea so that there is no clear distinction between the two. The rock in the foreground has been painted with browns, blues, and reds using a very fine brush to form a brownish mass that gives the impression of its porous composition.

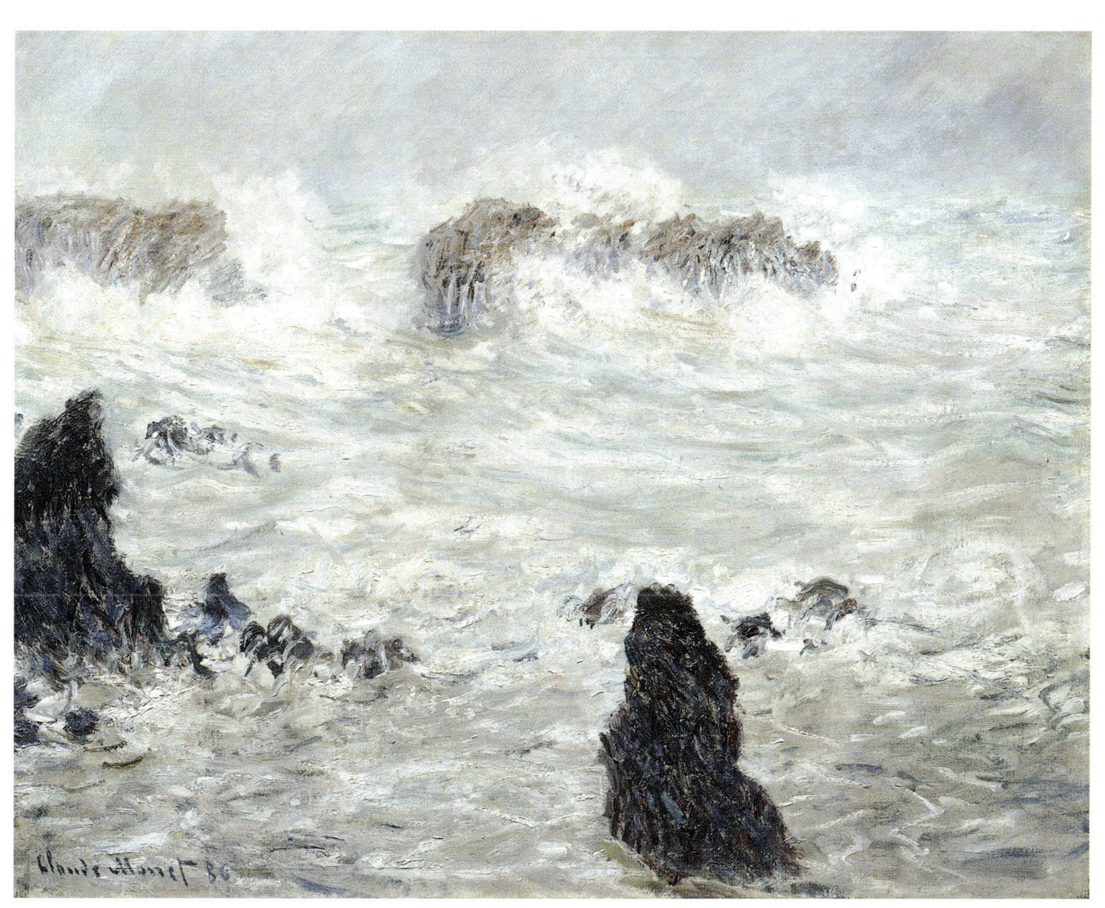

Haystack at Giverny

1886
Oil on canvas, 60.5 × 81.5 cm
St. Petersburg, The State
Hermitage Museum

The motif of the haystacks interested Monet in 1886 but it was only later that they became the subject of a series painted in 1890–91. The painting in the Hermitage was from several years earlier. It was conceived as a work of transition between the impressionist landscapes painted at Argenteuil and the more poetic and sentimental ones of the later period.

In this first depiction of a haystack, Monet used very pale colors that give the painting a tenuous, delicate atmosphere. The stack stands in the foreground but its presence does not block the view of the landscape behind. In later versions Monet shifted his attention to illustrate the haystack itself in a lyrical manner. The motif is completely interpreted in terms of both color and form. As his thoughts and studies of the haystacks progressed, his representations moved away from presenting a true resemblance toward creating chromatic harmonies. The procedure that Monet used in landscape painting was applied by Degas to the human figure, achieving in his pastels in the 1890s images totally removed from the academic concept of form. They were awkward and almost deformed but they were produced using such perfect tonal harmonies that they appear attractive and well-balanced.

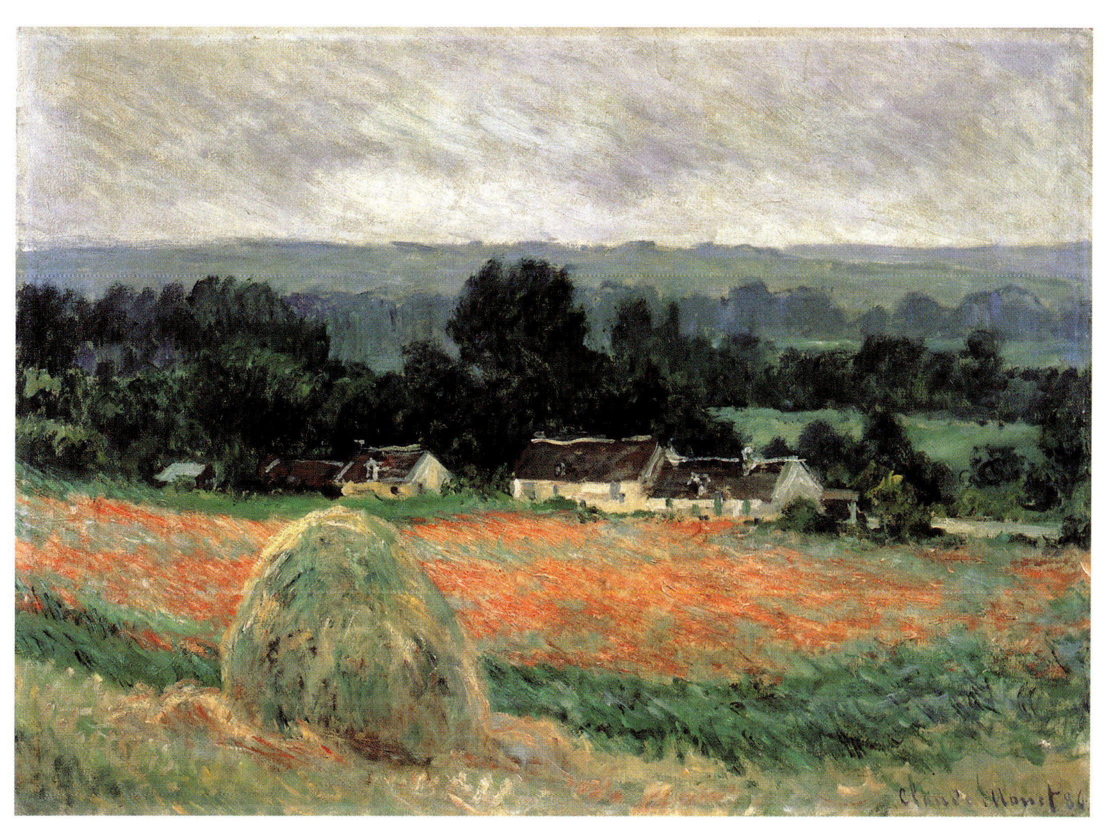

Woman with Umbrella Turned toward the Left

1886
Oil on canvas, 131 × 88 cm
Paris, Musée d'Orsay

This painting is the pendant to *Study of a Figure Outdoors (Facing Right)*. Both are full-length portraits of Suzanne Hoschedé, Alice's daughter, standing in a field and holding a parasol.

The two paintings are also titled *Study of a Figure Outdoors* because they were conceived as studies of the light in a figure portrait. The prevalent tonality is clear and bright but if we look closely the grass is formed by a wide range of colors: yellows, pinks, violets, and greens, as though it were possible to see all those different hues that the mind registers and then blends to create a single, uniform impression. This painting is one of the clearest examples of the marked attention the painter paid to the problem of formal values and the delicate balancing of colors.

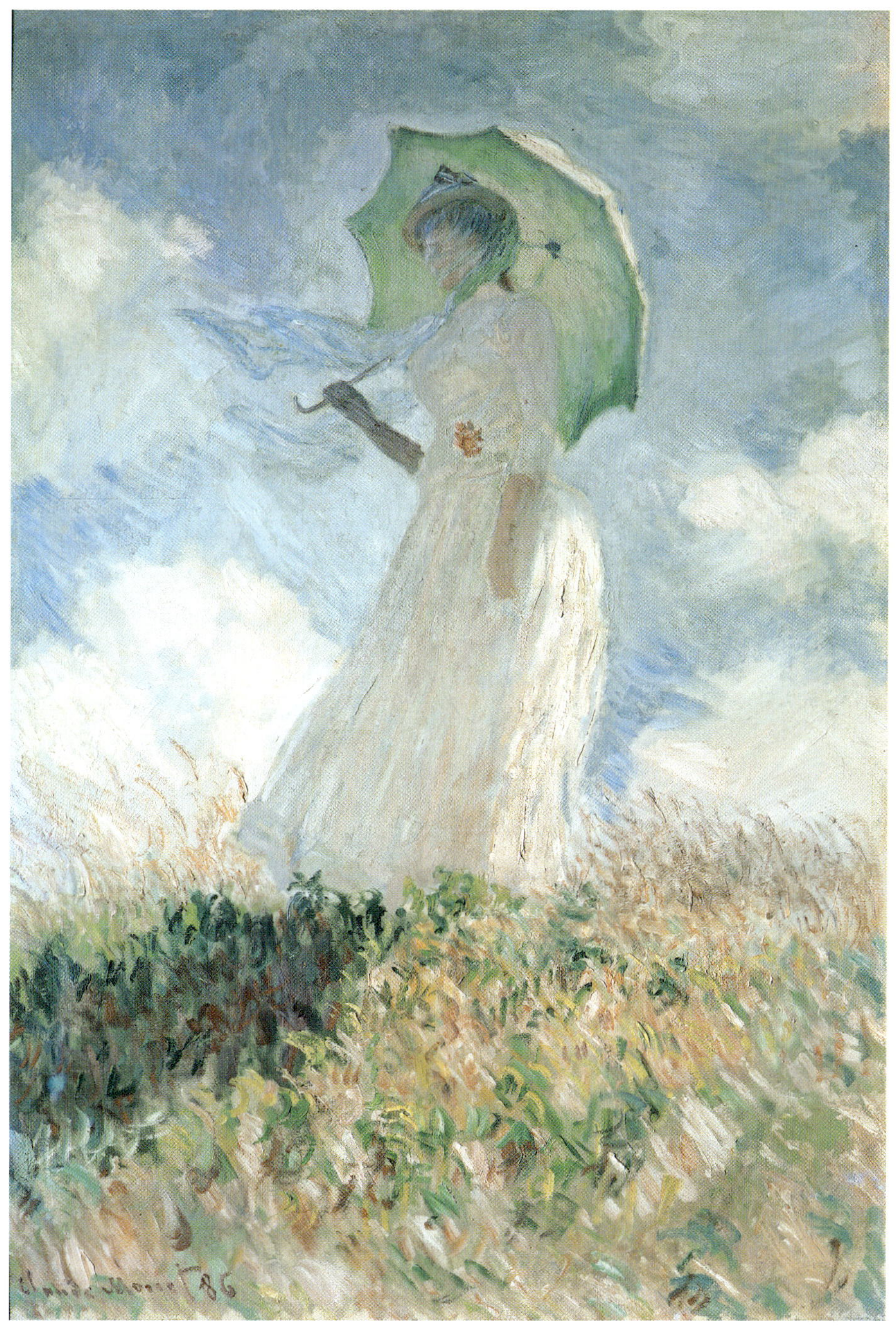

The Blue Rowing Boat

1887
Oil on canvas, 109 × 129 cm
St. Moritz, Thyssen Collection

When visiting an exhibition of impressionist paintings, Stéphane Mallarmé was fascinated by Monet's passion for water. The symbolist poet noted in 1876, "Claude Monet loves water and has the gift of representing its mobility and transparency, whether of the sea or river, gray and monotonous or the color of the sky. I have never seen boats suspended on the water with the lightness apparent in his paintings, nor air more mobile and light than his atmospheres in movement."

When he moved to Giverny, Monet spent most of his time on his own property. His passion for boats was transmitted to his family and he painted several pictures of Alice, his second partner, with her daughters Suzanne and Blanche fishing or chatting on the little rowing boat. They took their craft out on the river Epte close to the Monet home in Giverny. Their excursions on the river became a new opportunity for the painter to study nature, thereby combining work with the pleasure of spending time in close contact with nature.

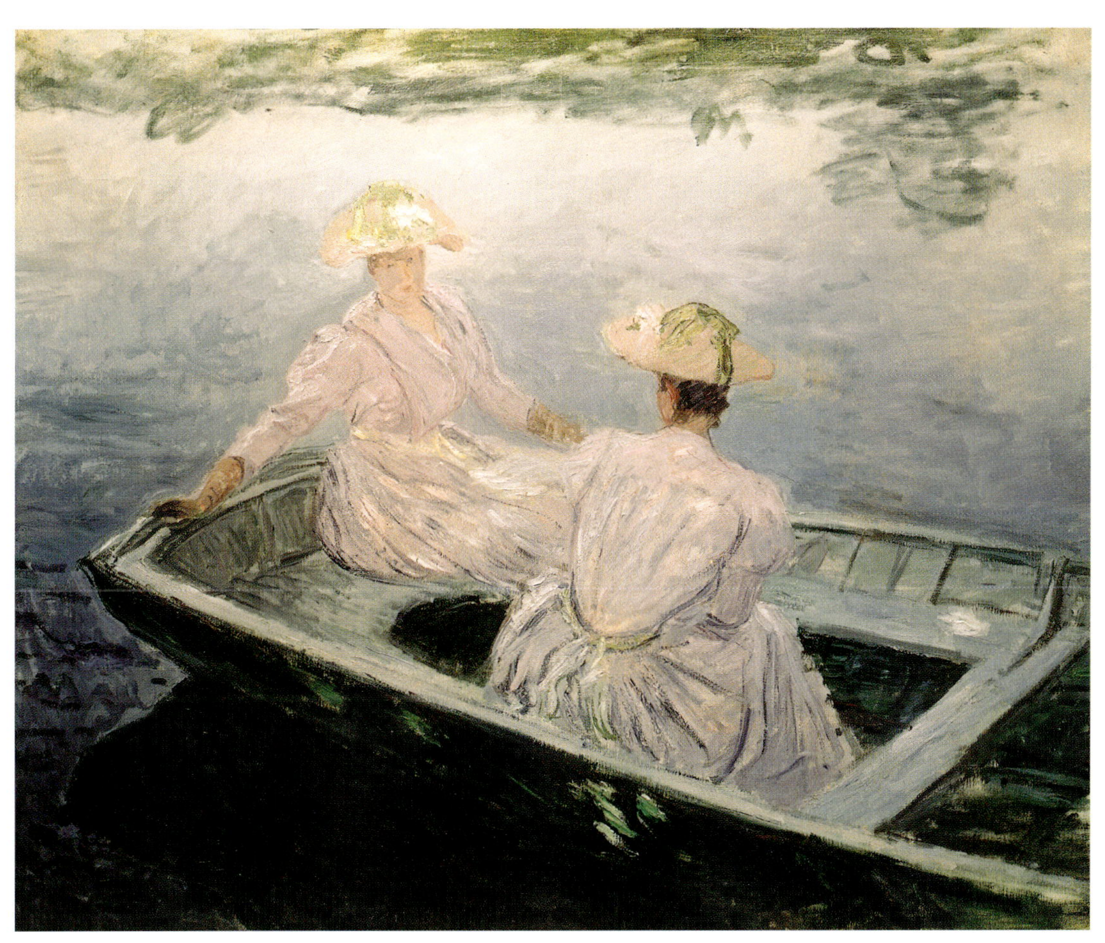

In the Boat

c. 1887
Oil on canvas, 98 × 131 cm
Paris, Musée d'Orsay

The atmosphere in this painting of a boat trip on the river Epte is unreal and dreamlike. Art critics of the period emphasized the romantic tone of representations of this type in which young bourgeois girls chat or dabble with fishing.

The general tone of the composition is a very deep blue made delicate by pink and blue highlights in the women's clothing. The individual brushstrokes in previous works had been fairly easy to distinguish on the canvas but in this painting are uniform. The scene is wrapped in a dreamlike atmosphere in which the boat glides slowly and silently on the still water of the river. Contemporary critics compared canvases like this to literary works such as *Search of Lost Time* by Marcel Proust and the music of Claude Debussy, such as his *En Bateau*.

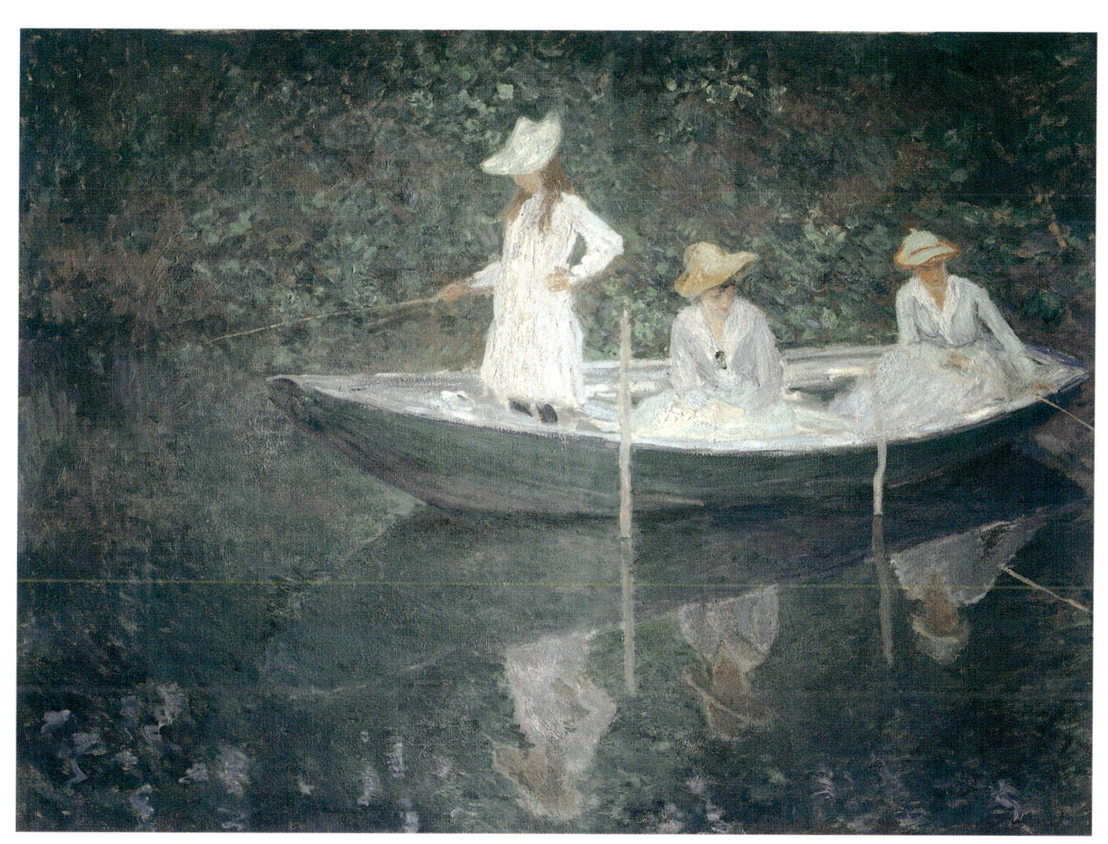

Meadow at Giverny

1888
Oil on canvas, 92 × 80 cm
St. Petersburg, The State
Hermitage Museum

Monet seemed never to tire of the countryside around his home in Giverny and claimed that he ceaselessly continued to portray nature without ever successfully pinning it down. At the end of the 1880s he was better off financially than previous years thanks to the close ties his dealer, Durand-Ruel, had with the American market. In reality Monet was not very happy that his works ended up in the "country of the Yankees," as he called it, but in the end he resigned himself to the fact because he received better money and this enabled him to build the lily pond in his garden that provided the basis for most of his works during his last years. Another outlet for his work, though much more restricted, was Russia. The painting *Meadow at Giverny* was bought by the collector Sergei Schukin of Moscow from Durand-Ruel.

The landscape is treated summarily with the foreground filled by a large green and yellow meadow lined by trees in the background. In this painting Monet approached the chromatic experimentation that he was to investigate in depth in the *Haystacks* series.

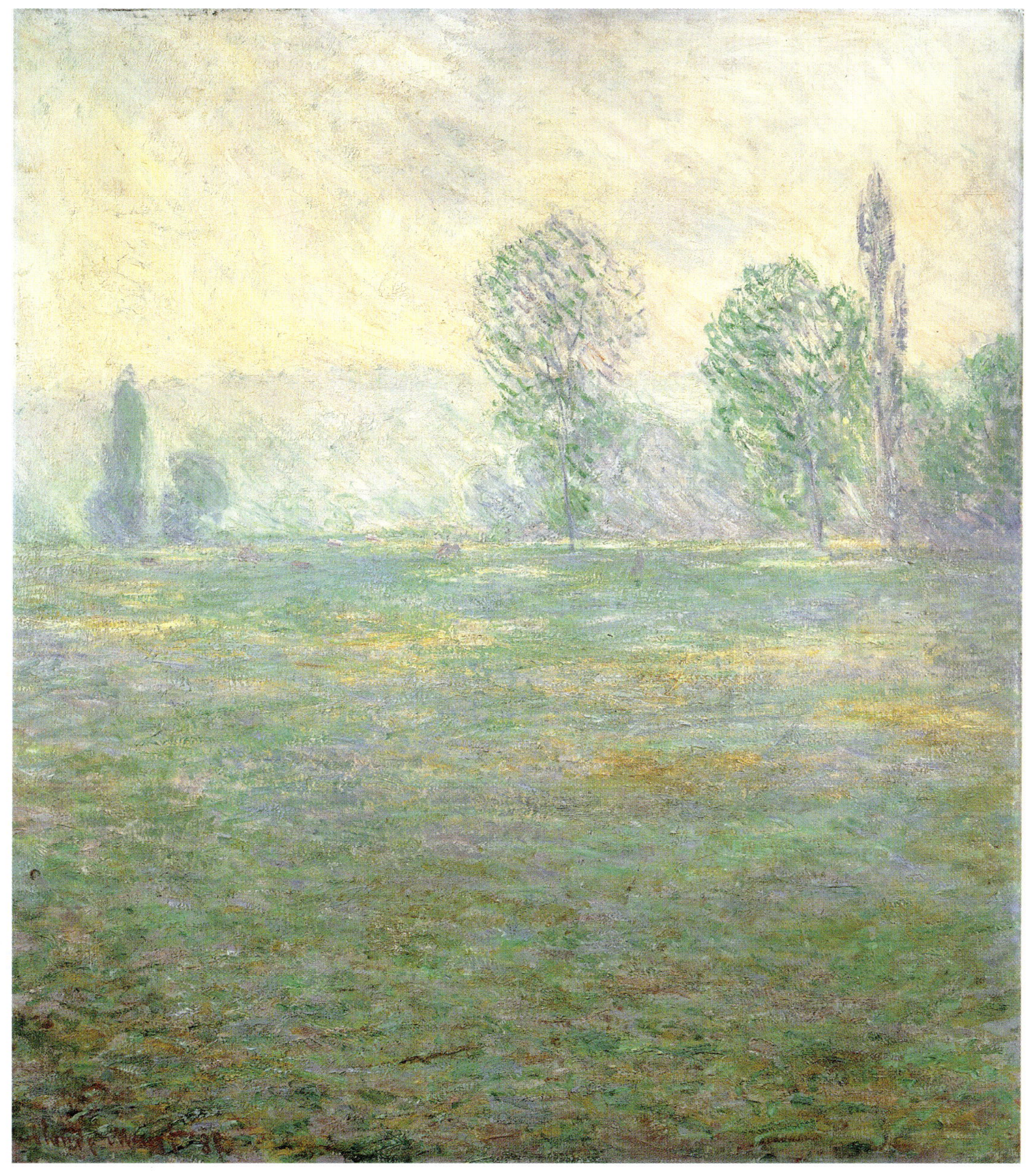

Haystack at Giverny

1889
Oil on canvas, 64 × 81 cm
Moscow, The Pushkin State
Museum of Fine Arts

In May 1891 Durand-Ruel organized an exhibition of twenty-two of Monet's works, fifteen of which were of haystacks painted at different times of the day. The paintings quickly sold at prices between 3,000 and 4,000 francs. Monet later explained that he had initially thought of producing only two paintings of haystacks—one in full sunshine and the other in bad weather conditions. However, as he painted them, he realized there were many more lighting effects he could record and decided to make a painting for each one. He stressed that it was important to abandon the canvas he was working on as soon as the lighting effect changed and work on the next one. Employing this method he was able to depict a particular aspect of nature and not a composite vision, which working on a single canvas for several hours continuously would have produced.

When one of the *Haystacks* was exhibited in Moscow in 1895, the young painter Wassily Kandinsky was overwhelmed and wrote, "Before I only knew realistic art [...]. Suddenly, for the first time, I saw a 'painting'. The catalog told me it was of a haystack but I wouldn't have recognized it [...]. I had, deep down, the impression that the object was missing in this painting, and I was quite overcome when [...] it etched itself in my memory without me expecting it, and it continued to remain there before my eyes in every tiny detail."

The *Haystack at Giverny* in The Pushkin State Museum of Fine Arts in Moscow is fresh and filled with light; the stack itself stands in the foreground and a line of poplars crosses the picture in the background.

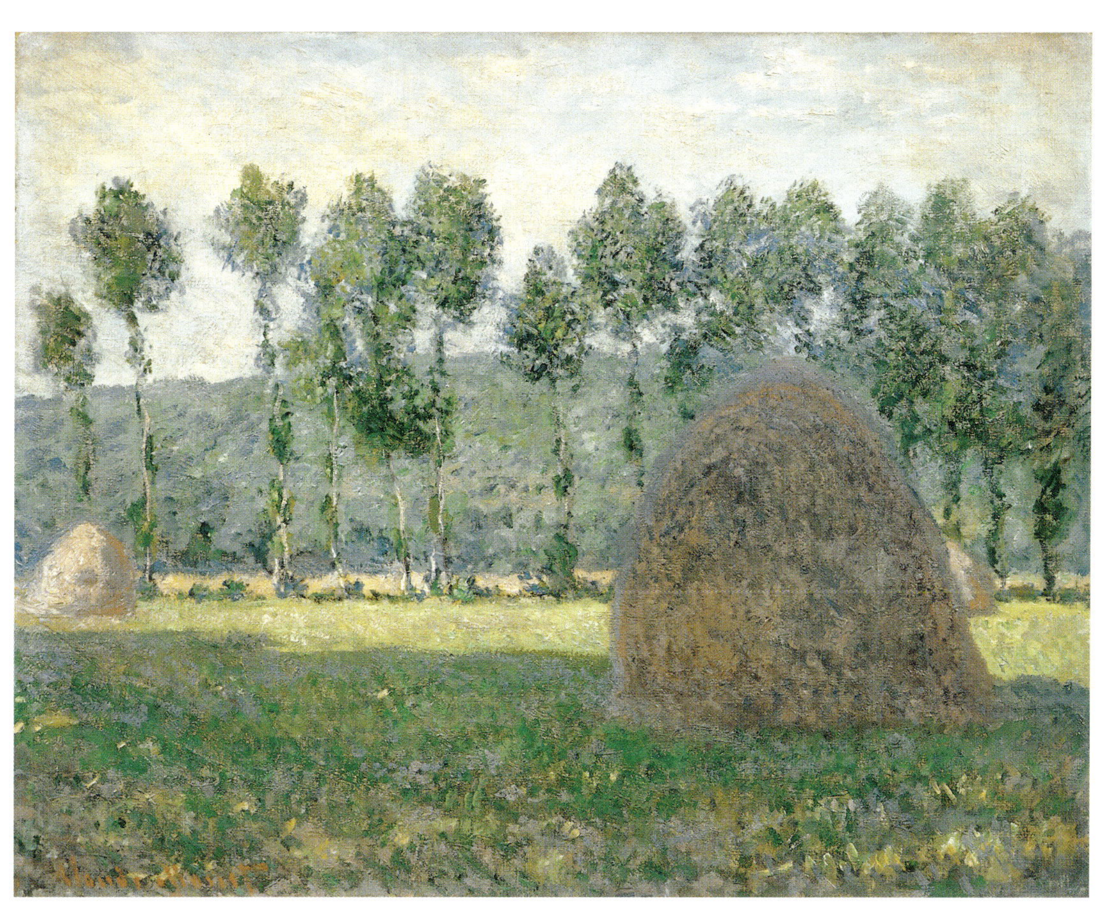

Rouen Cathedral, Evening

1894
Oil on canvas, 101 × 65 cm
Moscow, The Pushkin State
Museum of Fine Arts

In the cycle of more than fifty paintings of Rouen Cathedral, which Monet produced between 1892 and 1894, the artist investigated and reproduced systematically variations of light in the same manner he had in the series of *Haystacks*. This time his study was of architecture and made from different viewpoints and at different times of the day.

In this painting, the cathedral is shown at dusk and seems opaque and lifeless. The artist created contrasts of color using stippled browns rather than bright tones though shifted to dull yellows in the more luminous zones. Monet used a frontal, almost symmetrical view in terms of the space he used for the left and right sections. At the top of the painting the two towers stand out cleanly against a section of yellow ocher sky.

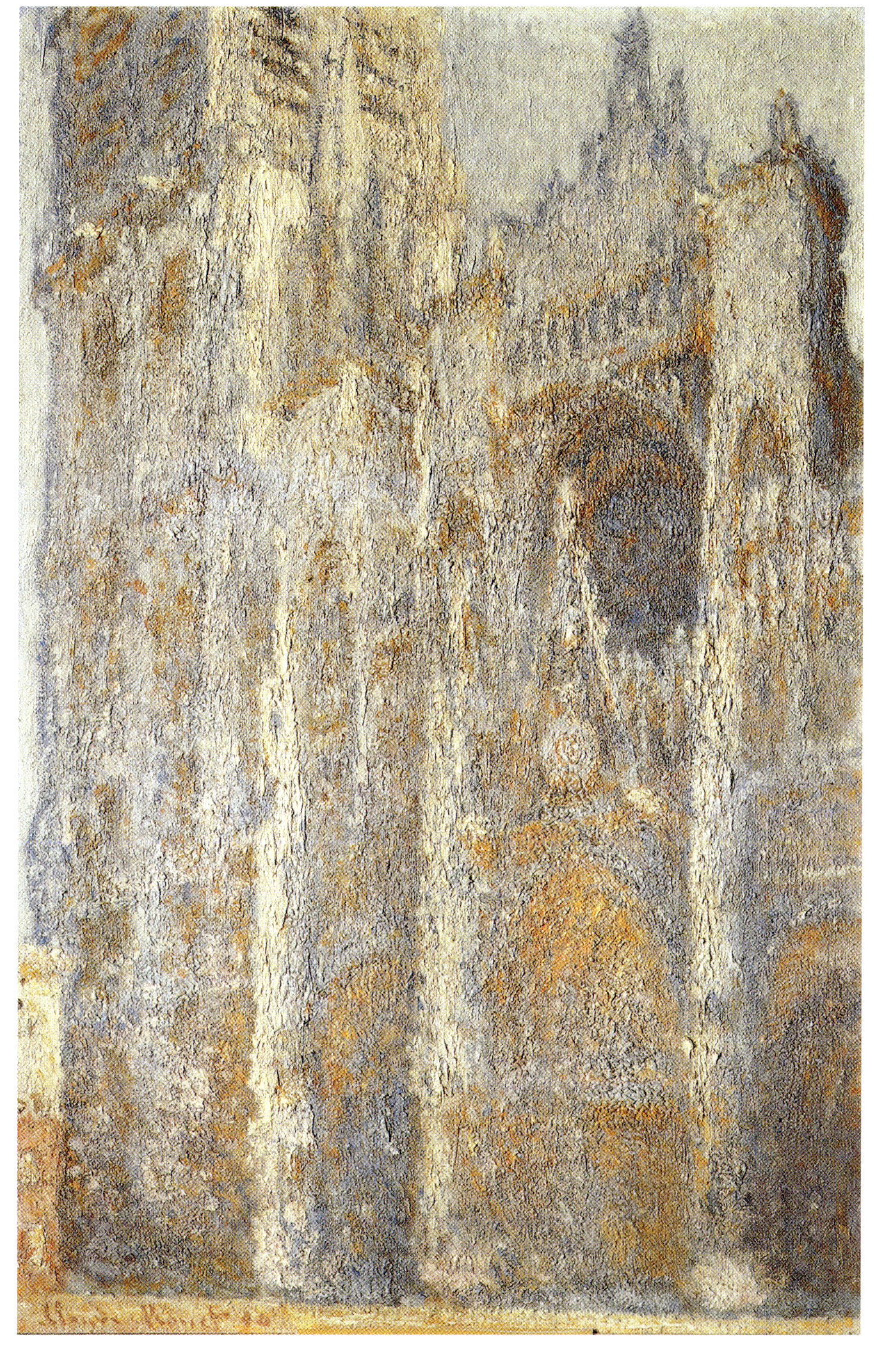

Rouen Cathedral, Midday

1894
Oil on canvas, 100 × 65 cm
Moscow, The Pushkin State
Museum of Fine Arts

Even more than previous series, the views of Rouen Cathedral represented a fundamental step forward in the development of modern painting. Monet's approach to painting was similar to that of Cézanne, who at that time was producing paintings of bathers and views of Mont Sainte-Victoire. In the lyrical description that Rainer Maria Rilke made of Cézanne's working method we find the same tenacity apparent in Monet's letters. "But in spite of everything, the next day [Cézanne] started once again with the same enthusiasm; every morning at six he was already up, he went through the city to his studio and stayed there till ten, [...] he ate and once again headed off, often half-an-hour by road away from his studio, *sur le motif* of a valley, in front of which Monte Sainte-Victoire rose with an indescribable effect, representing an unending challenge."

Accepting that perception was a dynamic rather than unambiguous phenomenon meant also accepting the notion of "possibility" in the study of visual phenomena—a philosophical concept debated in modern science. "Was it just chance," asked Umberto Eco when analyzing the problem, "that such poetics were contemporary with the physical principle of complementarity, in which it is not possible to indicate simultaneously the different modes of behavior of an *elementary* particle; in order to describe these different behaviors, different *models* are in force which are valid when they are used in the right place, but which contradict one another and are therefore called reciprocally complementary?"

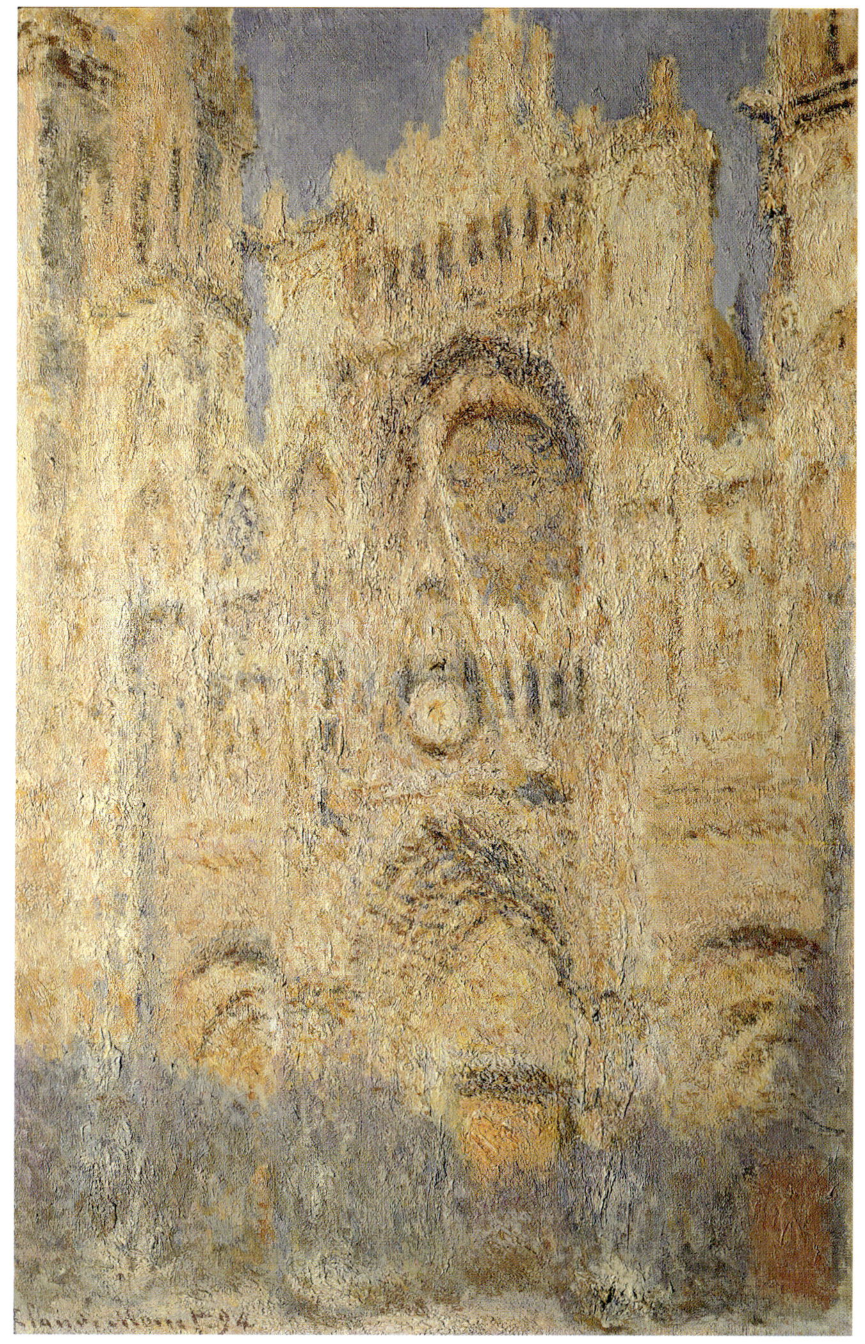

Rouen Cathedral, First Light

1894
Oil on canvas, 106 × 73 cm
Paris, Musée d'Orsay

On March 30, 1893 Monet confided to his dealer and friend Paul Durand-Ruel, "I am working very hard but I cannot think of doing anything else than the cathedral. It is an enormous task." We do not know on which canvases he was working at that time but he was once more unsatisfied at how the work was proceeding. It is clear that this continuous tension between Monet and his painting was part of his natural temperament. There is hardly any trace of satisfaction at his work in his correspondence, not even during the years that it was appreciated by the public.

Rouen Cathedral, First Light, harmonized on tones of blue and yellow, was one of the last variants on the theme he began in 1893. The light increases from left to right and is transformed from a dark blue to a diaphanous, vibrant yellow by the effect of the sun. The outlines are indefinite and the effect is of a metaphysical vision. The low vantage point gives the facade a sense of monumentality, the tower of which remains outside of the picture. At the top of the building the greater luminosity tends to blur the forms.

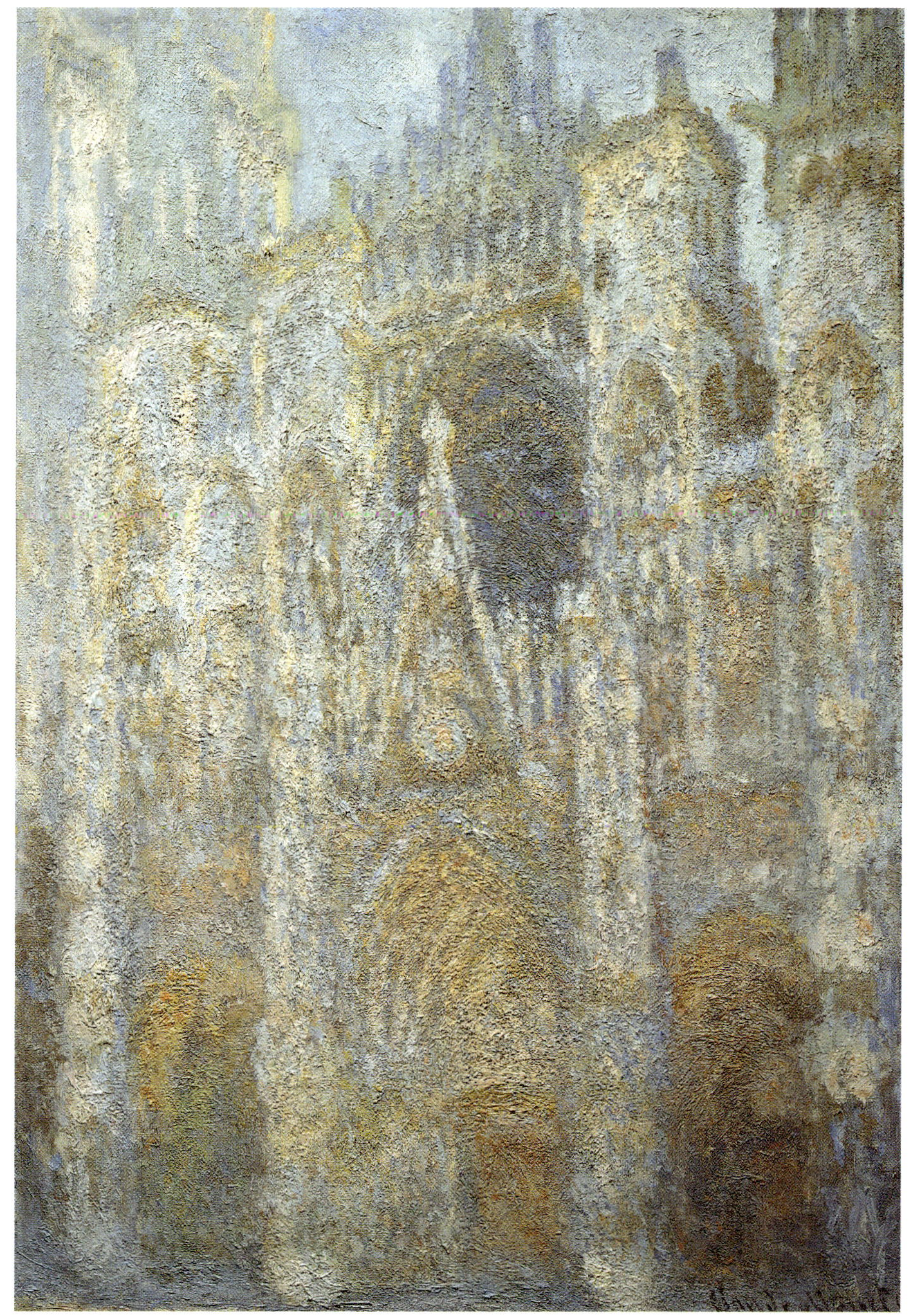

Rouen Cathedral, Morning Sun, Harmony in Blue

1894
Oil on canvas, 91 × 63 cm
Paris, Musée d'Orsay

In this painting Monet depicted Rouen Cathedral as it appears in the morning light. He chose a frontal view and the facade is too large to be contained in the space of the canvas. This approach diverged from the traditional notion of sizing an object to fit the space of the canvas and was completely innovative. The painter used it to give the impression that the observer is actually "seeing" the cathedral from very close up.

During the morning the sun softly enveloped the forms of the cathedral with the result that those sections in the lightest places seem almost distended. The Gothic portal with the tall spire above it can be clearly made out although the outlines are indistinct and tremulous. The filled and empty spaces of the volumes are easily perceived, making the building surface a hive of recesses and projections in which light and shade alternate. This representation of the building revolves around different tones of ocher and blue, with yellows in the more luminous zones.

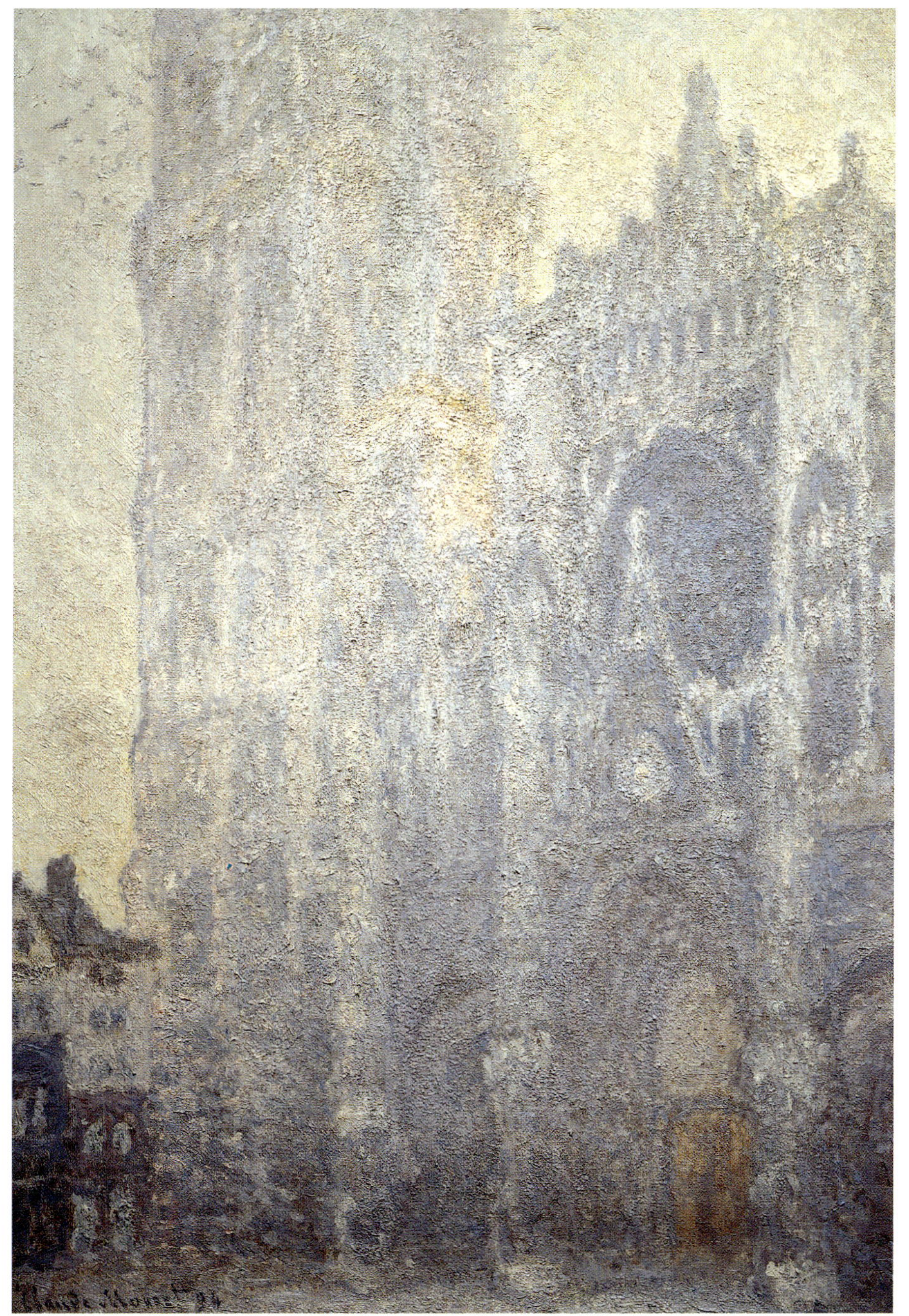

Rouen Cathedral, in the Sunlight

1894
Oil on canvas, 107 × 73 cm
Paris, Musée d'Orsay

The midday sun invades and transfigures the forms of the cathedral. In the parts of the building of greatest brightness the outlines have been completely dissolved by the light. The only zones that remain in shadow, and reinforce the three-dimensionality of the volumes, are the portals and the large rose window above. The viewpoint is very close to the building which rules out the tower and the sides of the facade. The colors used are mostly tones of yellow which create a spongy effect on the canvas that, if observed closely, suggests the paint has been trickled on. When viewed from a short distance the volumes seem mixed together but from further away they take on an extraordinary and vibrant definition. However, what to us appears lyrically perfect was a source of creative torment to Monet. His letters give the impression of the artist eager and anxious to see and represent what he considered far-off and elusive. "My stay here is going ahead: that does not mean that I am close to finishing my cathedrals. [...]. The more I see, the worse I succeed in rendering what I feel; and I tell myself that anyone who says he has finished a canvas is an arrogant so-and-so. [...] I work quickly but without making progress, searching and groping but without achieving very much though I am on the point of exhaustion."

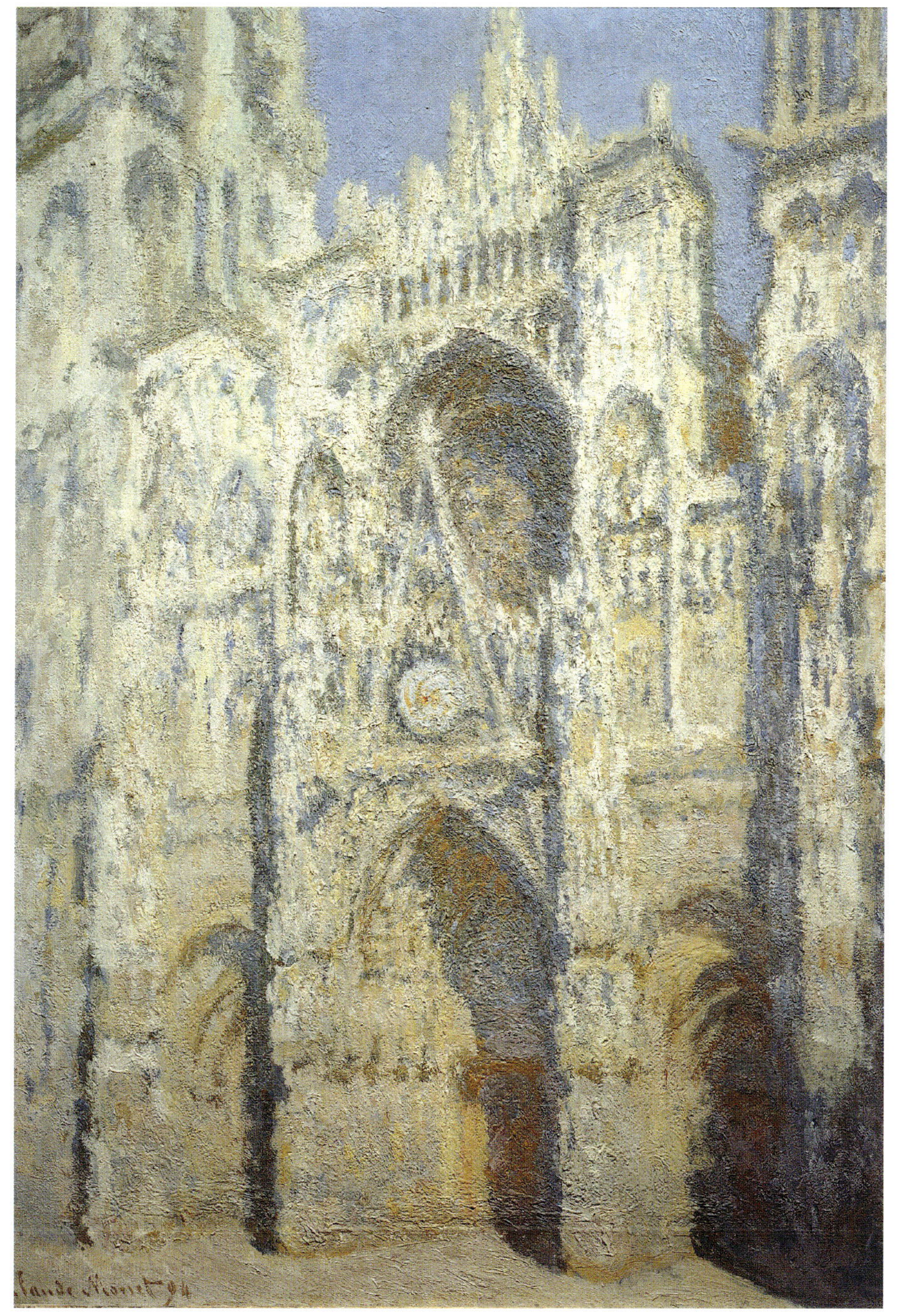

Arm of the Seine at Giverny

1897
Oil on canvas, 75 × 92.5 cm
Paris, Musée d'Orsay

Monet never gave up on the theme of water. At the end of the century he was still fascinated by views of the Seine valley, which had been one of his favorite subjects even in his earliest years. In this painting, filled with light and its reflections, Monet returned to the motif of iridescent light that he had started to explore in his commissions from Ernest Hoschedé in the late 1870s. A huge series of studies he had carried out in the past had made Monet a master in the rendering of forms and colors reflected in a sheet of water. Comparing this painting to his works from the 1870s we see that the older artist succeeded in creating effects of greater virtuosity and refinement. He portrayed the landscape in great detail but he was now fully able to handle it emotionally as well as technically. The result is extraordinary and, by this time, the public too had learned to admire the work of the fifty-seven year old painter.

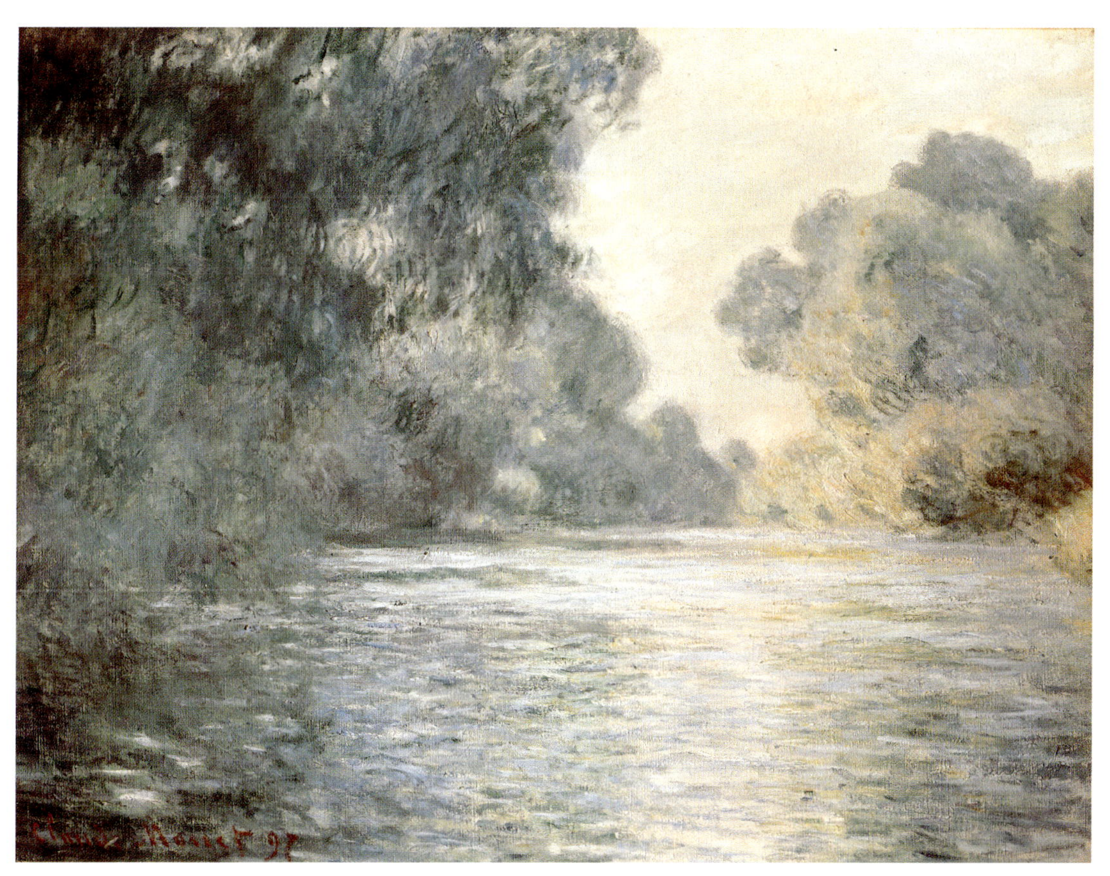

Pink Water Lilies

1898
Oil on canvas, 81.5 × 100 cm
Rome, Galleria Nazionale
d'Arte Moderna

This painting is one of the few examples of Monet's series of water lilies in Italy. The tonality of the painting centers on pale pinks. The plants are portrayed from very close up and seem to have rested on the water for centuries. In his garden Monet turned his back completely on the contemporary world. Since his youth he had been happy to paint city views but now he seems to have renounced the clamor and dynamism of the metropolis. His subjects now were still though he managed to capture the passing of time through depicting them in the cycle of their blooming and fading. This sense of transience is also expressed in his letters: "In the air I find a color I discovered yesterday and I throw down a quick version of it on one of the canvases: immediately the painting comes to me and I try to capture it as quickly as possible; but usually it disappears almost straightaway leaving a different color in its place, one that I had already recorded some days earlier on another canvas and which comes before me immediately. And so it goes on all day." The solitude that Monet shut himself up in during his last years was followed by a general silence by art critics on his work. He continued his experimentation but by that time the Parisian art world was being filled with new stars who attracted the attention of the extreme critics. It was only after his death that favorable opinions were expressed on the cycle of *Water Lilies*, his last great undertaking.

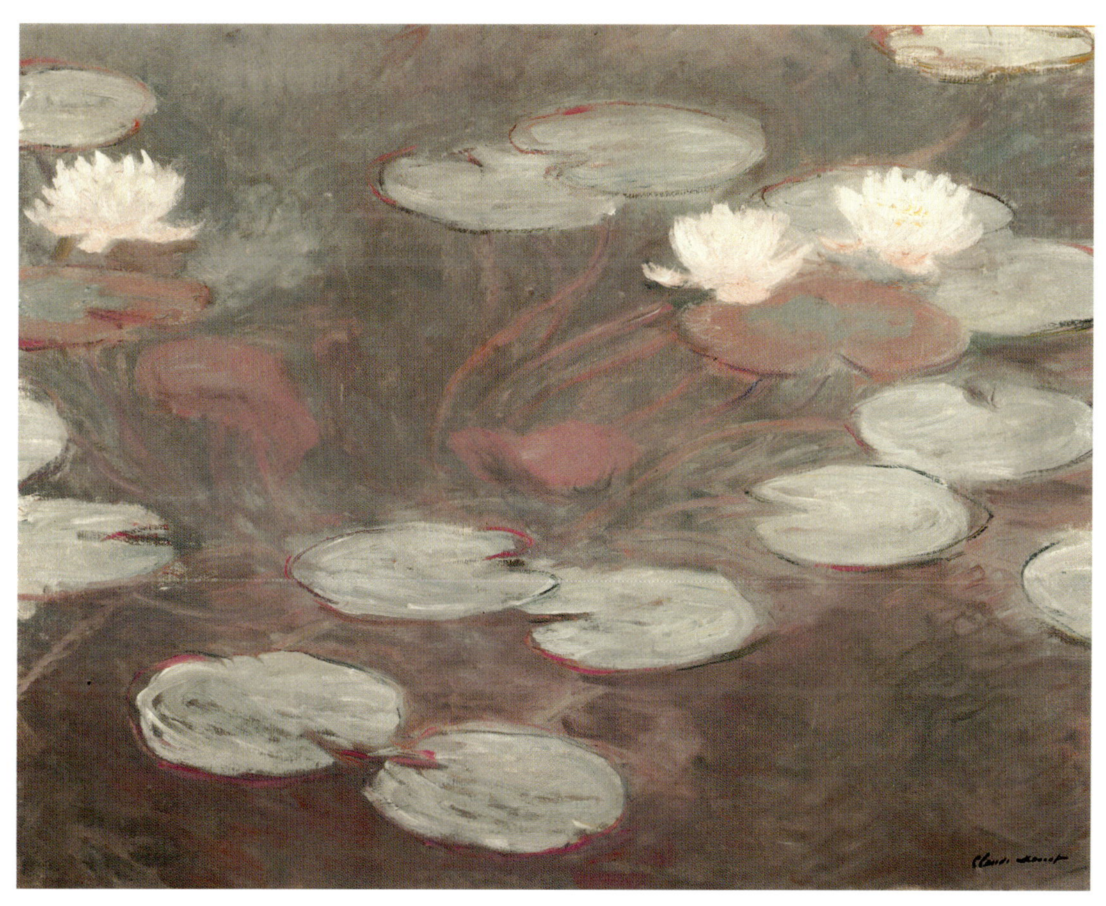

Waterlily Pond

1899
Oil on canvas, 89 × 93 cm
Moscow, The Pushkin State
Museum of Fine Arts

This painting in the Pushkin Museum is one of the most famous from his *Water Lilies* series. It is very similar to the version *Waterlily Pond, Symphony in Green* in the Musée d'Orsay. The thick vegetation fills the entire canvas, without either sky or horizon. To tell the truth, the term "decorative panel" would be more suitable for a work of this type since this is not the painting of a conventional landscape but a work in which surface values tend to predominate, created by the myriad interwoven living essences that make up the subject. Between 1910 and 1920 Monet returned to paint this part of his garden, but in the later versions the subject matter was done away with in favor of a whirl of colors used to represent the plants and bridge.

In 1939 the art historian Lionello Venturi wrote, "In the series Monet searched for exceptional motifs [...], he said he was disgusted by anything that succeeded easily and produced wonders of technical ability. The gradations are uniform and rigorously harmonized. But the more refined the gradations, the less they maintain their vitality; the more the light is carefully rendered, the less it bursts out from a haze that envelops everything and which effaces the object represented. [...] Unquestionably the study of the light in the series is a scientific program but its pictorial realization reveals sentimental tendencies."

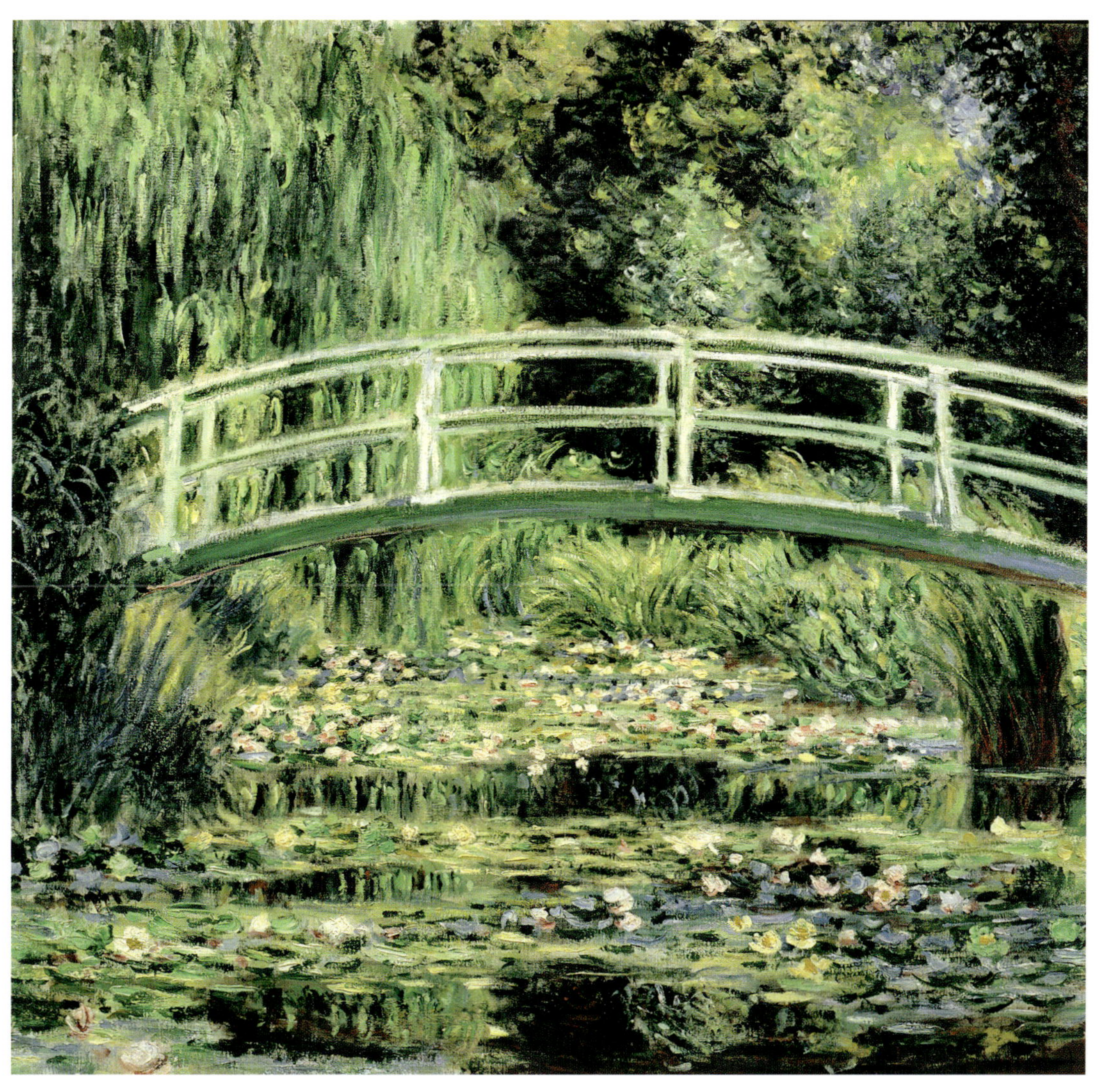

Waterlily Pond, Symphony in Green

1899
Oil on canvas, 89.5 × 100 cm
Paris, Musée d'Orsay

The painting is of a corner of Monet's garden in Giverny and was conceived as a harmony of colors in which the various tones of green prevail. The color is dense and mellow like in the cycle of paintings of *Rouen Cathedral*. The Japanese bridge at the center of the composition divides the pictorial space into two horizontal sections. No use is made of perspective effects and the artist has returned to the inspiration offered by Japanese prints, of which he had a large collection. One of the rooms in his house was entirely lined with Japanese prints that he had mostly purchased in Holland. In 1896 he wrote to a dealer friend, "Thanks for thinking of me for Hokusai's *Flowers*." It was from Japanese painters that he had learned to coordinate space using canons different to those in Western art. In addition, Oriental painting had taught him to conceive landscapes using decorative criteria.

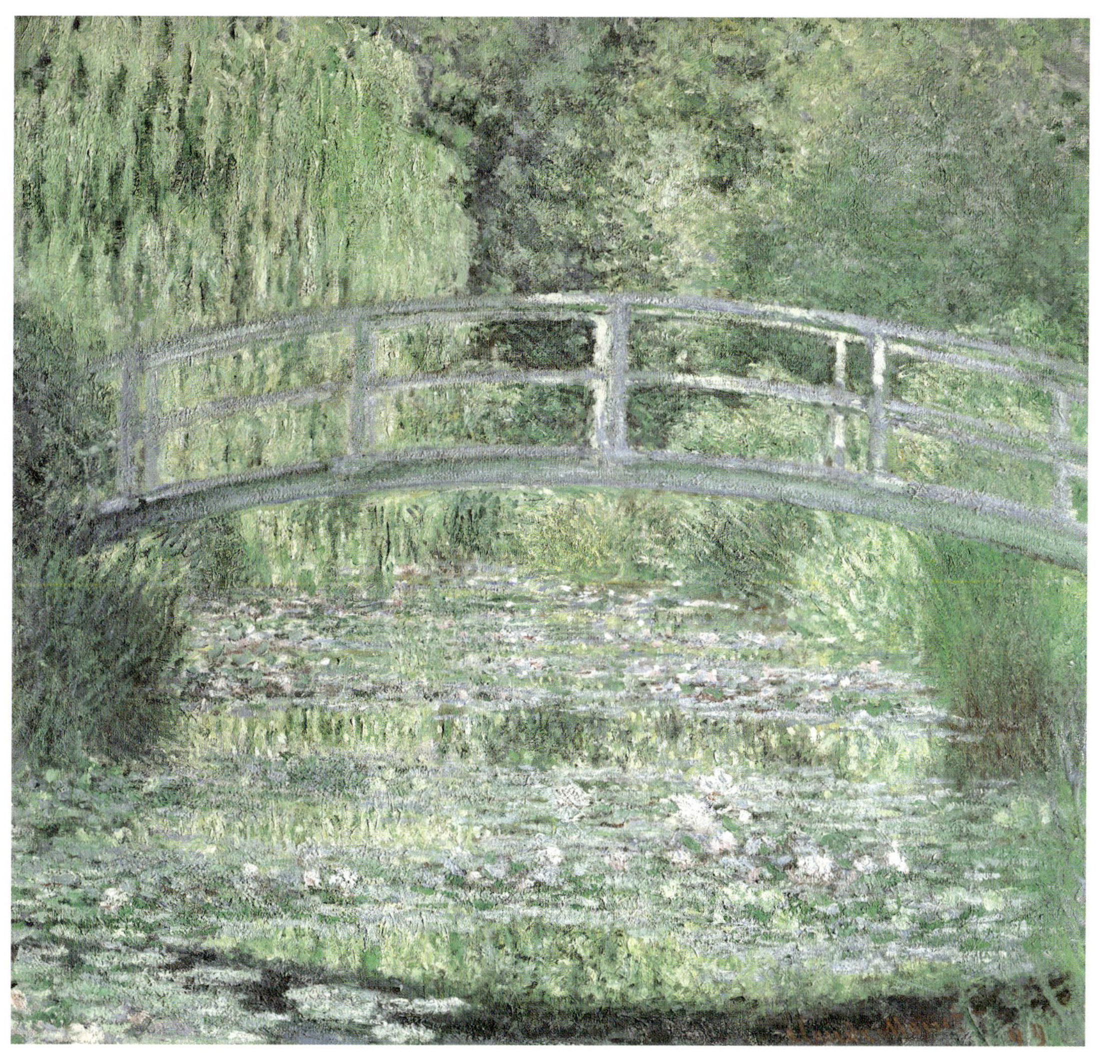

143

Waterlily Pond, Symphony in Pink

1900
Oil on canvas, 89.5 × 100 cm
Paris, Musée d'Orsay

This painting is of the Japanese bridge in Monet's garden in Giverny. The tonalities are modulated on dazzling chromatic harmonies, with red-mauve hues mixed with greens and yellows. The paint has been applied thickly with thin, disordered brushstrokes. The effect is of a highly colored pastel and it seems that in this version of the water lilies Monet is referring explicitly to the great colorist Renoir. The dazzling set of colors used seem to communicate the artist's passion for the delicate water lilies that he had chosen personally to decorate his private paradise, the place in which he had chosen to spend the serenity of his old age. However, we know that his work on the *Water Lilies* occupied him incessantly and gave him no peace. He wrote to his art dealer, Paul Durand-Ruel, on several occasions complaining that he was unable to capture the motif as he would like: "Know that I am absorbed by my work. These views of water and reflections have become an obsession. It is beyond my strength as an old man but I want to depict what I feel so strongly. I am worn down by it […], I keep starting over hoping that something will come out of so much effort."

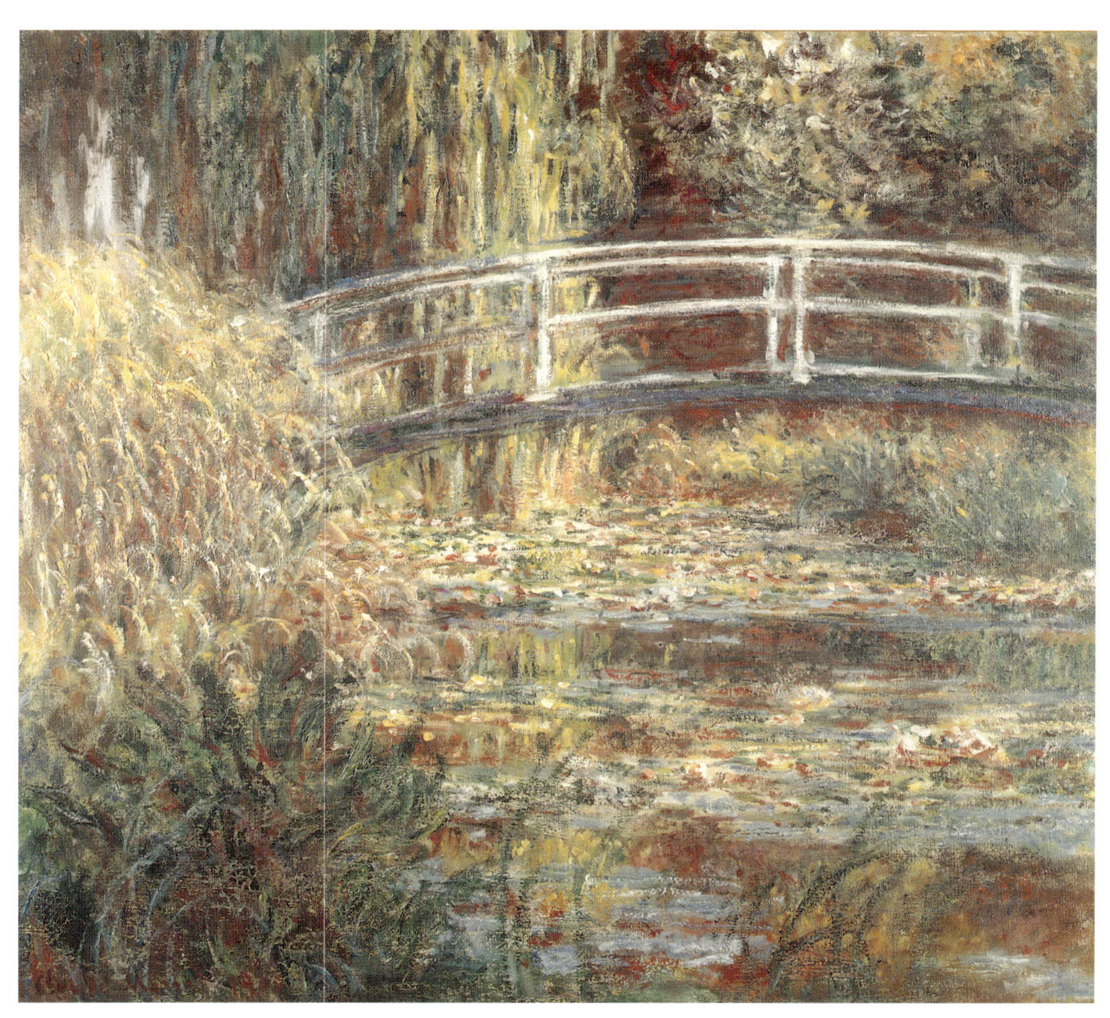

Waterloo Bridge, Effect of Fog

1903
Oil on canvas, 63.5 × 101 cm
St Petersburg, The State
Hermitage Museum

Monet returned to painting views of a city but no longer those of a chaotic and teeming metropolis. He substituted the Paris of the large boulevards for a silent London immersed in fog. The sublime voice of Coleridge seems to rise from the Thames and sing: "The silence of a City, how awful at Midnight! / […] And all the City silent as the Moon / That steeps in quiet light the steady vanes / Of her huge temples."

Monet's vision of the cityscape of London seems affected by the melancholic interpretation in the works of James Abbott McNeill Whistler. The two painters were in contact from an early period and in London they had the opportunity to renew the artistic partnership they had begun in Paris. Whistler was very well thought of by the impressionist group for his delicate use of color and the suffused atmosphere in paintings that visibly reflect the poetry of Mallarmé. With Whistler, Monet shared the ability to manipulate a single color to describe a city view, brightening it and darkening it to suit. The rarefied use of the paint achieved almost "abstract" effects, and confirmed Monet's interest in the symbolist aesthetics that had permeated the French world of culture at the end of the century.

The Houses of Parliament,
Effect of Sunlight in the Fog

1904
Oil on canvas, 81 × 92 cm
Paris, Musée d'Orsay

The pictures Monet painted of London at the start of the twentieth century marked a return to urban scenes, a genre he had abandoned long before. The sense of "modernity" that had infused the cityscapes of earlier years were no longer present at all in the views of London. The viewpoint was always distant from the subject and the landscape was set in a haze that blurs the shapes. There is no trace of human life in these mysterious views of the British capital and the outlines of buildings can hardly be made out. The predominant tones are pinkish oranges and blues veering to violet. The brushwork is compact and more visible in the lower section where the sun is reflected in the Thames. It follows a circular path that guides the observer's eye, from bottom right to the left and then coming back on itself to the center at the top.

In an attempt to describe the beauty of the painting, Octave Mirbeau wrote of Monet's views of London, "a unique theme in these canvases, unique and yet different: the Thames. Smoke and fog; forms, architectural masses, vistas. A muffled city enveloped by fog, the fog itself; the struggle of the light and all the phases of the struggle; the sun a prisoner of the haze or which pierces the colored, radiant, teeming depths of the atmosphere in disconnected rays; the multiple, infinitely changing and vague, obscure and fantastic, delicious, florid, anguished and terrible drama of the reflections on the water of the Thames."

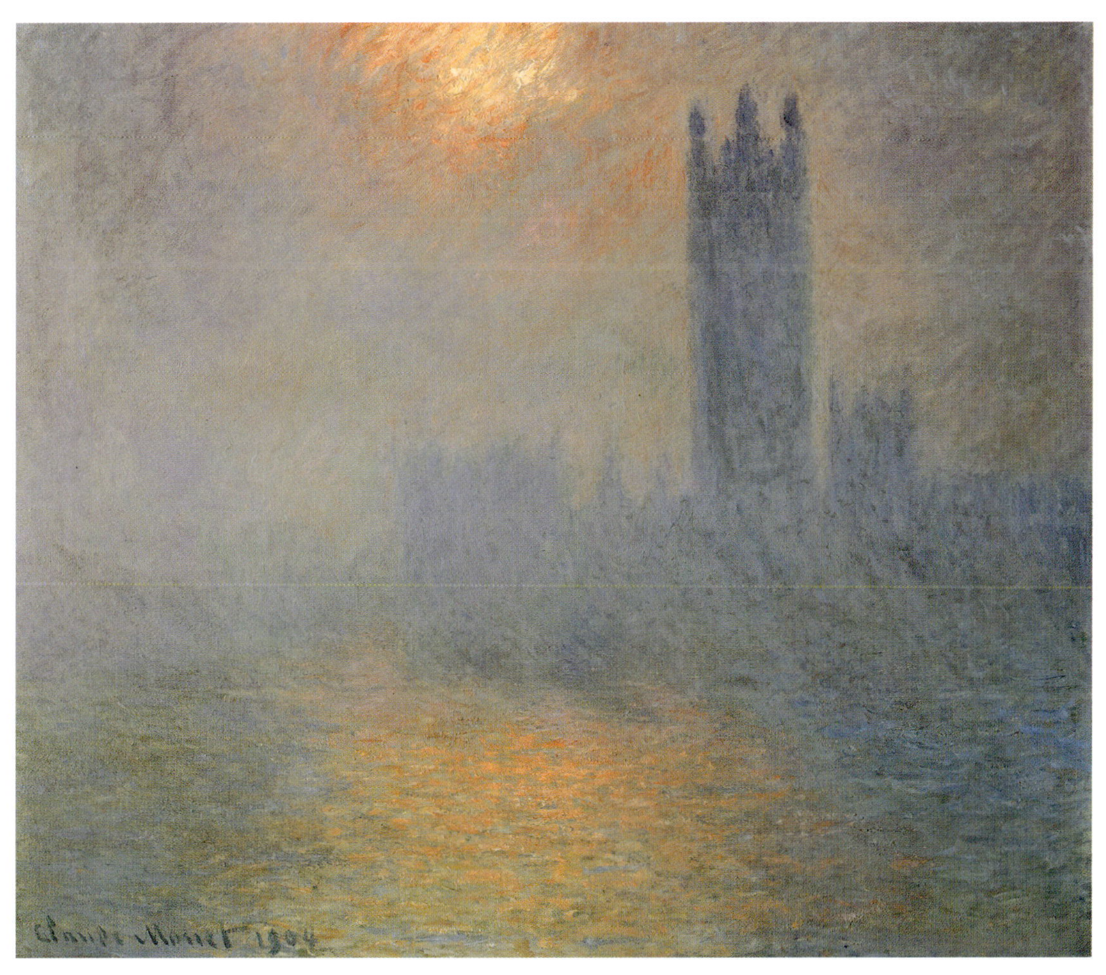

The Japanese Bridge

c. 1910
Oil on canvas, 89.5 × 115.3 cm
New York, The Museum
of Modern Art.
Grace Rainey Rogers Fund.
Digital Image © 2002
New York, The Museum of
Modern Art

The passion for Japanese culture that had swept Paris in the 1860s brought with it an enthusiasm for Japanese gardens. In 1890 Monet bought the house in Giverny and decided to build a garden with many different types of plants; he even had the seeds for his water lilies sent from Japan. Over the lily pond he built a small Japanese-style wooden bridge, at the ends of which he grew various exotic plants encircled by weeping willows. He depicted this corner of the garden in many paintings from 1899. In the first paintings he used a frontal view that allowed him to represent clearly the morphology of the prospect. As his studies of the water lilies progressed, so the views of the bridge—which he continued to paint every few years—took on different connotations. The perception of the colors altered, perhaps because of the cataract that prevented him from distinguishing forms and tonalities clearly. In his later years he produced decidedly abstract results. The paint was applied so thickly onto the canvas and the colors so intense that the vision seems to rise up out of the canvas. The artist seems to have discovered the pure matter that forms the quintessence of things, something that went beyond the possibilities offered by human vision.

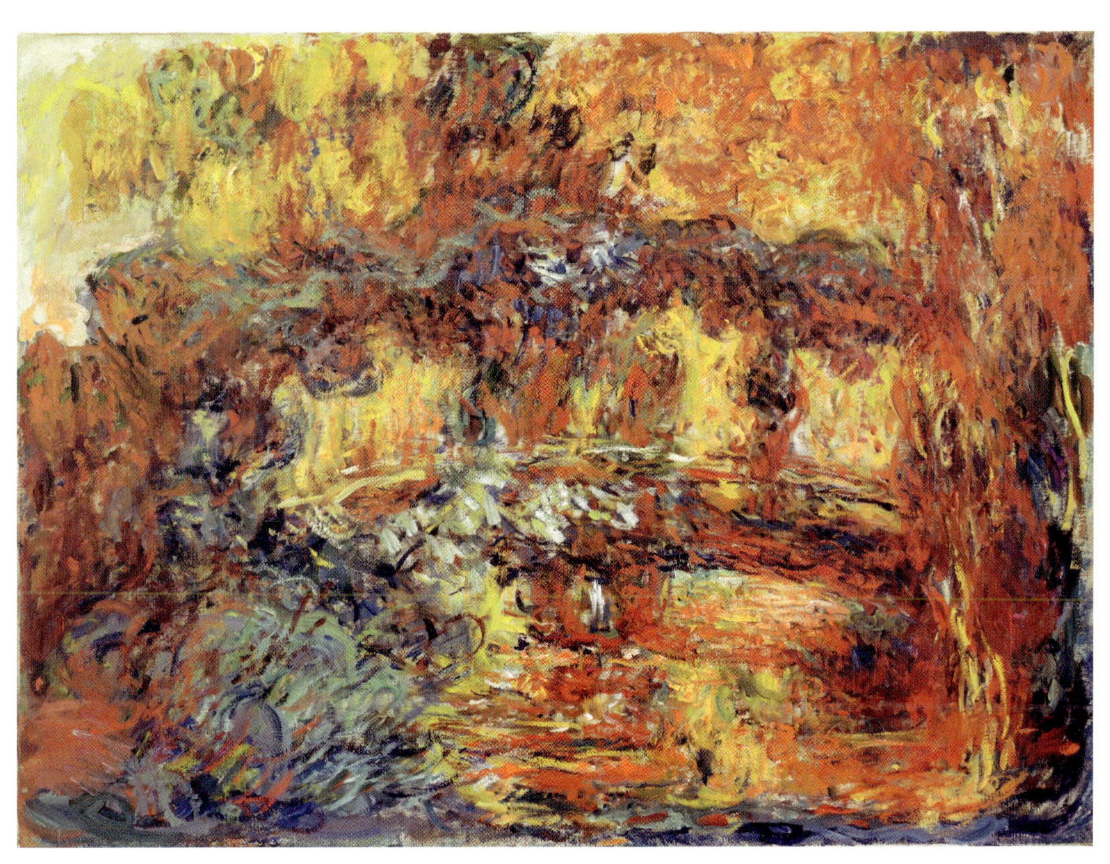

Self-Portrait

1917
Oil on canvas, 70 × 55 cm
Paris, Musée d'Orsay

With the exception of the reclusive Cézanne, Monet was probably the least worldly of the impressionists. He rarely allowed himself to be portrayed by his friends and seldom portrayed himself. Faces were unimportant to him, so he had little interest in his own. He painted this self-portrait at the age of seventy-seven, but it seems to be almost a sketch thrown down, without much care, between one lily and the next. It is of average size and the summarily depicted face has great expressive power. He painted his features at the center of the canvas, using a rapid and approximate technique, violet, pink, and orange for the flesh tones and greens and yellows for the beard. The face is framed by a hasty greenish-blue aura. The technique Monet used was in line with the rapid, emotional manner he was using on the *Water Lilies* of the same period.

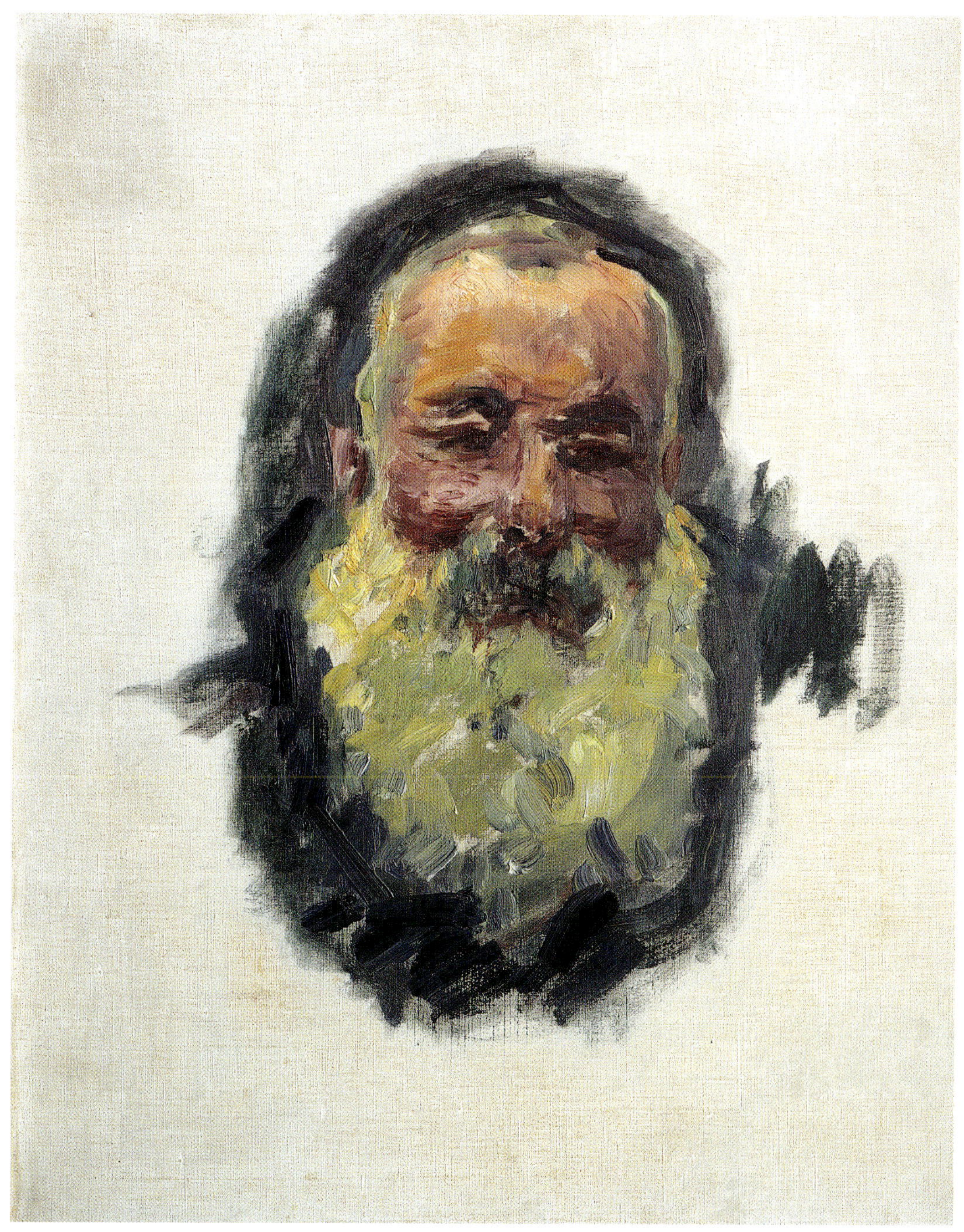

Waterlily Pond

1918
Oil on canvas, 199.5 × 599 cm
New York, The Museum
of Modern Art.
Mrs Simon Guggenheim Fund
Digital Image © 2002
New York, The Museum of
Modern Art

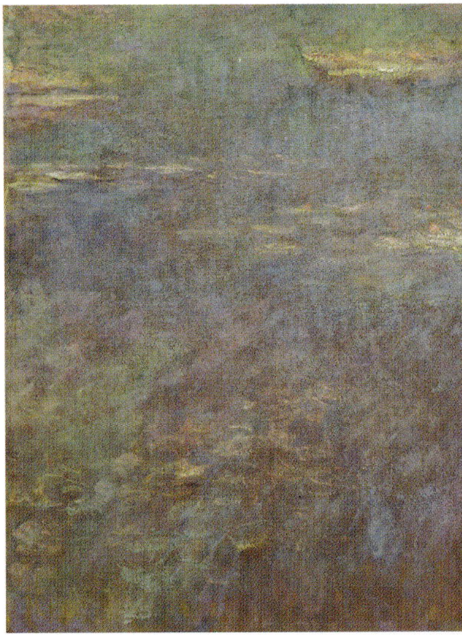

From the end of the 1890s until 1926, the year of his death, Monet painted uninterruptedly the water lilies in the pond he had had built in his garden in Giverny. He executed more than two hundred paintings with the lilies as subject. In the later canvases, the pond and flowers cover the entire canvas: there is no horizon, no depth and the sky is only seen in the reflections on the surface of the water. Monet chose particular intonations for each painting: some are pale and based on diaphanous pinks and blues, others are dark and intense, painted with deep blues and greens, and others are wan, modulated on yellows and pale greens.

Marcel Proust was amazed by the poetic beauty of the *Water Lilies*: "Land flowers and water flowers, these delicate water lilies that the Master has painted in sublime canvases [...] are like a first, delicious sketch of life."

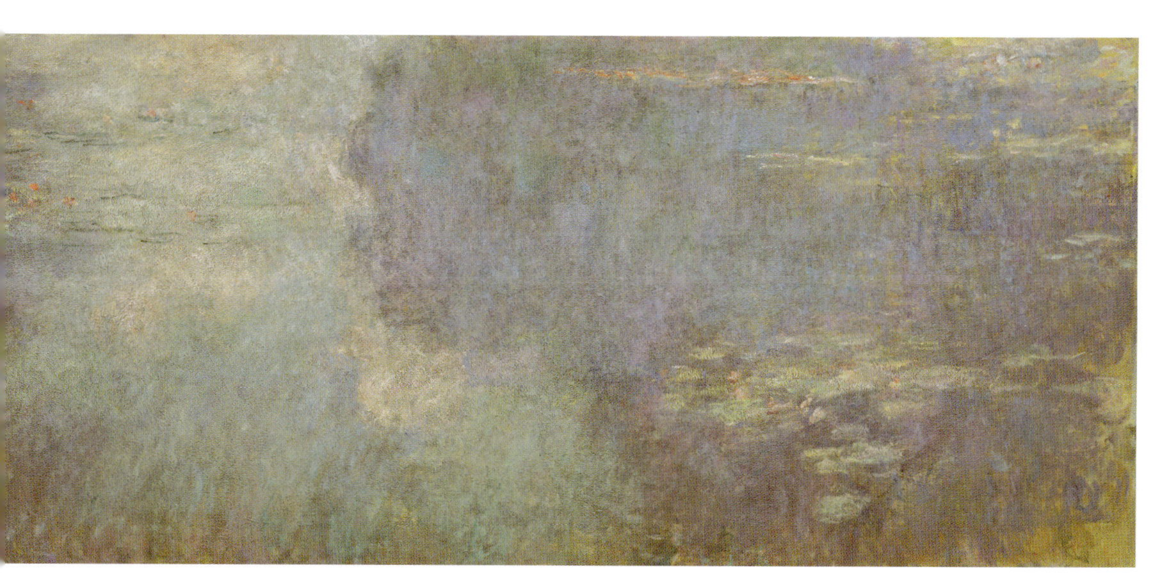

Water Lilies III

1918
Oil on canvas, 200 × 425 cm
New York, The Museum
of Modern Art.
Mrs. Simon Guggenheim Fund
Digital Image © 2002
New York, The Museum of
Modern Art

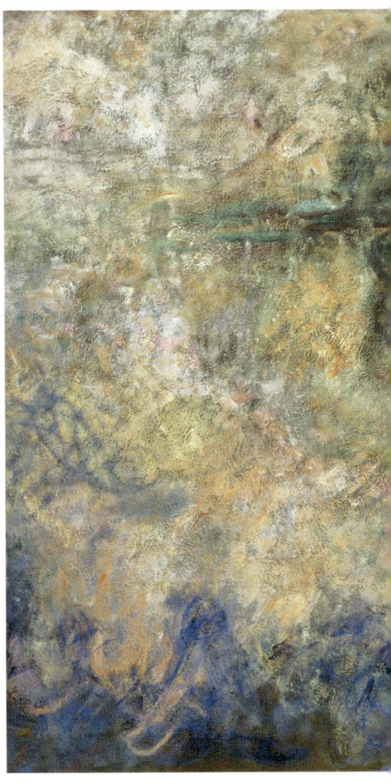

Claude Monet was an artist who, throughout his life, produced an enormous number of paintings. He painted them with regularity but without deriving any sense of complacency and was always unsatisfied by his achievements. Each new painting prompted new doubts and conflicts in himself but also caused new ideas to arise for how to go on. When he completed a painting outdoors and took it into his studio, he was unable to detach himself from it as he still thought it could be improved, so for days he continued to make alterations to it.

What he discovered in the end was that what he was searching for was no longer out there in nature but to be found in the concreteness of art. In the colors themselves there is a potential that is independent of what is being observed: that he did not realize this is not important. That he never explicitly recognized the non-figurative value of his last works does not exclude the fact that by looking at them we do not perceive the contrary. His experimentation and studies had in some ways become analogous to that of one of his colleagues, Cézanne, another painter who, by concentrating "too much" on nature, ended up by transcending it completely.

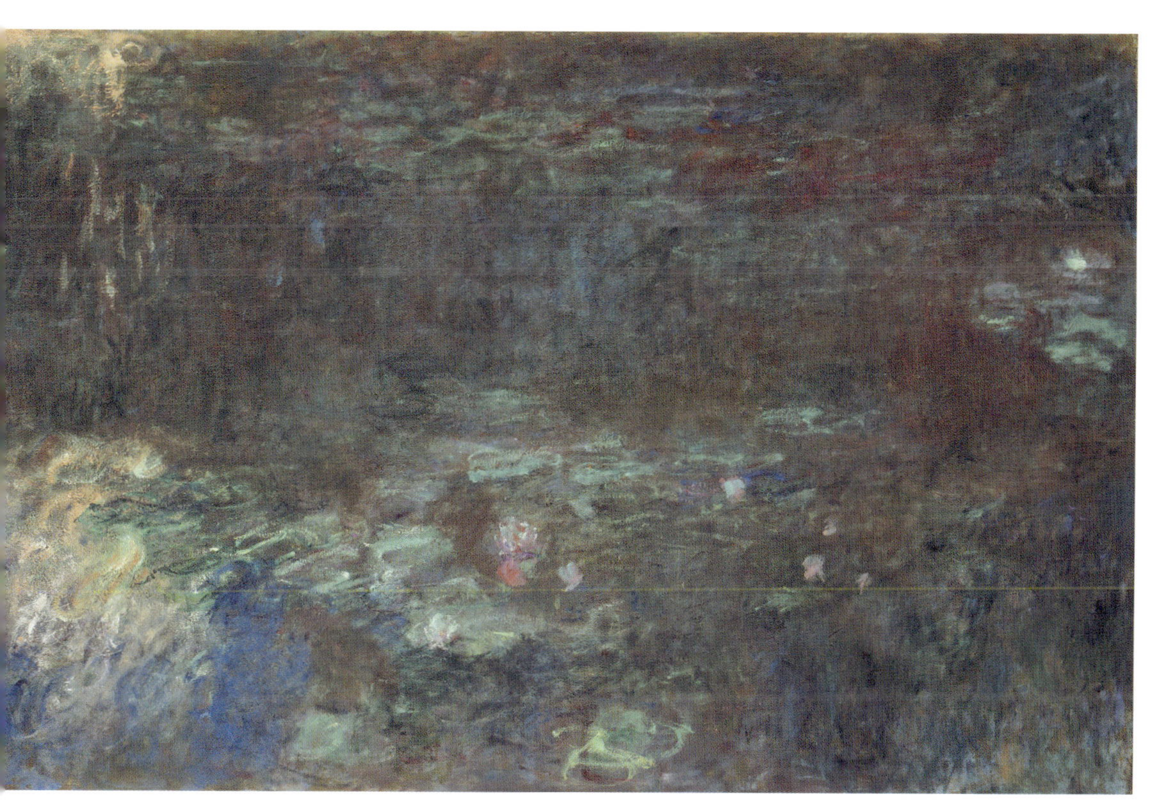

Water Lilies II

1918
Oil on canvas, 200 × 425 cm
New York, The Museum
of Modern Art.
Mrs. Simon Guggenheim Fund
Digital Image © 2002
New York, The Museum
of Modern Art

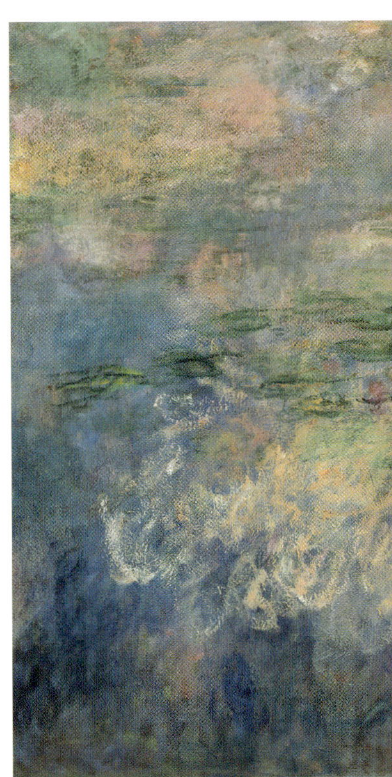

Paul Cézanne argued that no one before Monet had been able to paint water so well and its ineffable capacity to assimilate forms, colors, and light. From his early years as a painter, Monet had preferred marine views for his paintings. He had then moved to the banks of the Seine in search of places where the land gave way to water. In the pond in his garden in Giverny his experimentation continued ceaselessly, concentrating on the motif of water lilies and their changing effects of color and light. In this painting in New York he focused on pink and its variations, which he probably observed in the gossamer light of morning.

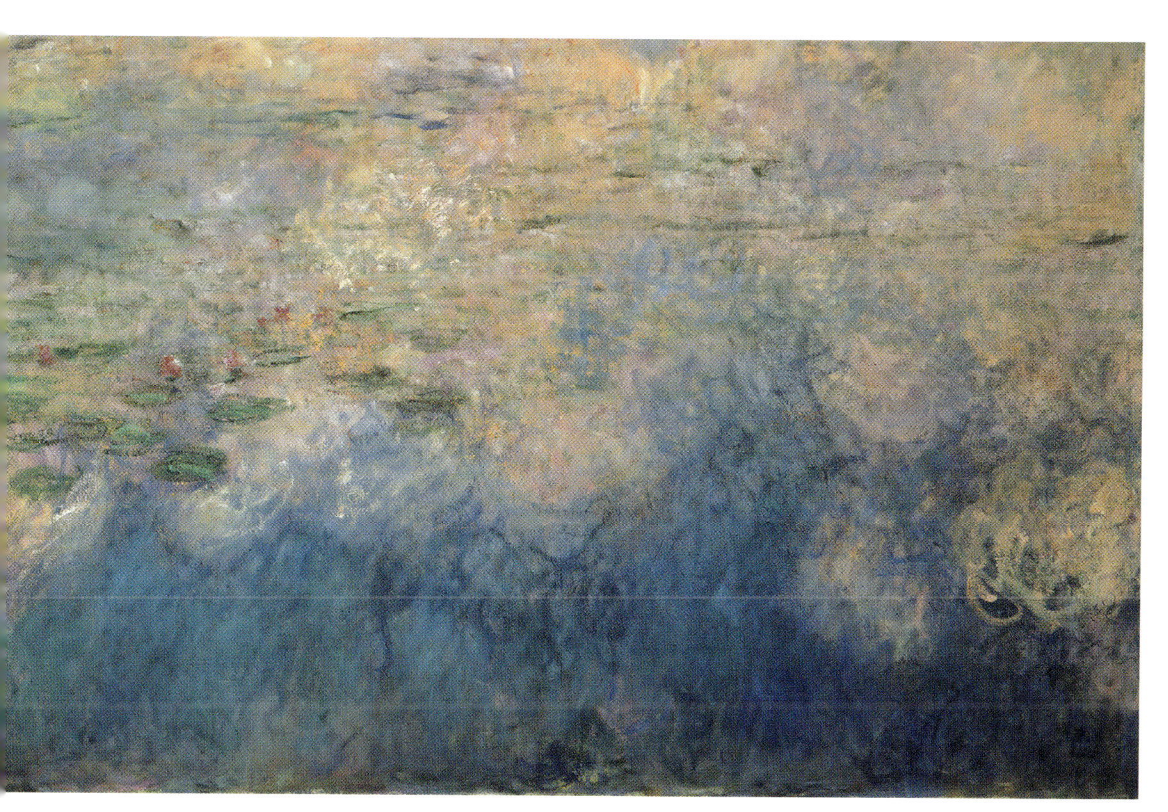

Water Lilies I

1918
Oil on canvas, 200 × 425 cm
New York, The Museum
of Modern Art.
Mrs. Simon Guggenheim Fund
Digital Image © 2002
New York, The Museum
of Modern Art

The artist concentrated on representing the surface of the water and the reflections that generated a confusion of the forms perceived by our vision. He explored the relationships between the depth of the actual field and its transformation, producing compositions that were increasingly detached from a recognizable relationship with objective reality. The canvases he painted increased in size and provided continuations from one another to create an entire vision. What he focused on during the last years of his life was the creation of a private universe in which the field of investigation centered on understanding the most intimate secrets of nature. William Seitz wrote in his biography of the painter, "Monet had always been aware of the presence of an internal reality that lay beyond the threshold of vision and to which it was inaccessible; but, with rare exceptions, his art had never crossed the boundaries between the world of appearances and the metaphysical, or between impressionism and expressionist or abstract painting." In the *Water Lilies* of his last years the boundaries between an "immediate" representation and reality are very blurred. However, when questioned about these paintings, Monet replied that he did not like to explain his art and that everyone could see in them what he or she wished.

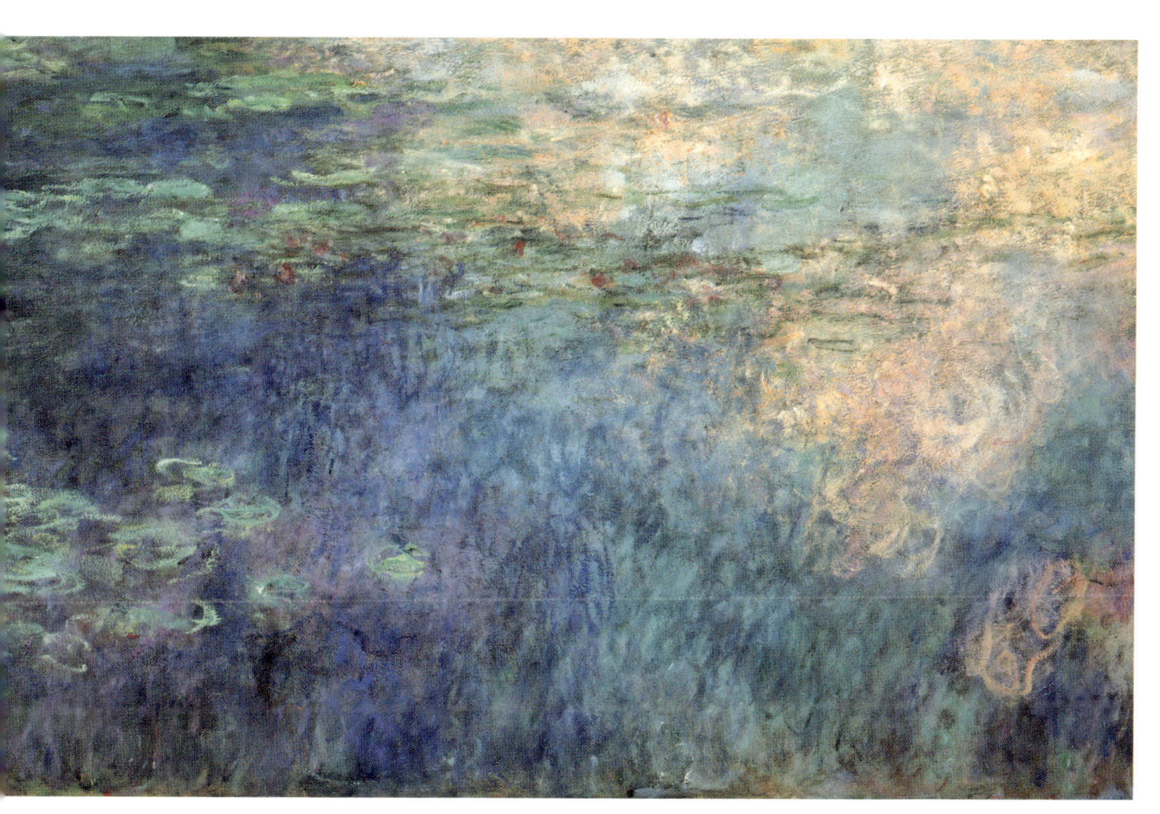

Grandes Décorations
The Clouds

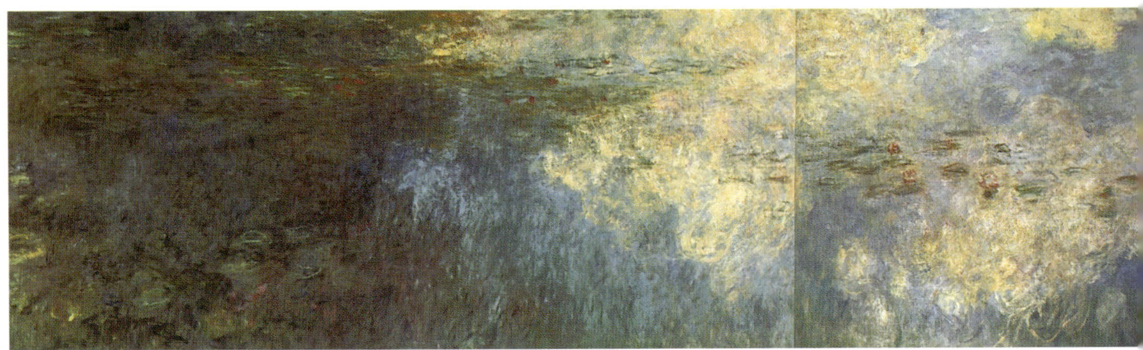

c. 1923–1926
Oil on canvas, 200 × 1275 cm
Paris, Musée de l'Orangerie

In October 1920 Monet thought of offering the French State twelve canvases, each almost four meters long, to be hung in a pavilion that was to be built in the garden of the Hôtel de Brion (this later became the Musée Rodin). The project never came to fruition and the canvases were hung in the Orangerie in the Tuileries, the garden in front of the Louvre. Almost blinded by cataracts, Monet worked on the last *Water Lilies*, which became the theme of a large decoration. He painted immense canvases that were housed in two oval rooms; there the large lily pond is studied and portrayed at all hours of the day, morning, afternoon, evening, and night. The painter concentrated on the surface of the water and studied its emotional qualities, intonations, and the reflections of the light. The result is a dreamlike spectacle in which every one of us—as the painter said—can see what he wants.

The canvases in the Orangerie are hung beside one another to form a single painting that rings the entire room. Visitors are spellbound by the colors that emerge from the depths of the water and blend with the reflected sky.

Shortly after his death on December 6, 1926, Monet's work was

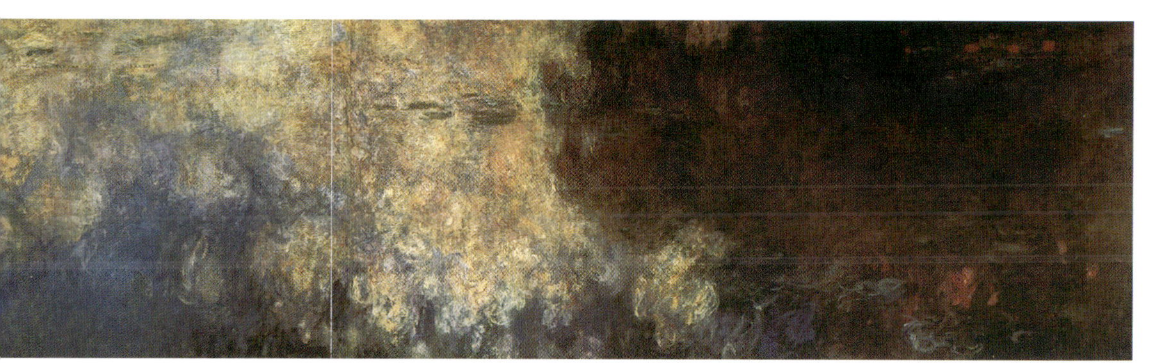

acclaimed by the critics and the masters of the avant-garde movements of the twentieth century.

In his *Mémoires* for June 27, 1931, Amédée Ozenfant wrote, "Monet dedicated his last years to the lyrical series of the *Water Lilies*. When I saw them I was amazed to see myself take off my hat to the man who had painted them. If reality can cause such an instinctive reaction, there is no way to deny it: Monet's work is noble and powerful."

The illustrations on the following pages are details from the large canvases hung in the Orangerie, the size of which does not permit the entire works to be illustrated:
Grandes Décorations, Sun at Dusk (200 × 600 cm, Room 1, wall 1)
Grandes Décorations, Clouds (three canvases, each 200 × 425 cm, Room 1, wall 2)
Grandes Décorations, Reflections of Trees (two canvases, each 200 × 425 cm, Room 2, wall 1)

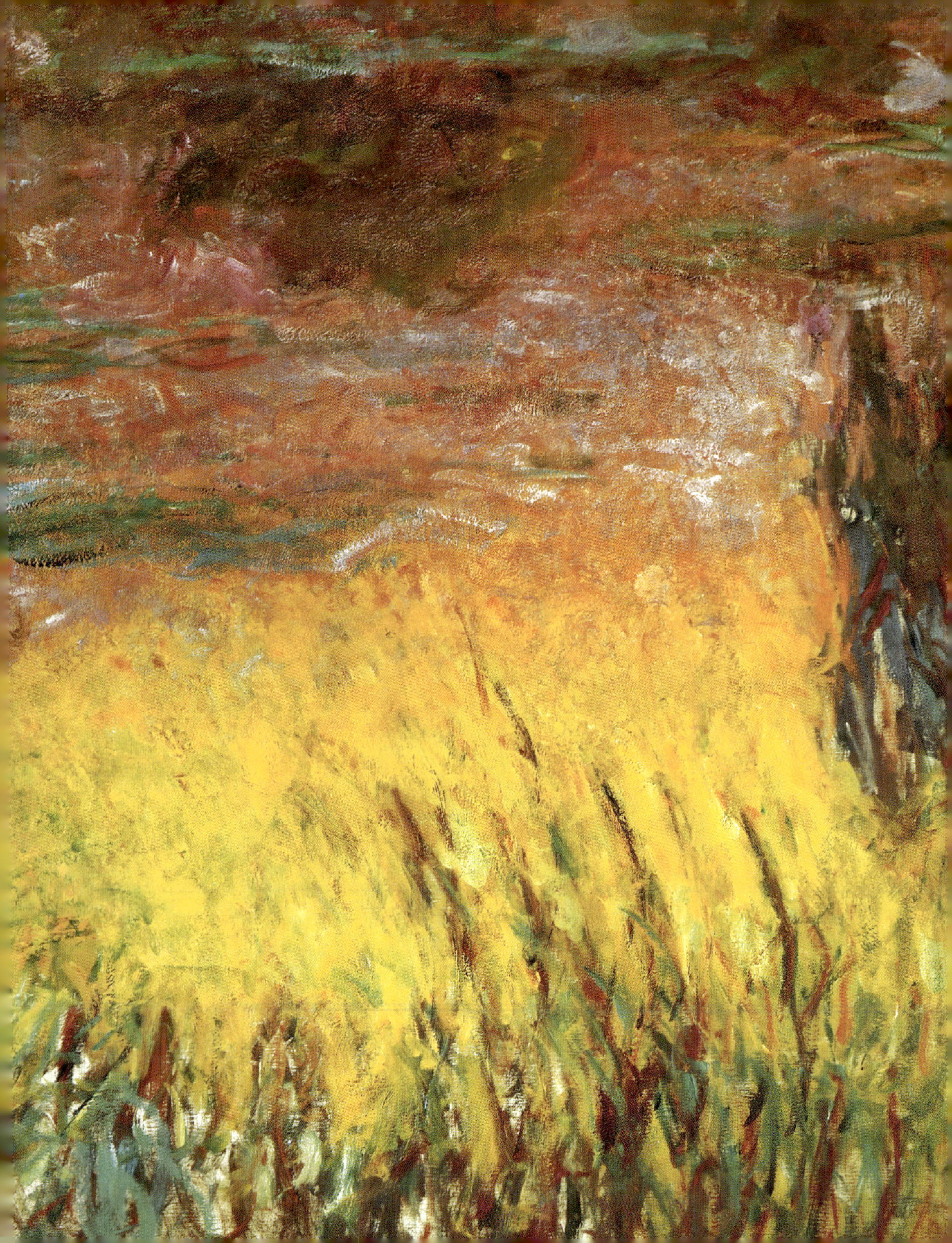

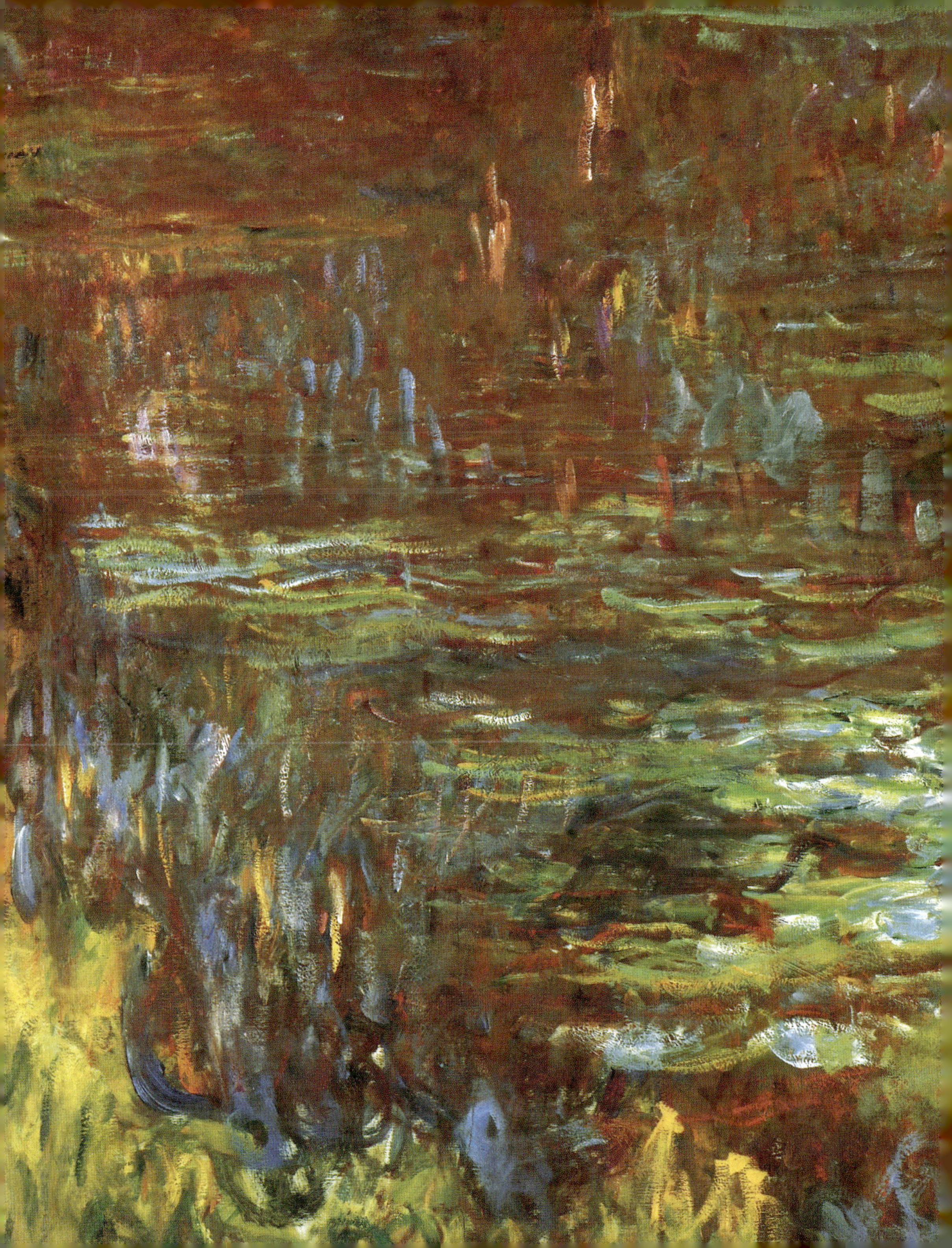

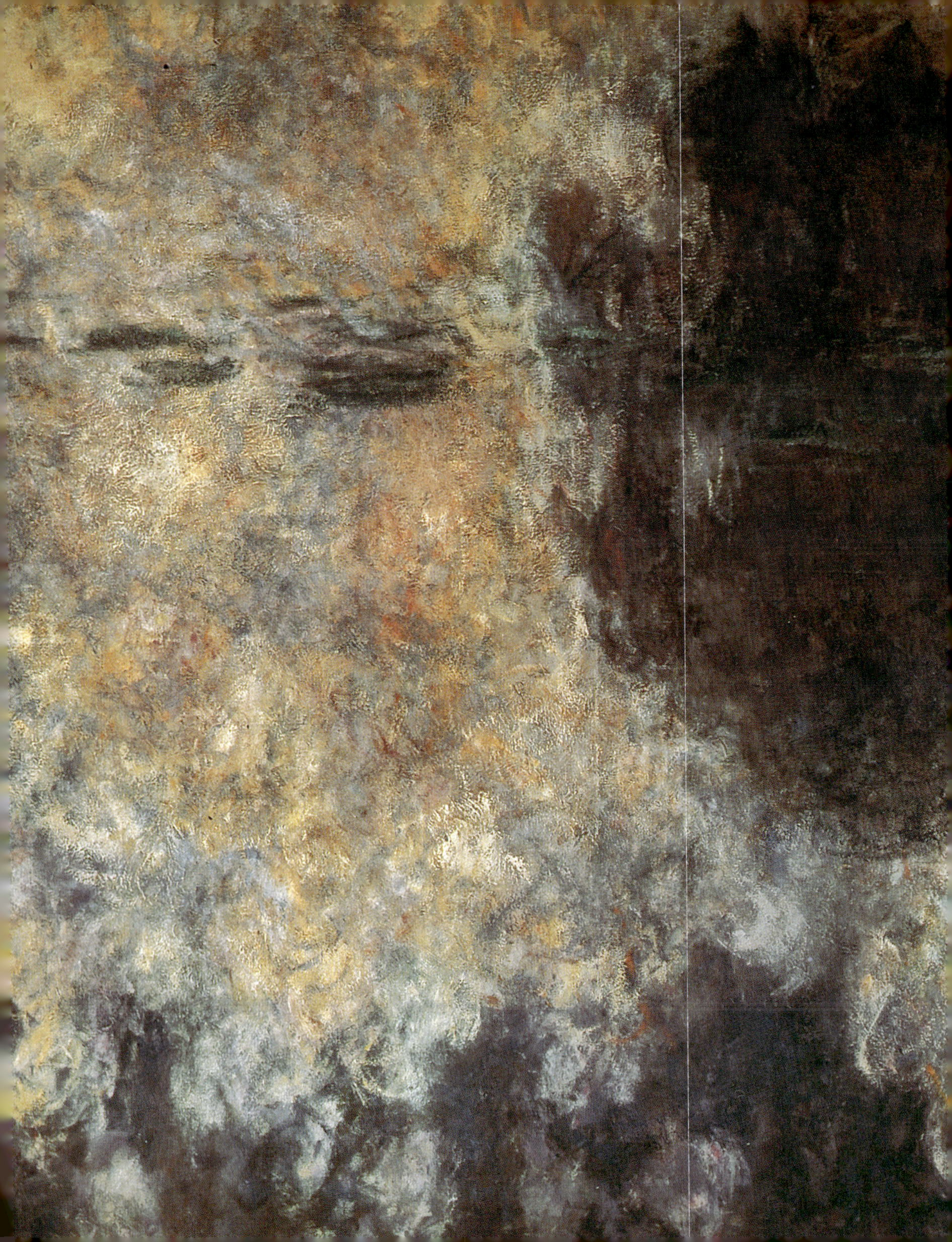

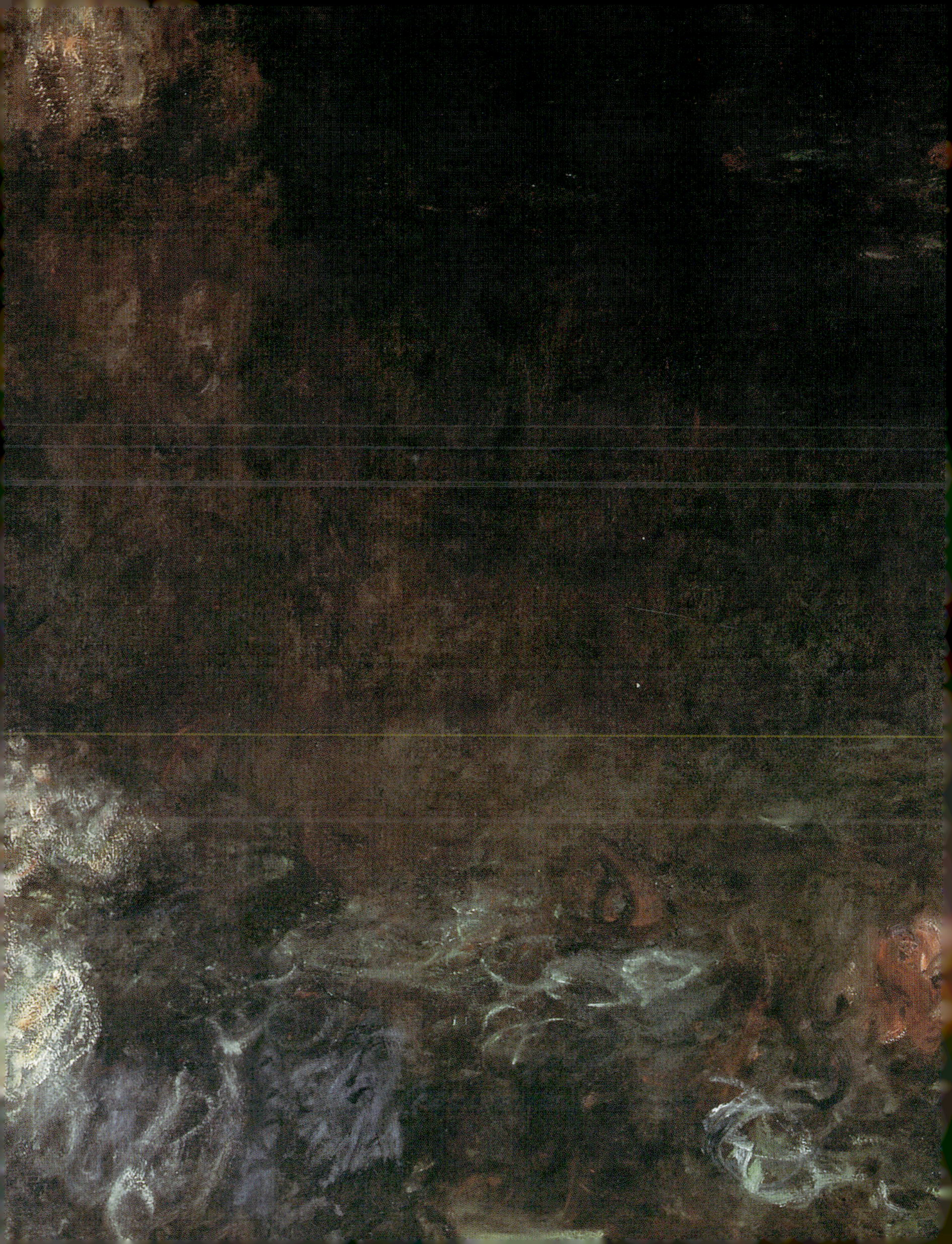

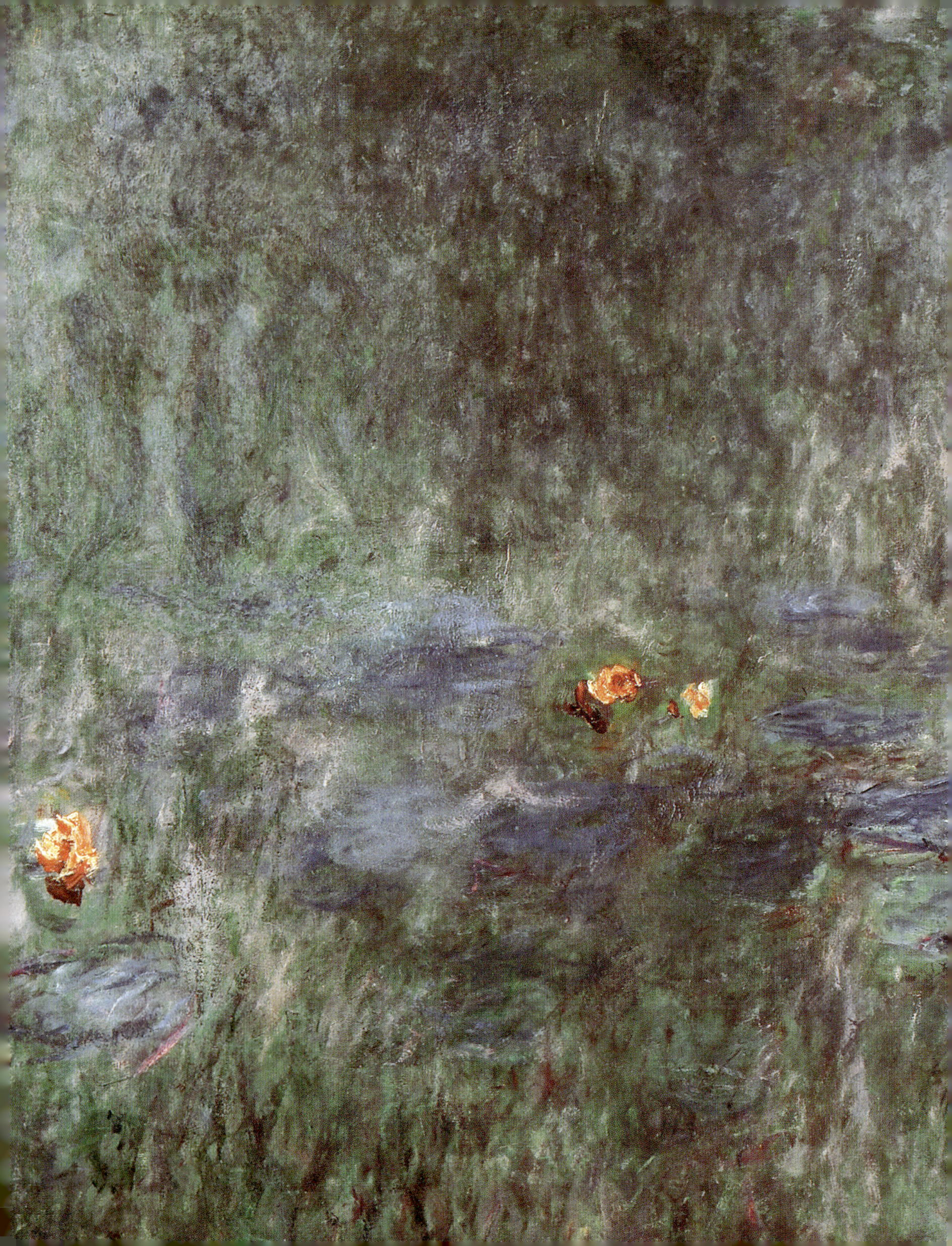

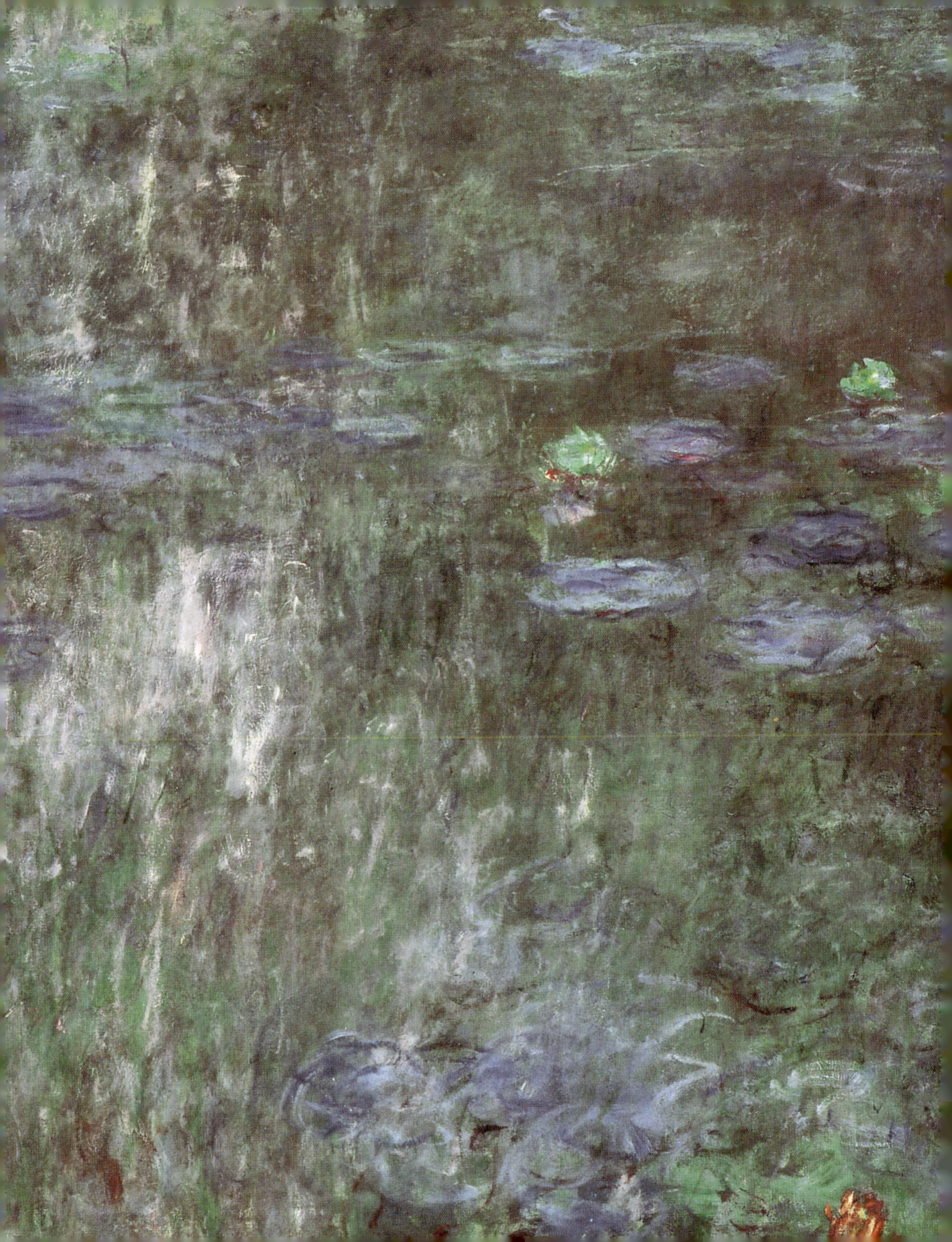

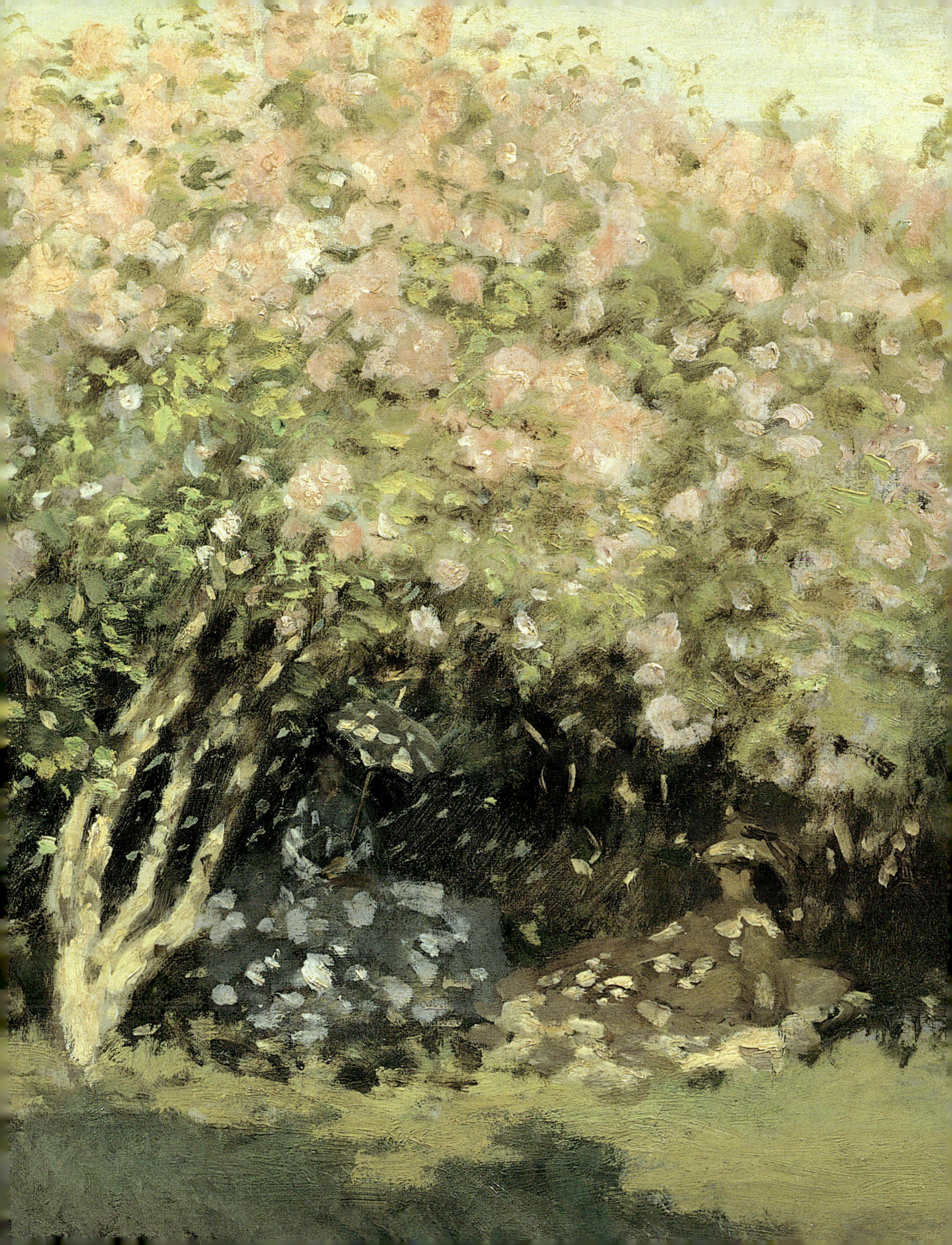

Appendix

Chronological Table

	Life of Monet	Historical and Artistic Events
1840	Claude Monet is born in Rue Laffitte in Paris on November 14.	
1845	The Monet family moves to Le Havre, in Normandy.	
1848		Louis Napoleon is elected President of the Republic.
1852		Louis Napoleon proclaims himself emperor.
1855	Monet wins some renown by drawing caricatures of the best-known figures in Le Havre.	Exposition Universelle in Paris. Courbet exhibits in the Pavilion du réalisme. Duranty prepares the periodical *Le réalisme*.
1856	He meets Eugène Boudin, who becomes his art master.	The painter Théodore Chassériau dies.
1859	Monet moves to Paris. He studies at the Libre Académie Suisse, where he meets Delacroix and Courbet.	Darwin publishes *The Origin of Species* and Hugo *La légende des siècles*. Manet is rejected by the Salon.
1860	In autumn he does his military service in Algeria.	Garibaldi lands at Marsala in Italy with his one thousand followers.
1864	He vacations in Honfleur with Jongkind, Boudin, and Bazille.	Cézanne is rejected by the Salon but Renoir is accepted. He later destroys the painting. Tolstoy begins to write *War and Peace*.
1865	He works on *Luncheon on the Grass*, his interpretation of the theme of Manet's famous painting. He meets Courbet and forms an attachment with Camille Doncieux, whom he later marries.	Manet exhibits *Olympia* at the Salon, which is savagely criticized.
1867	Busy painting landscapes at Saint-Siméon and Le Havre. In August Camille gives birth to Jean.	Marx publishes *Das Kapital*. Exposition Universelle in Paris with personal pavilion exhibiting Courbet and Manet. Ingres dies.
1869	Monet lives with Renoir in Saint-Michel. The two paint side-by-side. Like Cézanne and Sisley, Monet is rejected by the Salon.	The Suez Canal opens. Degas leaves for Brussels and then goes to Italy. Pissarro settles with his family in Louveciennes.

	Life of Monet	**Historical and Artistic Events**
1870	Monet is in Trouville in Normandy with Camille when news of the outbreak of the Franco-Prussian war arrives. He moves to London where he meets Paul Durand-Ruel.	On July 18 war breaks out between France and Prussia and the Third Republic is proclaimed on September 4. Courbet and Daumier refuse the Légion d'Honneur.
1871	After the end of the war and the repression of the Paris Commune, Monet returns to France via Holland, partly in response to the news of the death of his father. He settles in Paris once more but then moves to Argenteuil.	Paris Commune (March–May). Nietzsche publishes *The Birth of Tragedy*.
1872	He paints *Impression, Sunrise*. He works with Renoir in Argenteuil.	Manet, Jongkind, Pissarro, Cézanne, Renoir, and others sign up for another Salon des Réfuses.
1873	Following Daubigny's example, he works on a floating studio in Argenteuil.	Death of Napoleon III. Courbet flees to Switzerland and Cézanne settles in Auvers-sur-Oise.
1875	Still in Argenteuil he paints several important landscapes. This is a time of great financial straits.	The impressionists organize an auction at the Hôtel Drouot on March 24. Pissarro collaborates on the foundation of a new society of artists called L'Union.
1876	Second impressionist exhibition in April. In Montgeron Monet falls in love with Alice, the wife of collector Ernest Hoschedé.	Rivière writes the first article on the impressionists. Mallarmé publishes *L'après-midi d'un faune* illustrated by Manet.
1878	In June there is a forced sale of the Hoschedé collection, including fourteen paintings by Monet.	Exposition Universelle in Paris. Durand-Ruel exhibits 300 works by Barbizon painters. Duret publishes *Les Impressionistes*. Cézanne works in Aix-en-Provence and then L'Estaque.
1879	Monet spends the year in Vétheuil. Camille dies in September.	Fourth impressionist exhibition. Fifteen participants.
1880	He exhibits at the Salon for the last time. In June he exhibits at Charpentier's gallery (Renoir's patron). His work is well received by the public and critics.	Dostoevsky publishes *The Brothers Karamazov*. Fifth impressionist exhibition, eighteen participants.
1881	He works at Fécamp on the Normandy coast. In spring disagreements within the impressionist group lead to a split.	French protectorate in Tunisia. Sixth impressionist exhibition, thirteen participants. The French State renounces its control of the Salon. Foundation of the Société des artistes français.

	Life of Monet	**Historical and Artistic Events**
1882	In March Monet exhibits in the seventh impressionist exhibition. He works in Poissy with brief stays in Dieppe, Pourville, and Varengeville.	Triple Alliance between Germany, Austria, and Italy. Georges Petit founds the Exposition Internationale. Courbet retrospective at the École des Beaux-Arts.
1883	After inaugurating a solo exhibition in Durand-Ruel's gallery, he moves to Giverny.	Manet dies. Durand-Ruel exhibits works by the impressionists in London, Berlin, and Rotterdam.
1884	Monet stays in Bordighera (Italy) until April. On his return to Giverny he participates in the third Exposition Internationale organized by art dealer Georges Petit. In summer he returns to Étretat.	The Société des Vingt is founded in Brussels, and the Groupe des artistes independants in Paris. Manet retrospective at the École des Beaux-Arts. *La Révue Indépendante* is founded.
1885	He exhibits once again in Georges Petit's gallery and works on the decoration of Durand-Ruel's house. In November he moves to Étretat.	Delacroix retrospective at the École des Beaux-Arts. Victor Hugo dies. Éduard Dujardin founds *La Révue Wagnérienne*.
1886	He exhibits thirteen canvases at the fifth Exposition Internationale. After a short trip to Holland, he returns to Étretat.	Last impressionist exhibition, seventeen participants. Zola publishes *L'œuvre* and Fénéon publishes *Les impressionistes en 1886*.
1888	He stays in Antibes and exhibits in two Paris galleries through the offices of Theo van Gogh.	Émile Bernard is in Pont-Aven, where he becomes friend with Gauguin.
1889	He opens a large solo exhibition in Petit's gallery. He is now a widely admired artist. He heads a subscription to purchase Manet's *Olympia* to donate it to the State.	Opening of the Exposition Internationale in Paris. The critic Roger-Marx includes Manet, Monet, Pissarro, and Cézanne. Bergson publishes *Essay on the Immediate Data of Consciousness*.
1890	He moves permanently to Giverny.	First celebration of the First of May. Van Gogh dies.
1891	The art dealer Ernest Hoschedé dies in March. Monet makes a short trip to London in December.	Exhibition of the Nabis painters in December at Le Barc de Boutteville. Death of Seurat, Théo van Gogh, and Rimbaud. Aurier publishes the *Manifesto of Symbolist Painting*.
1892	On July 16 Monet finally marries Alice Hoschedé. He begins work on the cycle of paintings, *Rouen Cathedral*.	The Berlin Secession is formed. Second Nabis exhibition at Le Barc de Boutteville. Aurier dies.
1895	He spends the first part of the year in Sandviken (Norway) where he paints many landscapes. In summer he makes a trip to the Pyrenees.	The world's first commercial cinematographic show, run by the Lumière brothers. First solo exhibition by Cézanne at the Vollard gallery.

	Life of Monet	**Historical and Artistic Events**
1897	Solo exhibition in Stockholm (Sweden) in February. Until March Monet paints in Pourville.	First exhibition of the Viennese Secession.
1899	Suzanne Hoschedé, Alice's daughter, dies. In summer Monet is in London. In Giverny he begins work on the *Water Lilies*, which he will continue to paint for the rest of his life.	The Boer War. Wireless telegraph invented by Marconi. Essay on *Classic Art* by Wölfflin. First issues of the *Die Fackel* magazine edited by Kraus.
1900	He returns to Vétheuil in summer to paint the Seine but an accident causes a temporary loss of sight in one eye.	In Italy King Umberto I is assassinated. Exposition Universelle in Paris. *The Interpretation of Dreams* published by Freud.
1903	He exhibits his London paintings in Durand-Ruel's gallery. He continues work on the *Water Lilies*.	Pissarro, Gauguin, and Whistler die. Salon d'Automne founded.
1904		Universal Exposition in St. Louis (USA). Weber begins *The Protestant Ethic and the Spirit of Capitalism*.
1905	Large exhibition by the impressionists in London.	Einstein's theory of relativity.
1906		Cézanne dies.
1908	In September he goes to Venice and returns the following year. His eyesight worsens.	Austria annexes Bosnia–Herzegovina. The Psychoanalytic Society of Vienna is founded.
1909	Alice dies.	First Futurist manifesto.
1911	Death of Jean, his son by Camille.	*On the Spiritual in Art* is published by Kandinsky and the *Theory of Harmony* by Schönberg.
1914		June 28: assassination of Franz Ferdinand in Sarajevo, which causes the outbreak of World War I.
1916	He builds a new studio in Giverny where he works on the *Water Lilies*.	Battle of Verdun. Franz Josef dies and is succeeded by Karl I. Dada is born.
1918	Visits to Le Havre, Pourville, Dieppe, Honfleur, and Étretat to paint.	Proclamation of the republic in Austria and Germany. Schiele, Klimt, Moser, and Hodler die.
1926	Monet dies on December 6 from a tumor. Among those present at the funeral in Giverny are Clemenceau, Bonnard, Vuillard, and Roussel.	Rilke dies. Hirohito ascends the imperial throne in Japan.

Geographical Locations of the Paintings

Italy

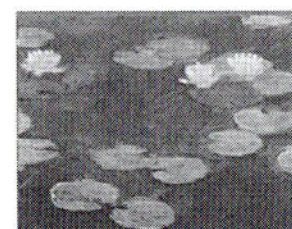

Pink Water Lilies
Oil on canvas, 81.5 x 100 cm
Rome, Galleria Nazionale
d'Arte Moderna
1898

France

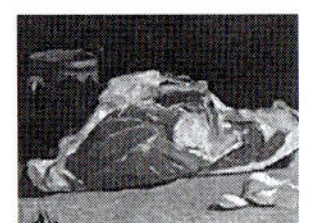

Still Life with Meat
Oil on canvas, 24 x 33 cm
Paris, Musée d'Orsay
1864

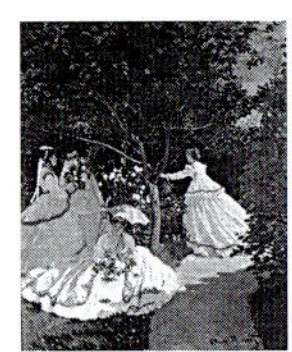

Women in the Garden
Oil on canvas, 255 x 205 cm
Paris, Musée d'Orsay
1867

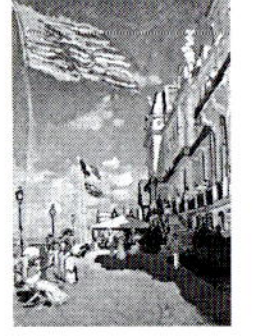

*L'Hôtel des Roches Noires
à Trouville*
Oil on canvas, 81 x 58.5 cm
Paris, Musée d'Orsay
1870

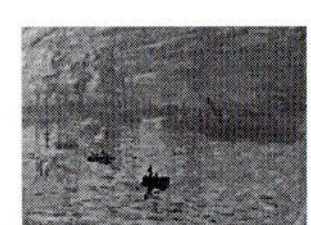

Impression, Sunrise
Oil on canvas, 48 x 63 cm
Paris, Musée Marmottan
Monet
1872

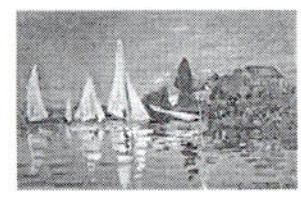

Regatta at Argenteuil
Oil on canvas, 48 x 75 cm
Paris, Musée d'Orsay
1872

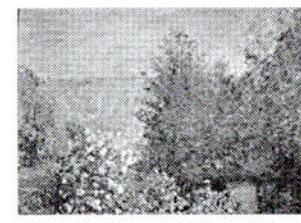

The Port at Argenteuil
Oil on canvas, 60 x 80.5 cm
Paris, Musée d'Orsay
c. 1872

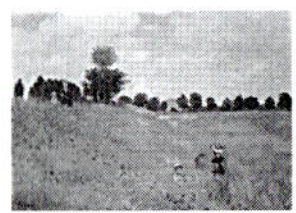

Poppies at Argenteuil
Oil on canvas, 50 x 65 cm
Paris, Musée d'Orsay
1873

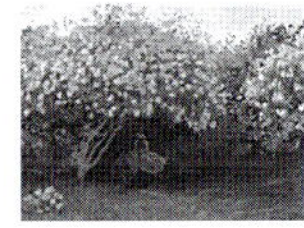

Lilacs in the Sun
Oil on canvas, 50 x 65 cm
Moscow, The Pushkin State
Museum of Fine Arts
1873

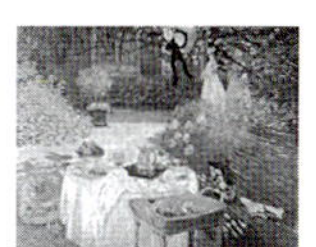

The Luncheon
(decorative panel)
Oil on canvas, 160 x 201 cm
Paris, Musée d'Orsay
c. 1873

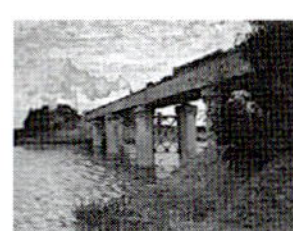

The Railway Bridge
at Argenteuil
Oil on canvas, 55 x 72 cm
Paris, Musée d'Orsay
1873-1874

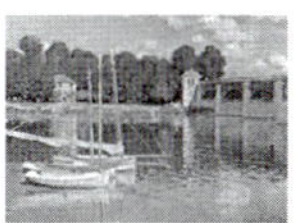

The Bridge at Argenteuil
Oil on canvas, 60.5 x 80 cm
Paris, Musée d'Orsay
1874

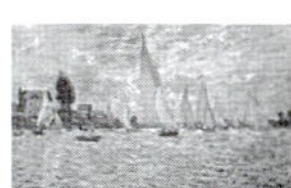

Regatta at Argenteuil
Oil on canvas, 60 x 100 cm
Paris, Musée d'Orsay
1874

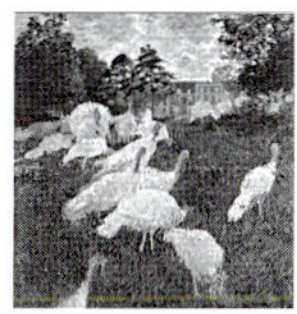

Turkeys
(Les dindons)
Oil on canvas, 174.5 x 172.5 cm
Paris, Musée d'Orsay
1877

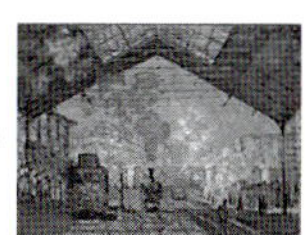

The Saint-Lazare Station
Oil on canvas, 75.5 x 104 cm
Paris, Musée d'Orsay
1877

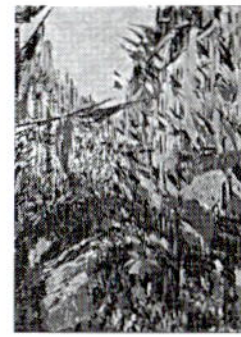

The Rue Saint Denis.
Celebration of June 30, 1878
Oil on canvas, 81 x 50.5 cm
Rouen, Musée des
Beaux- Arts
1878

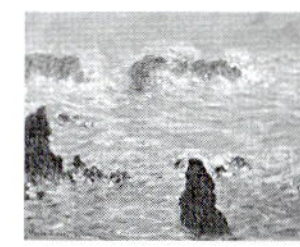

Storm off the Belle-Île Coast
Oil on canvas, 65 x 81.5 cm
Paris, Musée d'Orsay
1886

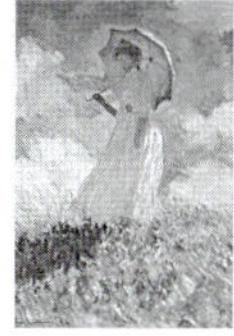

Woman with Umbrella
Turned toward the Left
Oil on canvas, 131 x 88 cm
Paris, Musée d'Orsay
1886

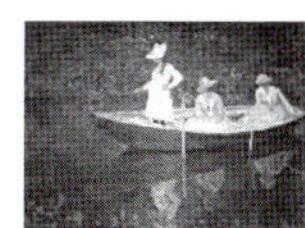

In the Boat
Oil on canvas, 98 x 131 cm
Paris, Musée d'Orsay
c. 1887

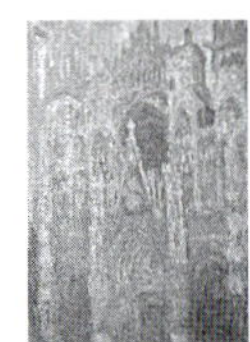

Rouen Cathedral, First Light
Oil on canvas, 106 x 73 cm
Paris, Musée d'Orsay
1894

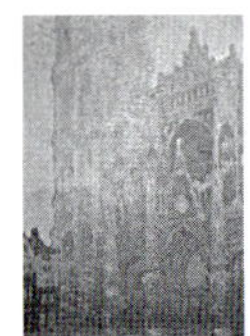

Rouen Cathedral, Morning Sun, Harmony in Blue
Oil on canvas, 91 x 63 cm
Paris, Musée d'Orsay
1894

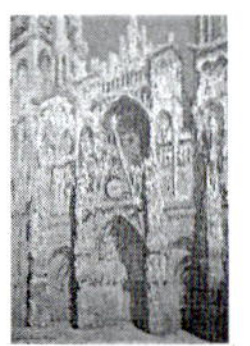

Rouen Cathedral, in the Sunlight
Oil on canvas, 107 x 73 cm
Paris, Musée d'Orsay
1894

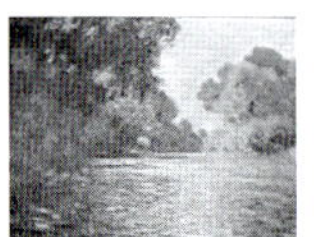

Arm of the Seine at Giverny
Oil on canvas, 75 x 92.5 cm
Paris, Musée d'Orsay
1897

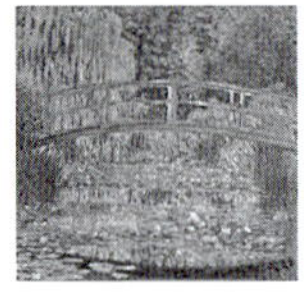

Waterlily Pond, Symphony in Green
Oil on canvas, 89.5 x 100 cm
Paris, Musée d'Orsay
1899

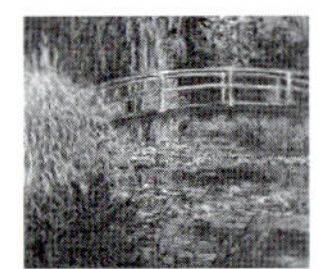

Waterlily Pond, Symphony in Pink
Oil on canvas, 89.5 x 100 cm
Paris, Musée d'Orsay
1900

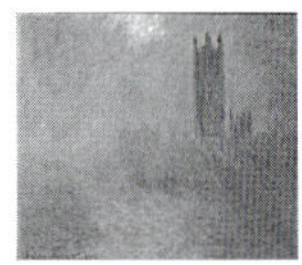

The Houses of Parliament, Effect of Sunlight in the Fog
Oil on canvas, 81 x 92 cm
Paris, Musée d'Orsay
1904

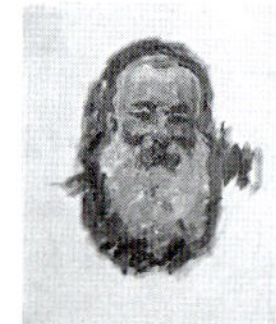

Self-Portrait
Oil on canvas, 70 x 55 cm
Paris, Musée d'Orsay
1917

Grandes Décorations. The Clouds
Oil on canvas, 200 x 1275 cm
Paris, Musée de l'Orangerie
c. 1923–1926

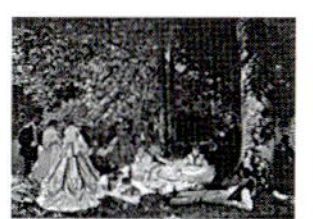

*Luncheon on the Grass
(Déjeuner sur l'Herbe)*
Oil on canvas, 124 x 181 cm
Moscow, The Pushkin State
Museum of Fine Arts
1866

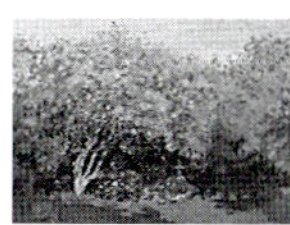

Lilacs in the Sun
Oil on canvas, 50 x 65 cm
Moscow, The Pushkin State
Museum of Fine Arts
1873

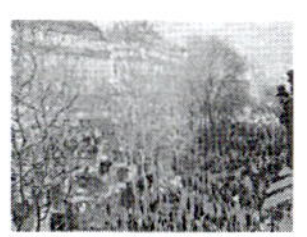

*The Boulevard
des Capucines*
Oil on canvas, 60 x 80 cm
Moscow, The Pushkin State
Museum of Fine Arts
1873

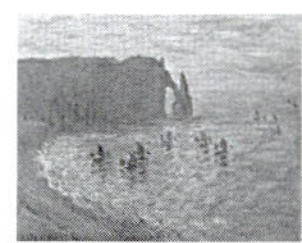

Cliffs at Étretat
Oil on canvas, 65 x 81 cm
Moscow, The Pushkin State
Museum of Fine Arts
1886

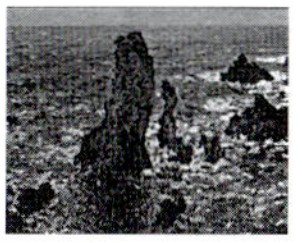

*Pyramids at Belle-Île.
Rough Sea*
Oil on canvas, 65 x 80 cm
Moscow, The Pushkin State
Museum of Fine Arts
1886

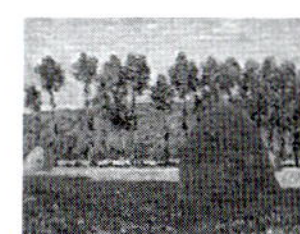

Haystack at Giverny
Oil on canvas, 64 x 81 cm
Moscow, The Pushkin State
Museum of Fine Arts
1889

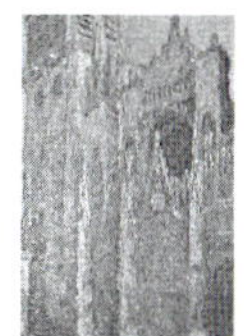

Rouen Cathedral, Evening
Oil on canvas, 101 x 65 cm
Moscow, The Pushkin State
Museum of Fine Arts
1894

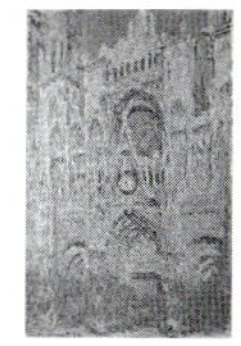

Rouen Cathedral, Midday
Oil on canvas, 100 x 65 cm
Moscow, The Pushkin State
Museum of Fine Arts
1894

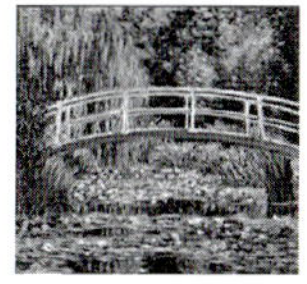

Waterlily Pond
Oil on canvas, 89 x 93 cm
Moscow, The Pushkin State
Museum of Fine Arts
1899

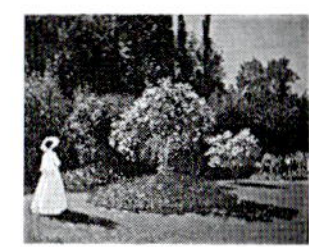

*Jeanne-Marguerite Lecadre
in the Garden at Sainte-
Adresse*
Oil on canvas, 82.3 x 101.5 cm
St. Petersburg, The State
Hermitage Museum
1867

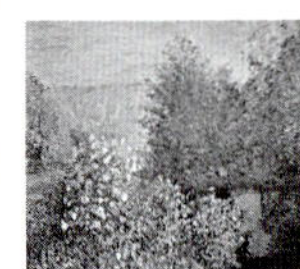

The Garden at Montgeron
Oil on canvas, 172 x 192 cm
St. Petersburg, The State
Hermitage Museum
1877

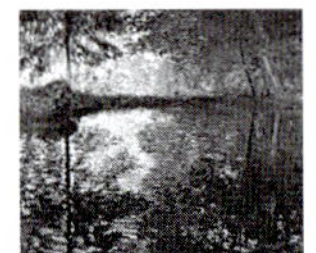

The Pond at Montgeron
Oil on canvas, 172 x 193 cm
St. Petersburg, The State
Hermitage Museum
1877

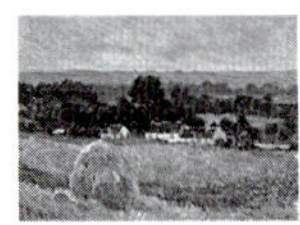

Haystack at Giverny
Oil on canvas, 60.5 x 81.5 cm
St. Petersburg, The State
Hermitage Museum
1886

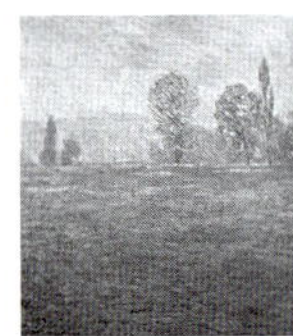

Meadow at Giverny
Oil on canvas, 92 × 80 cm
St. Petersburg, The State
Hermitage Museum
1888

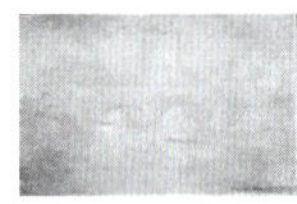

Waterloo Bridge, Effect of Fog
Oil on canvas, 63.5 x 101 cm
St. Petersburg, The State
Hermitage Museum
1903

United States

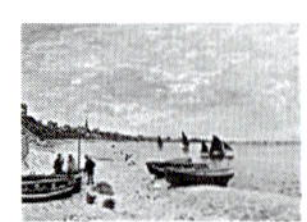

The Beach at Sainte-Adresse
Oil on canvas, 75 x 101 cm
Chicago, The Art Institute
of Chicago
1867

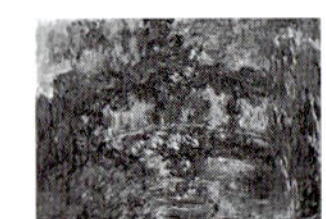

The Japanese Bridge
Oil on canvas, 89.5 x 115.3 cm
New York, The Museum of
Modern Art. Grace Rainey
Rogers Fund.Digital Image ©
2002 New York, The Museum
of Modern Art
c. 1910

Waterlily Pond
Oil on canvas, 199.5 x 599 cm
New York, The Museum of
Modern Art. Mrs. Simon
Guggenheim Fund Digital
Image © 2002 New York,
The Museum of Modern Art
1918

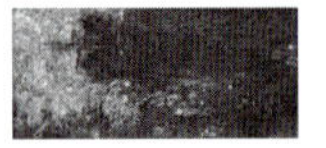

Water Lilies III
Oil on canvas, 200 x 425 cm
New York, The Museum of
Modern Art. Mrs. Simon
Guggenheim Fund Digital Image
© 2002 New York, The Museum
of Modern Art
1918

United States		*Water Lilies II* Oil on canvas, 200 x 425 cm New York, The Museum of Modern Art. Mrs. Simon Guggenheim Fund. Digital Image © 2002 New York, The Museum of Modern Art 1918		*Water Lilies I* Oil on canvas, 200 x 425 cm New York, The Museum of Modern Art. Mrs. Simon Guggenheim Fund. Digital Image © 2002 New York, The Museum of Modern Art 1918
Switzerland		*The Blue Rowing Boat* Oil on canvas, 109 x 129 cm St. Moritz, Thyssen Collection 1887		

Letter to Fréderic Bazille, 1864
It is indeed frighteningly difficult to do something
that is complete in every respect, and I believe there
are very few people who are satisfied with ap-
proximations. So my friend, I want to struggle,
scrape out, start again, because one can do what one
sees and understands, and it seems to me when I
am looking at nature that I ma going to do everything, write it all down, but then just try to ac-
complish it [...] when you're there before the canvas [...].

All of which proves that we must think of
nothing else. It is through observation and reflection that one finds.

Letter to Alice Hoschedé, Bordighera, 1884
I've been working non-stop today right up to
6 o'clock this evening, and took only an hour off
for lunch, but I worked well and am very satisfied
with what I've done today; what a lot of daubs I did
in the beginning, but now I've caught this magical
landscape and it's quite unreal and that I'm out of
my mind, but that's just too bad, anyway, that's
what they say when I paint our part of the world.

They may excite a bit the enemies of blue and
pink, because it is exactly the sparkle, this enchanted light that I am determined to render, and
those who haven't seen this country, or have seen
it wrongly, will protest, I'm sure, the lack of resemblance, although I am well below the tone:
everything is iridescent.

Letter to Alice Hoschedé, Etretat, November 1885
After another rainy morning I was glad to find the
weather slightly improved; despite a high wind
blowing and a rough sea, or rather, because of it, I
hoped for a fruitful session at the Manneporte;
however an accident befell me. Don't alarm yourself now, I am safe and sound since I'm writing to
you, although you nearly had no news and I would
have never seen you again. I was hard at work beneath the cliff, well sheltered form the wind, in the
spot which you visited with me; convinced that the
tide was drawing out I took no notice of the waves

which came and fell a few feet away from me. In short, absorbed as I was, I didn't see a huge wave coming; it threw me against the cliff and I was tossed about in its wake along with all my materials! My immediate thought was that I was done for, as the water dragged me down, but in the end I managed to clamber out on all fours, but Lord, what a state I was in! My boots, my thick stockings and my coat were soaked through; the palette which I had kept a grip on had been knocked over my face and my beard was covered in blue, yellow etc. But anyway, now the excitement is passed and no harm's done, the worst of it was that I lost my painting which was very soon broken up, along with my easel, bag etc. Impossible to fish anything out. Besides, everything was torn to shreds by the sea, that "old hag" as you sister calls her. Anyway, I was lucky to escape, but how I raged when I found once I'd changed that I couldn't work, and when it dawned on me that the painting which I had been counting on was done for, I was furious. Immediately I set about telegraphing Troisgros to send me what's missing and an easel will be ready for tomorrow [...].

Letter to Gustav Geffroy, Rouen, March 1893
My stay here is advancing, which doesn't mean that I'm near to finishing my "Cathedrals." Regretfully I can only repeat that the further I get, the more difficult it is for me to convey what I feel; and I tell myself that anyone who claims he's finished a painting is terribly arrogant. To finish something means complete, perfect and I'm forcing myself to work, but can't make any progress; looking for something, groping my way forward, but coming up with nothing very special, except to reach the point to where I'm exhausted by it all.

Letter to Alice Monet, March 1893
What terrible unsettles weather! I carry on regardless without a break. I'm feeling better, but, dear God, this cursed cathedral is hard to do! Since I've been here, a week tomorrow, I've worked every day on the same two paintings and

can't get what I want; well it will come in the end, with a hard struggle. I'm very glad I decided to come back, it's better like this [...].

Letter to Alice Monet, Rouen, 1893
I'm working away like a madman but, alas, all your words are in vain, and I feel empty and good for nothing. It all happens at once, the weather isn't very predictable: wonderful sunshine yesterday, fog this morning, sun this afternoon which disappeared just when I needed it; tomorrow it will be a dark grey day or rainy, and once again, I'm very much afraid I'll leave everything and come home on an impulse [...].

What's the good of working when I don't get to the end of anything? This evening I wanted to compare what I've done now with the old paintings, which I don't like looking at too much in case I fall into the same errors. Well, the result of that was that I was right to be unhappy last year; it's ghastly and what I'm doing now is quite as bad, bad in a different way, that's all. The essential thing is to avoid the urge to do it all too quickly, try, try again, and get it right once and for all [...].

Things went a little better today and I'll finish with this cathedral eventually, but it will take time. It's only with hard work that I can achieve what I want; I wouldn't be surprised if once again nothing definitive comes of it, and I might have to come back next year. I'll certainly do all I can to pull through this time; it depends on the weather, but in any case I don't want to prolong work endlessly or alter my paintings as the sun gets higher. Anyway I'm a little happier today, but I'll have deserved my Sunday off [...].

Letter to Alice Monet, London, February 1900
In the early hours of this morning there was an extraordinary completely yellow fog; I did an impression of it which I don't think is bad; otherwise it's still fine, but very variable; so I had to start lots of canvases of Waterloo Bridge and the Hous-

es of Parliament; I also resumed work on several paintings done on the first trip, the least good ones. I'm mostly working here for the time being, and don't go to the hospital until 4 in the afternoon. Unfortunately the fog doesn't seem to want to lift and I fear the morning will be wasted.

Monet's notes to his gardener, Giverny, 1900
Sowing: around 300 pots Poppies—60 Sweet pea—around 60 pots white Agremony—30 yellow Agremony—Blue sage—Blue Waterlilies in beds greenhouse—Dahlias—Iris Kaempferi.— From the 15th to the 25th, lay the dahlias down to root; plant out those with shoots before I get back.—Don't forget the lily bulbs.—Should the Japanese paeonies arrive plant them immediately if weather permits, taking care initially to protect buds from the cold, as much as from the heat of the sun. Get down to pruning: rose trees not too long, except for the thorny varieties. In March sow the grass seeds, plant out the little nasturtiums, keep a close eye on the gloxinia, orchids, etc, in the greenhouse, as well as the plants under frames. Trim the borders as arranged; put wires in for the clematis and climbing roses as soon as Picard has done the necessary. If the weather's bad, make some straw matting, but lighter than previously. Plant cuttings from the rose trees at the pond around manure in the hen huts. Don't delay work on tarring the planks and plant the Helianthus cariflorus in good clumps right away. If anything's missing such as manure, pots etc, ask Madame if possible on a Friday so as to have it on Saturday. In March force the chrysanthemums along as the buds won't open in damp conditions; and don't forget to put the sulphur sheets back over the greenhouse frames.

Letter to Gustav Geffroy, Giverny, 1907
Like you I'm sorry not to be able to exhibit the "Water-lilies" series this year, and if I made this decision it's because it was impossible. Perhaps it's true that I'm very hard on myself, but that's better than exhibiting mediocre work. And I'm not delaying the exhibition because I'm keen to show a lot of work, far from it, but too few were satisfactory enough to trouble the public with. At the very most I have five or six that are possible; moreover I've just destroyed thirty at least and this entirely to my satisfaction.

I still have a lot of pleasure doing them, but as time goes by I come to appreciate more clearly which paintings are good and which should be discarded. All the same, this doesn't effect my eagerness and confidence that I can do better.

Letter to Durand-Ruel, Giverny, 1907
You must know I'm entirely absorbed in my work. These landscapes of water and reflections have become an obsession. It's quite beyond my powers at my age, and yet I want to succeed in expressing what I feel. I've destroyed some […]. I start others […] and I hope that something will come out of so much effort […].

Letter to Durand-Ruel, Venice, 1908
Absorbed as I was in my work, I was unable to write to you and so I handed my wife the task of giving you the news. She no doubt told you of my enthusiasm for Venice. Well, it increases by the day and I'm very sad that I'll soon have to leave this unique light. It's so very beautiful, but we must resign ourselves to the inevitable; I have many pressing obligations at home. I comfort myself with the thought that I'll come back next year, since I've only made some studies, some beginnings. But what a shame I didn't come here as a younger man, when I was full of daring! Still […] I've spent some thoughtful hours here, almost forgetting that I'm now an old man […]. Best wishes from my wife and myself.

Letter to Gustav Geffroy, Giverny, 1920
Really, you never seem to lose interest in me. I am honoured indeed; however, it's Boudin who concerns us here. On this matter, concerning my relationship with the "King of skies," I think I already told you that I consider Boudin as my Master.

You are quite right, I did meet Boudin, my senior, I believe, by about fifteen years, in Le Havre, while I was struggling to earn my reputation as a caricaturist. It's true that I was fifteen or so at the time. I was known throughout the town of Le Havre. I charged between 10 and 20 francs for my portraits and signed them Oscar, my second name. I often exhibited them with Boudin, whose painting I didn't appreciate at first, influenced as I was by academic theories. Troyon and Millet also frequented the gallery shop. One day Boudin said to me: "You're talented, you should drop this kind of work which you'll tire of sooner or later. Your sketches are excellent, you're not going to leave it at that. Do what I do, learn to draw well and appreciate the sea, light, and the blue sky." I took his advice and together we went on long outings during which I painted constantly from nature. That was how I came to understand nature and learnt to love it passionately and how I became interested in the high-keyed painting of Boudin. It should be remembered that he had received some training from a master, Jongkind, whose work (his watercolours in particular) lies with Corot's at the origin of what has been called Impressionism. I've said it before and can only repeat that I owe everything to Boudin and I attribute my success to him. I came to be fascinated by his studies, the product of what I call instantaneity.

"Science and Philosophy in Art": A Review of the work of the Impressionists of Paris exhibited at the American Art Association Rooms, New York, during the Spring of 1886

The mainspring of happiness to the philosophic mind is to penetrate into the internal structure of things, and to analyze the complex to its ultimate elements. This principle has been accepted consciously or unconsciously, and underlies the works of the best representatives of the impressionist school of painting. The truths of geometry and the laws of force have been also recognized by them, whether consciously or unconsciously, as the only correct basis upon which to proceed, in order to produce on the mind of the observer those subjective effects which are the highest expression of Art, and of which this school, *par excellence,* is the most able exponent. The pictures of Claude Monet come first as the latest art expressions of scientific and philosophic thought.

This is clearly shown both by the treatment and by the subject. The simplest elements are introduced and managed with such consummate skill as to form a combination in the highest degree complex. These pictures are the work of a genius, of a master thinker, who feels the power of the infinite, and can reflect it to others. This familiar association with the eternal problems, is where the master spirit of Claude Monet manifests itself. None in art before him has ever approached so near the domain of the philosopher. The inflexible principles of geometry give the form to his charming color harmonies. The line between the aesthetic and the intellectual is so lightly traced in his creations, that the slightest touch effaces it, and thus almost proclaims their identity. Nature is rendered more lovely by this revelation of her mechanism and the sources of her activity, which are clearly brought out by study of his pictures; though to those minds unprepared for and incapable of grasping the laws of the universe, these pictures will offer little of interest. But to the thinker, the canvases of Claude Monet are records of what the sensitive mind sees in nature. It is not the pitiless laws of growth and decay which present themselves, but humanity with its hopes and fear shining forth, with which the true soul alone can sympathize.

The compositions of Claude Monet are animated evidences of what some one has said, that the true source of knowledge can be derived alone from the subjective. He does not paint what nature is, or as she presents herself to the ordinary mind through the medium of the imperfect sense, but he paints those thoughts which she impresses upon him by means of subtle forces to which only the sensitive mind responds.

The idea of *triangulation* is clearly expressed in the works of most of the followers of the impressionist school. It would be difficult for one acquainted with this school's teachings to say if this is purely unconscious or by design. It is not accidental. Of this there can be no doubt; for in each picture of Monet's, as well as those of other painters whose pictures have been studied, the same theory is expressed. It is along the hypotenuse of the right-angled triangle that the attention of the observer is, as a rule, directed. This line is used as a framework upon which to construct the picture. The lights and shadows and objects, when introduced for the main effect, are always along this line, but a parallel series, always running at the same angle. So with shadows, trees, elevations, depressions, or with whatever objects the picture is composed. Numerous examples can be brought forward from his pictures. One may refer to *Le Jardin de Monet à Vetheuil.*

It represents a garden rising from the foreground. This is occupied by an open space a little to the left of a right line drawn from the median line of the canvas. This space is very high light, with deep shadows of dark blue. On each side are blue figured vases filled with flowering plants, the shadows on the space and vases being along the diagonal line. A staircase, which is interrupted by a narrow terrace, leads from the space upward to the right, to a second terrace on which are the houses. Nearly the entire canvas is occupied, and the narrow space above is a deep blue sky. On either side of the staircase are numerous tall plants, their yellow flowers rising one higher than the other, like a flight of steps. This ended by a lattice work running along the second terrace. The light falls along the hypotenuse line through the flowers to the lefts, across the stone steps, and vanishes beyond to the right-hand lower corner. The same is true of the shadows. The lattices of the little fence around the terrace are distinctly seen only where the slats are arranged in the direction of the hypotenuse. The left-hand corner, which corresponds to the right angle of the triangle, is where the objects are most clearly represented, and the coloring is richer in tone. As the right-hand corner of the picture is examined, it will be seen that the objects are less distinctly painted, but the lines which correspond to the direction of the hypotenuse are more distinct, and the color of the picture seems to fade away, and only the geometrical basis remains. The sky is cloudless, but a vapor-like effect can be detected by close observation, draped over the sky's form, in directions corresponding to the hypotenuse. This light drapery is a most appropriate clothing for the heated sky. The coloring of the sky is remarkable; the appearance is one familiar to those who have seen it in southern France and Spain. The rich colored vault is apparently brought almost within reach. On gazing at it steadily, the eye becomes fatigued, and the sky is no longer blue, but of a leaden color. This can also be seen on examining the picture by gaslight; the sky, by artificial light, loses its blue tone and assumes the dull, leaden hue. It may be noted that the skies of Monet are the most carefully painted of any parts of his pictures.

Two little children stand on the flight of steps leading to the dwelling, in a diagonal line. The immediate impression conveyed by this scene is one of warmth and vitality. Rich tones of green, blue, red and orange, are used with wondrous skill. It is a mid-summer scene; the vegetation is at its highest; the air sultry and heavy with heat. It is a picture of the present moment, and the only pause to check the joy which such a surrounding offers, is the sky, by its depth suggestive of the impenetrability, to human understanding, of the termini of life.

Everywhere is seen this *triangulation.* It is the painter's guide for composition. In these color idylls, drawing is scarcely present. The artist's mind rests upon this simple geometric foundation, and his thoughts are turned into a perfect form, because true to nature. Frequently the pictures can be divided into several triangles; these triangles are formed by shadows, lights, clouds, fields, the sea, houses, or lines of trees; and are always significant of the underlying truths of life, which these painters have felt. In *Mail Post at Étretat,* the roll of the waves, the dip of the rock, and the direction in which the clouds are flying, are all expressed in lines corresponding to the hypotenuse. The oblique parallelism of the picture is indicative of movement. Motion is expressed by every stroke of the knife. The sunlight is coming from the same direction as the lines run; and the shadow of the great rock upon the water is in motion. As the observer move from one to the other side of the picture, the shadow seems to change its position. The effect is strange. The sea is shimmering in the sunlight and seems to be many fathoms deep. Its lovely transparency, which is finally lost in depth, reminds us of how we are lured on in our search after truth—simplicity and clearness at the start, ever increasing dimness following. The high swells of the sea are coming on in stately procession, each bending before the mighty rocky arch, and then rushing upon its as if to reach its summit. These great billows are composed of small waves, and upon them rise smaller ones still, until the little ripples come, as a bright smile upon a loved face. The prevailing color tones of greens, blues and pinks, offer a harmony of incomparable composition. One can sniff the fresh salt breezes, and hear the heavy thud of the waters coming against the rock. On viewing such a scene, we cannot but feel that we are looking upon more than nature has to offer in her cold way. It is the thoughts which the artist had on painting this picture which we see and feel, in addition to the sea, rock and waves.

The theory of *triangulation* should be considered at this stage. It was stated above, that in *Mail Post at Étretat* movement is forcibly expressed, by all the objects in the picture being painted along parallel diagonal lines. Motion can only be represented by ideas of force. Force is always exerted in straight lines, whether as initial or deflected force. The triangle is selected as the simplest figure enclosing space, and thus represents the lines of force in their simplest elements.

[...] Many of the tricks which painters of other schools employ to give motion to their pictures, are disregarded by the Impressionists. They have penetrated to the source of motion, and they recognize force as the cause. This fact that force manifests itself in straight lines is not only expressed in generality, but in the details or technique of their pictures. On close inspection, their pictures are masses short, straight lines, and all their effects are produced in this way. Curved lines are only employed when it is desired to express the idea of retardation, and when curves are used, they are formed of short, straight lines, much as, in modern geometrical teaching, a circle is held to be formed of innumerable straight lines.

The right angle of the triangle, which includes all the elements of the picture, falls sometimes outside the canvas. The hypotenuse, however, is never absent. Without it, there could be no basis for the composition. Sometimes the right angle of the triangle is occupied with the most prominent objects of the painting, and to these the focal point of vision is directed. *The Setting Sun* by Monet, is a conspicuous example of this. The focal point of vision is thrown entirely to the left, where are seen the coast line and the setting sun; to the right is a vast expanse of sea. A mistiness pervades the picture; the sky and sea blend to shut off forever from the soul the knowledge of what lies beyond.

Another extraordinary picture is *Fog Effect near Dieppe.* The sandy bank and trees are to the right. The technique and coloring of these trees are startling; straight lines mark the canvas, reproducing this mood of nature with a masterly insight. The sea dashes with violence against the coast. A faint light shines through the waves, and the foam rests on their proud, crested heads, like a bridal wreath. On just such a coast line might life have originated, as the sport of accident, by the cruel sea, indifferent to the origin, progress and destiny of this life, to which she had given birth. The color tints of pinks and grays delineate the outlines. Monet's pictures are noticeable for the psychological effect they produce by their coloring. His colors are like an orchestra of instruments in perfect tune, and the pitch of his scale is given by the foundation tone of his pictures.

On close examination, it would be reasonable to conclude that the canvases were first coated by a uniform tint of paint; this is the pitch to which all the other colors are tuned, and the different effects in his pictures are produced by heavy straight lines of suitable colors, according with the pitch. For Monet's pictures are essentially harmonies of color tones, in distinction to Renoir's pictures, which are color discords.

The color scale of Monet's pictures is original, and essentially calculated to produce upon the observer an intense psychological impression. As the pitch is high or low, so his colors vary in strength. Some of his most beautiful water and sea effects are reached by combinations of pale nile green, blue and violet tints, of varying shades.

Some of his views are bathed in an atmosphere of magic grace and purity. The tone pitch is often taken from the visual forms. In Cap D'Antifer, the prevailing tones are violet and lilac colors. It is a late afternoon scene; with wonderful distinctness the cliff stands out; along its rugged edge runs the road, twisting and turning, but always true to a parallelism with the coast-line, our line of dissymetry. The light through the picture follows the same line, thought the light is symmetrical with regard to the oblique line, for it is equal in intensity on both sides, and it fades away equally towards the right of the picture.

To obtain their full effect, the pictures of the Impressionists should be studied in the light in which the scene was painted; and this is a very important point to remember in judging the works of these artists. A noticeable example of this was a picture by Besnard, *By Cande Light.* The light of day detracts a great deal from the beauty of this painting.

Not only does Monet excel in painting water in motion, but also in representing it when at rest. *Breaking of Ice on the Seine* is an example. The middle distance is the point to which the eye is attracted. We feel how cold the water must be. Its marvelous transparency and depth are startling, and in contrast with the opacity of the blocks of ice floating on its surface. It is like a slivered mirror, with here and there the coating effaced. The foreground is rough, and in blue, green and gray tints. The picture is constructed on the principle of dissymetry, and the effects of distance, depression and rising ground are well portrayed. The valley, between the lines of trees which follow the bend of the river and the distant hills, is only observable after long study.

The Low Tide at Pourville, by Claude Monet, shows the facility of this artist. The cloudy sky is reflected in the moist sands, and the eye is carried along the beach to the distant blue sea, which is painted with much distinctness.

In many of Monet's pictures, the middle or far distances are brought out with great force. It is a natural inclination of the mind, on viewing a scene, to gaze beyond the immediate foreground. Consequently, Monet's foregrounds are usually indistinct, and especially in his highest psychological studies, where this indistinctness of foreground has a philosophical bearing.

In point of fact, it is impossible to see clearly more than one object at a time; all surroundings are less distinct, or reflect the color of the focal visual object. Monet's *Cabin at Pourville* illustrates this statement. The central object of interest is a little shrimp-colored house. The atmospheric conditions doubtless influence the mind of the observer, but the tone most deeply impressed on the house is reflected on the entire scene, on the hill beyond and even in the sky. This same idea is brought out in Renoir's pictures, where the background, though often very indistinct, echoes the prevailing rich colors of the figures which occupy the foreground.

Monet's *The Seine at Giverny* is a picture which at once attracts attention. The view suggests calmness and purity. A delicious fragrance steals over the senses, and the delicate perfume of lilacs permeates the mind. The transparency and depth of the water are finely represented. The shadows of the trees growing along the banks are reflected in water, and again carry out the theory of dissymmetry. For clearness and crispness of coloring, this picture is excelled by none in the collection.

Scene at Port Villers carries out several of the originalities of Monet's style. The canvas is covered by a thin layer of pale gray tint. In places there is apparently an absence of all color, and it is the canvas that shows. The prevailing tones are pinkish grays. The last layers of color are laid on very heavily, and thus the scene is admirably represented. The theory of triangulation and dissymmetry is clearly expressed by the lines of trees to the right, forming the hypotenuse. The edge of the bank is a transverse line, prominently shown, and the ground rises above it in ragged outline against the sky, broken, dissymmetrical. The hill is reproduced by in the river by reflection. This general effect is one of the best illustrations of symmetry in any of Monet's works. The subjective side of this picture is produced by adherence to simple and exact principles. The ground-plan is triangular, and the tints are in those colors which subjectively produce the sensation of chilliness.

Monet's *Morning at Pourville* is an interesting study of shadow effects. The rock which boldly rises in the foreground is reflected in the rolling sea as a triangle. Here let us note how frequently any distinct object in the foreground of Monet's pictures is sure to be inorganic, inanimate, massive, stable, recalling the blind, immutable forces of unsympathetic nature. The extraordinary sheen of the water is most noticeable; straight lines of light aid the mind to realize that it is real water upon which the observer looks. The delusion is complete. The gallery and all surroundings vanish, and it is the sea which spreads before you, with its restlessness. Innocence is depicted upon the siren's countenance. In the past, how many adventurous mariners she has lured on to repose upon her trustful bosom, only to drag them to her distant abode, the dwelling of death.

Concise Bibliography

Courbet, Gustave. *Letters of Gustave Courbet.* Ed. and trans. Petra ten-Doesschate Chu. Chicago: University of Chicago Press, 1992.

Gordon, Robert, and Sydney Eddison. *Monet the Gardener.* New York: Universe Publishing, 2002.

Herbert, Robert L. *Monet on the Normandy Coast: Tourism and Painting, 1867–1886.* New Haven: Yale University Press, 1996.

Levine, Steven. *Monet, Narcissus, and Self-Reflection: The Modernist Myth of the Self.* Chicago: University of Chicago Press, 1994.

Lochnan, Katharine A., and Ian Warrell. *Turner, Whistler, Monet: Impressionist Visions.* London: Tate, 2004.

Pissarro, Joachim. *Monet and the Mediterranean.* New York: Rizzoli International Publications, 1997.

Rewald, John. *History of Impressionism.* New York: Museum of Modern Art, 1973.

Tucker, Paul Hayes. *Monet in the Twentieth Century.* New Haven: Yale University Press, 1998.

Wilson-Bareau, Juliet. *Manet, Monet, and the Gare Saint-Lazare.* New Haven: Yale University Press, 1998.